THE ANXIETY GAP

Between

Hope & Fear

Neil Breakwell

To my Mom, my Dad, and my Brother.
And their families.
Family is always important.

Contents

Preface

We all know when we are scared. We also usually recognise what scares us. Fear is easy. It's a built-in protection mechanism that makes us freeze or run away from something that we expect to harm us, and, if needs must, prepares us to fight for our lives. But we always know what we are running from. Whether it be a pack of wild dogs, an axe-wielding maniac, or a tsunami, anything that we perceive to be a clear and present danger to our safety, or to that of our family, we have learned to automatically fear.

But anxiety is strangely different. Anxiety is more anonymous. While many of us may recognise similar physical feelings within anxiety as we find in fear, they are not the same, and there are always odd subtle differences that we find difficult to put our finger on. Very often it is a gnawing sense of dread; a fear without fear and no obvious cause; a sense of doom with no purpose. Anxiety creeps up on us from the shadows and seeps into our bones. It is insidious and subtle in a way that the brash drunken frat boy of fear is not.

Fear hits us hard and then leaves. It leaves nothing behind. It does exactly what it says on the tin. But anxiety? Well, anxiety is anything but straightforward. Anxiety can lie patiently for hours eating away at our minds, trying to warn us of hidden dangers, speaking a language too obscure to understand. We know it is there for a reason, but it is a reason that is impossible to fathom when its grip is tight.

The problem with anxiety, then, is that it is difficult to see what stirs it. Unlike the jack-in-a-box of fear that leaps into action every time a trigger is pushed, anxiety often seems to lurk in the background attacking whenever it feels like it. Any triggers, if present at all, seem impossible to find. So, what is it that drives anxiety? Are there specific things in our lives that provoke anxiety to bite, or is anxiety just the rabid dog of emotions?

Much of the consumer content that I have read about anxiety offers wildly different reasons for the existence of anxiety. Some imply that anxiety is based on ancient fears from our "lizard brains" that are being applied to modern-day society. Fears that have become misplaced and misdirected onto the mundanity of our lives where they fester and grow as anxiety. Some mention that anxiety is a future-based fear where anxiety grows as a fear of the unknown, a fear of potential future events. Others lay the blame for anxiety on unseen adversaries, where our brains conjure imaginary fears onto imaginary foes and the dangers are anything but clear or present. Then, of course, there is the over-sensitive amygdala, which screams at us every time it deems something to be a threat, no matter how insignificant.

While these are all plausible, and possibly even accurate, descriptions of anxiety, they are, in my view at least, inherently flawed as explanations to anyone who has suffered from excessive anxiety. They are just not useful. No explanation is offered for the reason for any specific episode of anxiety. There is never anything that an anxiety sufferer can pinpoint as the true cause of their problems. People just want to know: "What are the triggers of MY anxiety, why are they there, and what can I do about them?"

Abstract ideas about anxiety are too often purposefully left hanging in the air like a cloud of smoke, engulfing sufferers and giving them just enough knowledge so they know the cloud is there, but not enough for them to break it down into anything useful. If I were a cynic, I might say that this was done by design, but it is more likely the lack of a useful model or a true understanding of anxiety. This lack of real understanding of what is causing anxiety creates this amorphous enemy which can be blamed for everything that goes wrong. Trying to predict what it might do next is a catalyst for generating even more anxiety. This limited understanding, and lack of details, is often more dangerous than complete ignorance. As they say, a little knowledge is a dangerous thing and, with anxiety, this is true.

This is the reason I decided to take what I had already learned about anxiety, a subject that I have been researching since 2012, and try to build upon it to form a coherent model for the average anxiety sufferer. A model that could provide a better understanding of an individual's anxiety rather than the generalisations that are most often pushed upon us. I wanted people to be able to "see" their anxiety. This is what the anxiety gap is—a visual representation of anxiety.

Very few of the fundamental ideas in this book are mine. I'm certainly not the first to use the idea that anxiety is based on conflict and uncertainty, as this has been around since the days of Kierkegaard, and even the conflict being formed between positive and negative drives is nothing new and is based on a popular modern scientific theory. All I have done is group these ideas together in a form that I hope is more useful to anxiety sufferers than the usual abstract ideas that are thrown around, and I have tried to create a visual model that I hope will make the whole concept of anxiety more tangible and more practical to people who experience it every day.

This model is based on modern-day scientific theories of personality and motivation that simplify anxiety by distilling it into a basic form that everyone can understand and hopefully can explain every single form of anxiety experienced. It is a model that exists to give anxiety a face—a visual representation—in the hope of breaking down the intimidatingly amorphous cloud of anxiety into a series of simple pictures. I wanted to find a way that anyone, anywhere, could explain their anxieties, specifically in graphical form, to themselves as much as to anyone else, without the need for a psychologist to translate it. That is where this book came from.

I hope it will be clear, that the models that I have developed for this book are intended solely to help people visualise and tackle their anxiety and are in no way intended as scientific or medical theories of any kind. It is simply a bringing together of other scientific theories and ideas about nature and the human condition into a form that might be of more use to us.

This book is not intended, unlike many anxiety books, to give you techniques to cope with individual anxiety episodes. There is plenty of literature out there that will help with calming the mind during anxious episodes and coping with serious anxiety attacks. This book is not that. This book is aimed at providing a framework with which you can view your anxiety and be able to see the problems involved. It is aimed at trying to overcome the base causes of out-of-control anxiety and show you a possible way out. There are no tricks or tips that will help you quieten your anxiety at any given time, there is only a model to help you re-evaluate what you think your anxiety is and ways that you can use this knowledge to help you bring your anxiety back down to manageable levels. It is recognised that this will take time and effort to achieve, but in the long run I am very confident it will be worth it.

I want to warn you ahead of time about the first part of this book: The chances are that you're reading this book because you, or someone very close to you, is suffering from an anxiety disorder of some description or anxiety levels that are way above those that you find acceptable and you are looking for help, and so when you read the first few sections of the book that discuss the anxiety present in all people, you may feel that this is not addressing the problems that you face daily. I assure you, I am not trying to make light of anxiety disorders in any way at all, but I feel it is important to discuss the anxiety that is present in all of us, and what it is for, before we can delve into what makes anxiety disorders different. I also think it is important for anxiety disorder sufferers to see that anxiety is everywhere and is essential for our well-being and development, and that it helps us grow as people, as many sufferers view their anxiety as a monster that is ruining their lives. Of course, anxiety disorders do ruin lives, and it is not your run-of-the-mill anxiety in these cases, but we must start somewhere, so I hope you will indulge me a little as I think it will all become clear later. And I think it will even help.

The book also contains a little of what some people might call mathematics and some simple equations that might seem daunting to begin with. I believe that applying numbers to this system helps to explain it better and to make it more robust as a theory, and therefore more helpful. I have tried to keep the numbers to a minimum and keep it as simple as possible, but if you are math-averse then you might find it a little overwhelming to start with. I ask that you stick with it and not let it put you off the main concept of the book. It might be worth re-reading the more number-heavy parts several times if you find it difficult, as I think it is important in fully understanding the gap model. I believe assigning numbers makes the model more concrete, and practical, and removes the traditional abstract nature of most anxiety theories. I also believe that once you understand how it works, it will be more useful to you. Which is, after all, the whole point of this.

Part 1: The Anxiety Within Us All

"To venture causes anxiety, but not to venture is to lose one's self.... And to venture in the highest is precisely to be conscious of one's self."
Søren Kierkegaard

Chapter One: The Beginning

Hedonic Motivation

Since the beginning of time in the early primordial waters of the Earth, life's single goal has been to survive and reproduce and ensure that the genetic code of each species is passed on. To do this, all living things have developed ways to solve the problems that stand in the way of their survival—they must obtain food and nutrients, regulate fluids and temperature, and of course avoid harm. This is as true for bacteria and amoeba as it is for insects, reptiles, and humans, and it is essential for survival.

It can be observed in microorganisms, insects, and fish, as much as it can in mammals that living organisms will move towards things that they need for their survival, such as food, water, or a possible mate, and will move away from things that could jeopardise their survival by causing them harm, such as a predator, fire, a superior aggressive rival, or a passive-aggressive friend. It is important to note that, contrary to common belief, a brain is not needed for these behaviours. Bacteria have no brain, or even a nervous system, and yet they will still move towards things that they need and move away from things that will harm them, although passive aggressiveness does seem beyond them. But who am I to judge?

These are the basic behaviours of survival and are automatic and innate. This is one reason why the behavioural scientist Theodore Schneirla wisely stated that behaviour is "a decisive factor in natural selection." Without these basic survival behaviours, living things would not survive to reproduce and therefore only those that had these behaviours could pass on their genes. How well an organism can approach positive things and avoid negative things plays an extremely important role in the survival of that species and is a driving force of evolution. While the mechanics and sophistication of how such behaviours are instigated differ between organisms, the basic outcomes are the same.

Even in humans, with our supposedly "superior" brains, the motivation to approach the things that we need is innate and non-conscious and driven by chemicals such as dopamine, serotonin, and oxytocin, while the equally innate motivation to avoid harm is driven by other chemicals within the brain, such as cortisol.

These drives are so powerful that they have been the fundamental building blocks of behaviour and personality research for decades, and while the methods of approaching and avoiding are different between the species, and most certainly learned behaviours in humans, the basic drives to move towards or away are in-built and ubiquitous in living things. As Theodore Schneirla also pointed out, *approach and avoidance are the most fundamental and universal classes of behaviour.*

Even before Schneirla, though, the idea that pleasure and pain, or reward and threat, play major roles in human motivation has filled history: From Epicures of Samos (341-270 BC), who contended that to achieve tranquillity and freedom from fear we must seek out modest pleasures and avoid physical pain where possible, through to a more contemporary Jeremy Bentham (1748-1832) who formulated his theory of "utilitarianism" and said "Nature has placed mankind under the governance of two sovereign masters—pain and pleasure. It is for them alone to point out what we ought to do as well as to determine what we shall do."

The idea that we are hard-wired to approach things that we deem good for us (pleasure) and avoid things that we deem bad for us (pain) is not a new one, then, and it has been backed by some of the greatest thinkers in history. These two fundamental behavioural drives have been the bedrock of behaviour and personality research throughout the last century. Hedonic motivation, as it was called, argued that a person's personality was built around their predisposition to pleasure and pain and how fervently they would move towards things that brought pleasure and move away from things that brought pain. With hedonic motivation, the drive to move towards things that will benefit us is often called "approach motivation" while the drive to move away from things that could harm us is often called "avoidance motivation". These two motivations are incredibly powerful in sculpting our overall behaviour, but while hedonic motivation is still a very intriguing and persuasive theory, it is incomplete when it comes to describing more complex responses such as anxiety. For that, we need to look at a more modern scientific theory built on the foundations of hedonic motivation.

Should I Stay or Should I Go?
The Revised Reinforced Sensitivity Theory

I hate fairgrounds! I have always hated fairgrounds. Every year, when I was young, the travelling fair would come to my hometown and camp out for a week or so on the town sports field. The kids in the area would get excited when they saw the Waltzer and Big Wheel rides being built on-site and the tired, old, haunted house being constructed. There was always a buzz in the air. My stomach, however, would sink. The weekend would roll around and my friends would be building up to head to the fair. I would feel sick. I'm still not sure why, whether it was the tightly packed crowds, the screams, whoops, and sirens of the rides, or just the rides themselves, something about the fairground scared the life out of me. And yet I still went. The longing to be with my friends, part of the group, and to share the "fun" they had there was stronger than my fear of the fair itself, and so I went along. (As we will see later, there is a little more to it than this, but it will do for now).

Once at the fair, I had a churning in my stomach somewhere between excitement and fear and I could never quite decide which it was, or which would win out. It was often a battle to remain with my friends and not make up some excuse to run home, but remain I always did. I can't say I ever really enjoyed fairgrounds, but I endured them and felt better afterwards for going.

This, then, is a simple modern-day example of what psychologists now call an approach-avoidance situation: The lure of some reward that makes us want to approach a certain thing (fun with friends), while at the same time offering a possible threat that we would like to avoid (fairgrounds. I can't be alone in this surely). If the reward is much greater than the punishment, then the decision is for an easy approach. Likewise, if the punishment is far more severe than the gain from the reward, then the decision is for easy avoidance. What happens, though, if the reward and the punishment seem almost equal? What happens if the possible reward is so good that it has us positively drooling, but to get it we must endure an unimaginable pain? How is the decision made? What is the deciding factor?

This question was answered by Jeffery Gray in 1982, when he proposed his theory of personality that he called the Reinforcement Sensitivity Theory, and again in 2002 when he updated the theory to fit more in line with the behavioural experiments of the time and renamed it (rather unimaginatively it could be said) the **revised Reinforcement Sensitivity Theory**[1], or rRST. The basis of Gray's theory was that the personality was mainly shaped through the motivations of approach and avoidance, which he assigned two conceptual networks of the nervous system that he called the Behavioural Activation System (BAS) and the Fight, Flight, or Freeze System (FFFS).

Whenever a possible reward was detected, the BAS would activate, and the subject would be motivated to approach the reward. If, on the other hand, a threat to survival was detected, then the FFFS would be activated, and the subject would be motivated to escape the danger. This we already knew, as it has simply given us names for systems in the brain that cause the approach or avoidance that constitute hedonic motivation. The interesting bit, though, is what happens when the approach and avoidance motivations are activated at the same time which hedonic motivation does not address. What happens when the BAS and the FFFS are activated together?

Place a hungry mouse at one end of a laboratory box and place food at the other end of the box that has been laced with cat odour and you will see a demonstration of inner conflict. The mouse can see the food, and cannot see a cat, but its olfactory senses are ringing bells that a cat is near. The mouse is torn between the motivation to approach

---

[1] Gray & McNaughton, 2000

and ease its hunger, and the obvious fear of being a cat's lunch that is motivating avoidance. There is a standoff between the BAS and FFFS.

This conflict that arises from approach and avoidance being in impasse requires us to introduce a third conceptual neural system that Gray called the Behavioural Inhibition System (BIS). This system is the arbiter, the judge, that decides upon the next move when the BAS and FFFS are in stalemate. The BIS puts things on hold while it performs a full risk assessment of the situation—scanning the current predicament, along with the options and the environment, and comparing it to memories of any similar situations or related cases that may have occurred in the past. It may even promote careful and slow approach behaviour to try and gather more information.

Once the BIS has its decision, then either approach or avoidance will be set in motion. In the case of the mouse in the feline-smelling box, the BIS may motivate the mouse to slowly inspect its surroundings until it is sure that no cat is present. Once the mouse is sure it is alone in the box, then the FFFS will diminish, and the BAS will promote approach to the food. If, however, the BIS finds no previous examples from experience with which to make a decision, and careful investigation yields no answers, then it will err on the side of caution and plump for avoidance. After all, it doesn't really matter how good the reward is, if the mouse is going to get eaten when it goes to get it, it won't last long as a species.

This is a rough overview of the rRST, and the differences in the way that each system performs were suggested to be a basis for different personality traits. It should be noted that the rRST is not an obscure theory that was proposed and never used. The theory has been a mainstay in modern motivation and personality research for years, and it has been backed up in many scientific studies[2]. It has been used

---

[2] Corr, P. J., & Cooper, J. E. (1998). The revised reinforcement sensitivity theory of personality. Personality and Individual Differences, 25(2), 303-312.

to develop many personality tests within psychology and is, without a doubt, a heavy-hitting and mainstream theory within the motivation and personality areas of psychology.

What interests us here, though, is Gray's idea that the BIS, in its duties as conflict negotiator, brings with it anxiety, and the weighing-up and evidence-sorting of the risk assessment process can lead to the worry and rumination that we associate with it. This means that the rRST has also become a major player in modern anxiety research and the BIS, itself, a prime suspect in the creation of all anxiety.

It is easy to see how a mouse that is torn between a meal and possibly being eaten by a cat is going to be filled with anxiety as it tries to decide its best course of action, and there is no doubt that a human in a similar situation (but with a slightly bigger cat) would also feel anxiety, but it is very unlikely that you or I, or anyone else for that matter, will ever be put in the situation where we have to choose between going hungry or possibly being torn to pieces by an oversized cat. Our anxieties aren't typically based around real life-threatening situations, they tend to be based on our finances, our security, and our social positioning. Can the rRST explain where these anxieties come from? Can the approach-avoidance conflict, or something like it, still be the basis of our modern-day anxious thoughts and feelings? Well, I'm hoping to show that it can, but to do so we must begin at the beginning with a deeper look into the systems of the rRST.

Behavioural Activation System - BAS

The Behavioural Activation System (or BAS) is a conceptual brain system that deals with reward. The reason we call it conceptual, is that

2 Harmon-Jones, E (1998). Behavioral approach and behavioral inhibition systems: Neuropsychological evidence for two independent motivational systems.
Gray, J. A. (1987). The psychology of fear and stress.

it is highly doubtful that there is a single brain system that deals with reward. After all, we have many kinds of rewards that motivate us, and many different chemical incentives are released by our brains to give our bodies the actual physical "reward" that motivates us. It is highly doubtful, then, that there is a single neural system in the brain that deals with these processes, and it is much more likely that there are several different areas of the brain and processes involved. This is why, for the sake of simplicity, all these different motivating systems are grouped together in this conceptual system that we call the BAS. It is both elegant and easy.

The BAS, then, is the conceptual system that leads mammals towards goals. It makes us strive for the necessities in life and the things we need to survive. It makes us search for food and shelter, social bonds, financial success, and cheesecake. Everything that we deem good and important and useful in life is achieved through the activation of the BAS. When a lion feels thirsty, it is the BAS that makes it search for water. When a human needs more financial security, it is the BAS that will lead him to the job interview. When a cat wants to attack your feet for no reason whatsoever—yep, you guessed it—BAS. When our lives have a need to be fulfilled, it is the BAS that will motivate us to fulfil that need. While the BAS may not be a single system biologically, we can count it as a single system conceptually as the outcome is the same.

As with most things in the brain, the BAS does this through the release of chemicals: The main chemical used in motivation is dopamine, which is the bread and butter of the BAS and the chemical that is involved in most goal achievement, but other chemicals can also be involved. Dopamine is a neurotransmitter and is probably most famous as the "feel good" chemical that is drip-fed into the brain when we anticipate meeting a goal or satisfying a need, and then "fuel-injected" when that goal or need is about to be realised. Other chemicals that are used in motivation, and often in conjunction with dopamine, are oxytocin—the social bonding hormone, and serotonin—a neurotransmitter/hormone that, amongst its many roles, plays a part in social ranking and connection.

There are certainly more chemicals that play roles in approach motivation, but in this book, I am not going to dwell on the roles of the neurotransmitters or hormones beyond this, as I feel that they just complicate the issue unnecessarily, especially when the BAS has already been simplified so elegantly. All we need to know here is that when our brain detects a reward, it activates the BAS for us to approach the reward for our survival. How the BAS works, which chemicals are released, or which parts of the brain are used, would be overkill and would muddy the waters unnecessarily.

If the BAS is activated in the brain, and only the BAS, then the behavioural response from the body will be to approach the reward. Nice and simple.

It is a good idea, here, to take some time to get used to this overall idea and what it implies. It is not an idea that is easy for everyone to accept, but it is true: We are, none of us, truly motivated by the things around us. It is not money that motivates us, or security, or even love, it is the BAS, the drip of neurotransmitters and hormones in our brains, that is the motivation. Of course, things that we value trigger these chemical motivators and keep us moving towards them, but it is important to make the distinction: Without dopamine, oxytocin or serotonin, there would be no motivation. People don't check their mobile phones every 2 seconds because of the phone or its contents, they do so for the drip of dopamine that accompanies it.

Fight, Flight, or Freeze System - FFFS

The FFFS, or the Fight, Flight, or Freeze system, is a conceptual threat response system and is activated when our brains detect a threat. As the name implies, the response has three main actions: freeze - to stay still to avoid detection; flight - to run away and avoid

23

the danger; or fight - to actively engage the threat for survival. In most situations, the action taken is not a choice but an automatic response to the situation and level of threat. The freeze is the first reaction and is to try and avoid detection. If an animal has already been detected and the threat is too close, then the animal will flee. If on the other hand, the animal has no opportunity to run, then it will also have no option but to fight. The cornered animal can be a dangerous thing.

This can be seen more clearly if we use an example of a cat and a mouse. When a mouse senses the presence of a cat, it will freeze in the hope that the cat does not see it and will move away without further action. If, however, the cat has already seen the mouse and is moving towards it, then the mouse will attempt to run to get away. On occasion of course, the mouse may well be cornered and have no possible escape routes. In this situation it might attempt to fight back against the cat. If the mouse deems none of these a plausible safety attempt, then it may choose a 4th option, which is fawn - basically to play dead in the hope that the cat gets bored. Fawning is not a response for every species though, and not so much in humans, although I guess it is sometimes used during warfare where playing dead might have its advantages. It is usually a last resort anyway and not always successful against hungry predators.

All animals have some kind of threat response. Even bacteria and other single celled organisms have responses that will cause them to move away from predators or harmful chemicals, but of course their systems are not of the same sophistication as the systems in ourselves and other mammals. In mammals, when this fight or flight response is activated, hormones and neurochemicals such as cortisol and adrenaline are released that prepare the body for action. The heart starts pumping faster and the breathing increases all to get more oxygen to the cells and the muscles to make the animal faster and stronger (useful for running or fighting); the vision becomes tunnelled, to focus on the threat, and blood is drained away from the extremities to minimise damage to the limbs if attacked.

This is the physiological response of the FFFS system in mammals and is completely automatic requiring no mental cognition whatsoever. It is often called the fear response, and when it is activated on its own by a threat, it results in what we usually characterise as fear, with the most common behavioural response being active avoidance, or as it's known by most people, getting the hell out of there. As we will see later, though, what we know as the fear response is different from the feelings of fear that we experience, and it will be important to make that distinction.

Behavioural Inhibition System - BIS

There are, of course, occasions when a situation offers pure reward, like a glass of cold water after a long run on a hot day, and other occasions that offer pure threat, like a cobra spooning you in bed. Often, though, a situation will involve both a possible reward, and a possible threat, together, at the same time. This is where the Behavioural Inhibition System (BIS) comes into play. The BIS is the conflict resolution system and the decision maker in the BAS vs FFFS conflict. The BIS will instigate risk assessment, which will search through memory for similar situations to help in the arbitration of the conflict.

Sometimes the reward will far outweigh the possibility of threat, for example an animal seeing a delicious meal but noticing that it might have to walk over some precarious terrain to get it. In these situations, the BIS will easily award the BAS the result and instigate an approach but will also make sure that the animal treads with care. Other times, the threat will far outweigh the reward, such as if a cat can see a lovely fishy snack but it is laying in the middle of a burning building. In this case, the BIS will not take long to deem the fishy snack unworthy of the risk of being barbecued to a crisp and will award the outcome to the FFFS and prompt the cat to slink away and find a fishy snack elsewhere.

There are other times, however, when the outcome is not so obvious. Times when the reward and the threat hold almost equal sway. In these situations, one system does not obviously override the other, and a conflict between the two is created. In these situations, the BIS must work much harder to determine the best result, after all, the wrong decision could be disastrous for survival. The BIS must use all the tools at its disposal, from scouring the environment for clues, weighing up all possible outcomes and their probabilities, and scanning the memory banks for any remotely similar memories that could give a clue as to the most beneficial response. Once the BIS has a result, it will either instigate a tentative approach (while still on high alert for changes in situation), passive avoidance, which means that the animal will basically do nothing and will decide that the reward is not worth the risk, or it will activate the FFFS, which will result in active avoidance (running away, presuming it has legs). If the BAS and FFFS are equally matched and the BIS is unsure what to do, it will usually opt for avoidance of some description, as the old mantra of "he who fights and runs away, lives to fight another day" holds true for all animals. Sometimes it is not always as easy as that though.

The interactions between the approach motivations of the BAS, and the avoidance motivations of the FFFS and how a final decision can be made by the BIS is most graphically illustrated in real-life lab studies in mice that are caught between the reward of a desirable snack and the punishment of a mild electric shock. The mice are caught in the middle of the approach-avoidance conundrum as the motivations are balanced and therefore rely on the BIS to sort out the problem. But what is interesting in these scenarios is that the BIS originally opts for passive avoidance as it will often do as default in impasse situations, and the mice begin to walk away. But as they move away from the threat, the FFFS begins to diminish as the fear of the threat is reduced.

The lingering smell of the snack leaves a robust approach motivation in place, and with a smaller avoidance motivation present, the BIS has a change of heart and makes the mice turn around and head back for the snack. Of course, as they get closer to the snack the electric shock generates a renewed FFFS response and the BIS once again promotes avoidance.

This cycle results in the mice being stuck in an approach-avoidance loop. It has been shown in the studies that the mice have no way to get out of the cycle as the motivations are unconscious drives and would keep the mouse walking in circles forever (or at least until the hunger got so bad that a mild electric shock was no longer such a deterrent).

This is much like the cute Facebook videos that show people running directly away from each other to see which of them their dog loves the most. Usually, this results in the dog almost self-destructing with indecision. The only difference with the dog is that its indecision is caused by an approach-approach decision, which we will talk about later, and the fact that the dog is being tormented by its humans for clicks.

The Conflict That is Anxiety

As you may have already guessed, the conflict between the BAS and the FFFS and the subsequent activation of the BIS to determine a behavioural response to this conflict, is the foundation of anxiety and is why anxiety is always associated with uncertainty. If a reward is certain, then the BAS alone will function, and approach will occur. If physical peril is certain, then the FFFS alone will function, and active avoidance will occur. This is what we call fear. Only when there is a conflict between the BAS and FFFS, and therefore uncertainty between hope and fear, will the BIS activate, and anxiety be brought into play. This is why anxiety is profoundly different to the emotion of fear.

While anxiety is often confused with fear because many of the same chemicals of the FFFS are still in play, the uncertainty surrounding the rewards and threats characterise anxiety and makes it different to fear alone. The BIS also gives rise to the characteristic rumination and worry that often accompany anxiety. When the conflict between the BAS and the FFFS is closely contested and the uncertainty high, the BIS must delve into memory, both experienced and learned, and weigh up the likelihood and impact of all possible outcomes to decide what to do. This decision-making process between approach and avoidance is a crucial factor in our survival but is also one that creates the common issues with anxiety that give rise to books like this one.

The Role of Adrenaline

I mentioned adrenaline in the FFFS section above, but I thought it important to give a few more words to this neurotransmitter as its importance should not be underestimated. Adrenaline, also known as epinephrine, is the chemical that makes all the other drives more intense. It is the supercharger that gets our hearts pumping and our lungs working overtime to make us stronger and faster. Adrenaline by itself is not linked to any specific motivation but can be combined with the other chemicals to tell our bodies how important the motivation is. For example, adrenaline can be pumped up in readiness for us to run or fight if a threat is detected, but it can also be released when we see a positive reward and the BAS is activated, such as in situations of excitement or exhilaration. In this way, adrenaline never contributes to how good or bad something feels (the valence) but will determine the severity of that feeling (how aroused we are). This means, then, that adrenaline can be the difference between slight nervousness and abject fear, or mild hope and raging excitement. We will look more at how these emotions are formed later in the book.

The Problem

The rRST is a compelling and well backed scientific theory to explain the phenomenon of anxiety and has been used for years in studies about personality, motivation, mental health, and, of course, anxiety. The problem is that the rRST, as it stands, is still not very useful as an aid for individual anxiety sufferers to understand their own issues with anxiety, as it gives little insight into a person's real-life hopes and fears and how they are pitted against each other to trigger the BIS. This means that most anxiety sufferers would find no use for the theory and is probably why it has never gained any real traction in modern popular literature or the general anxiety field. But this doesn't mean it is wrong. Just not useful right now, in its current form, for the everyday anxiety conversation.

This is why I thought it important to take the main idea from the rRST and create a model that would be useful to any anxiety sufferer and give them the knowledge and know-how to apply this theory to their own individual anxieties.

This is why I created the Anxiety Gap.

Chapter Two: Mind the Gap

The Gap Model

The idea of anxiety being caused by conflict, as we have seen, is not a new one, but, even though we may now have a more scientific and specific conflict system to plant our flag in, it still does not help people with anxiety. It doesn't help people, like you and me, get a handle on exactly what anxiety is, help us visualise our anxiety, or allow us to apply our own hopes and fears to our anxiety to make sense of it all. It is still too abstract. Therefore, I was eager to make a visual representation—a model if you will—of this conflict system, which would allow anyone to plug their individual hopes and fears into it and be able to see immediately where their problems lie and place them in a stronger position from which to tackle their anxiety. This is the reason I created the "Anxiety Gap".

We can see the gap in action if we look at the simplest of conflicts—the simple approach-avoidance decision. As we will see later, this is an oversimplification, but it is a good place to start.

Simple Approach-Avoidance Gaps

The simple approach-avoidance conflict occurs when there is a simple case of a single reward and the possibility of a single threat. As the BAS and FFFS are in conflict, the BIS activates to perform a risk assessment and see which motivation—the approach or avoidance—should win out. This is a simple idea, and an easy one to understand as a concept, but it does not help us visualise or identify with the resultant anxiety. This is why I have found it useful to view the conflict between the systems as a gap between approach and avoidance. This gap is what I have termed the anxiety gap because it leads to the physiological processes that we perceive as anxiety. It is important to note that this is only what we can characterise as the physiological phenomenon of anxiety and not what we know as the *feeling* of anxiety, which I will discuss in a later chapter.

The "gap" I base around a neutral line, with the strength of the approach system determining how far above that neutral line the BAS line is, and the strength of the avoidance system determining how far below the neutral line the FFFS line is. If the gap only comprises an approach line, then the resulting physiological response will be pure hope or excitement with no apprehension at all. If the gap is only made up of the avoidance line, then the resulting expression will be pure fear (or despair).

The issues arise when both are present:

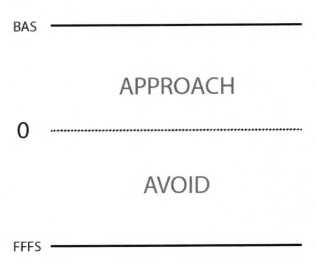

If a large approach line (denoting a strong urge to approach a reward) is combined with a large avoidance line (a strong urge to escape a threat) then a strong conflict is formed. This will mean first and foremost that many contrasting chemicals are released into the body and the strength of the body's physical response will be proportional to the size of the dominant gap i.e., the BAS or the FFFS. The valence of the response, (how good or bad it feels - which I will talk about in the emotions chapter) will be determined by which motivation is dominant and the difference between the two gaps. I will talk about this in more detail later. Of course, when a conflict exists and the body experiences both approach and avoidance motivations, it will be undecided on the course of action to take. This is where the BIS comes in and it will choose in favour of the dominant (largest) side of the gap.

But what if the BAS and FFFS are equally matched, how can there be a dominant gap? In these cases, where the motivations are of equal size to begin with, we know that the BIS will eventually choose a winner out of approach or avoidance, and therefore we decide on the size of the approach-avoidance gap in this model after the BIS has already completed its risk assessment and before it determines a winner. In other words, the side with the largest gap is the largest because the BIS has already deemed it to be the best choice. This makes our model simpler and more useful, as our decisions are made unconsciously by the BIS, and therefore drawing our own gaps consciously is always done retrospectively anyway. After all, we all know the results of our own gaps before we can consciously create them as we have either already approached, or already avoided. Drawing gaps before action has been taken is possible but takes some serious introspection and understanding of our own personalities and habits. This means that usually when we are drawing our own gaps, there is never a stalemate, and always a winner, as the BIS has already decided. Of course, if there is a decision to be made and you are unsure what to do, then following some of the tips in part 3 might help you build your gaps and make the decision.

If this is confusing, don't worry, it doesn't affect the overall idea here and you can safely brush over the last part with no issues. All you need to know, is the BIS always chooses the largest gap, whether that be BAS or FFFS.

Once the BIS has completed its risk assessment, it will result in a behavioural response. In other words, we will act in response to the stimuli creating our gap. If the BIS determines that the gains from approaching outweigh the possible negative consequences, then it will result in a cautious approach to the reward. On the other hand, if the BIS determines that a negative approach is more pragmatic, then passive avoidance might result. In extreme cases, the BIS can trigger active avoidance, whereby the BAS is completely inhibited, and a fight or flight response is initiated—this results in pure fear and a usual response of running away. If the BIS is unsure, then it will tend to err on the side of caution and instigate passive avoidance of the situation. I realise that I am repeating myself a little here, but it is an important concept, so worthy of repetition.

A simple example may help in this situation: the simplest example is that of a zebra that has just found some luscious grass on an African plain. The zebra is happy to have found such lush and tasty grass and its BAS will be rewarding it with dopamine for being so "clever". Its approach motivation will be well-sized as the animal is hungry and has found a new batch of grass to eat. Because the approach gap is the only gap present, the zebra will be happy that it has found such food and will move into the grass and start to eat contentedly.

BAS ────────────────────────────

APPROACH

0 ···

After a while though, the zebra senses a lion, either through smell, sight, or simply through the actions of other members of the herd and its FFFS will be activated. The zebra will now experience a conflict due to the gap between approach and avoidance systems, and because of this, the animal's BIS will be activated and will spur the animal to assess its surroundings by analysing the behaviour of the rest of the herd and trying to see the lion to see how much of a threat it appears to be. When the lion is seen to be lying down well out of reach, the BIS will determine that the lion is at a safe distance, and the risk assessment results in the zebra continuing to eat, albeit with greater caution and vigilance. This is the animal version of anxiety and is the same physiological response that we experience, although it is usually called vigilance instead of anxiety, and there is no evidence that the zebra experiences conscious anxiety as we do.

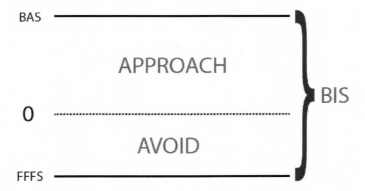

After a while, the lion stands, yawns, and begins to move closer. It is still quite far away, but the BIS has recognised danger and has alerted the zebra to be vigilant. The zebra stops eating the grass and waits to see what happens next, keeping all its senses on high alert. This is the BIS instigating passive avoidance of the grass due to the possible dangers.

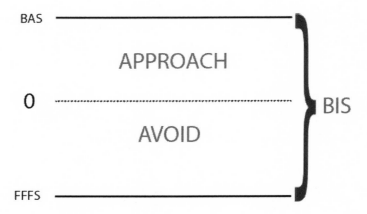

Suddenly, the lion starts to run towards the herd. If our zebra is the first to see the lion run, then it's FFFS will become increased in line with the threat. The BIS which is constantly performing risk assessment at this stage will note the increase in threat and the FFFS and alter the avoid gap accordingly. It will eventually decide that the risk is too great and outweighs the benefit of a good feed. Deciding that passive avoidance is no longer sufficient in this case, the BIS deactivates the BAS completely and activates a full fight or flight response—the zebra runs. Of course, the benefit of the herd mentality is that once our zebra runs, the action of our zebra will result in the same BIS decision in all the zebras, and the herd will run en masse. We have ourselves a stampede.

0   ···

AVOID

FFFS   ━━━━━━━━━━━━━━━━━━━━━━━━━━━━━━━━━

This is, in effect, how the BIS differentiates between the approach or avoidance motivations, but in doing so results in uncertainty and conflict as it undergoes its process of risk assessment.

What Causes the BAS and FFFS Activation?

It is important to note that the gap is not formed between the principles of do and don't do exactly. The gap is called approach vs avoidance and is built through the "reasons" for approach and/or avoidance. This is a subtle, yet important, distinction. It is not the conflict between drink and don't drink that causes anxiety in a thirsty human, because drink and don't drink have no skin in the game, it is the *consequences* of drinking or not drinking that form the gaps. If we drink or don't drink, there is something to be gained and something to be lost. It is not simply water that we gain or lose, it is the consequences of having or, more importantly, not having water that is important (i.e., dehydration and possible death). It is the needs to be gained and lost that are the driving forces, and it is these that cause the conflict, and hence the anxiety. Needs, then, are essential to understanding the nature of anxiety gaps, and must be looked at in more detail.

Needs

For there to be an approach drive strong enough to activate the BAS, and an avoidance (threat) drive strong enough to activate the FFFS, there must be something important enough to approach or avoid. These key factors can be categorised, at least at a base level, as our fundamental needs.

For most animals, these needs are basic and comprise the essentials of survival—safety, security, shelter, and the basic natural drives of hunger, thirst, warmth, oxygen, and reproduction. These needs are shared by almost all animals and will cause activation of a BAS when they are being pursued and an FFFS if they become under threat. The neurology of the systems may be different for each animal, but the effects are the same. If an animal sees an opportunity to fulfil one of its basic needs, for example it sees food, or fresh water, or a possible mate, then the BAS will be activated, and the animal will approach the need. If, on the other hand, an animal sees a threat to one of those needs, like a predator who could threaten its safety and security, or smoke from a fire making the air unbreathable, then the FFFS will be activated, and the animal will try to escape. If an animal detects something it needs but also suspects that a predator may also be present, then both BAS and FFFS will be activated. This of course will then activate the BIS that will assess the situation more vigorously to compare environmental context with experienced memories and will result in "anxiety" and the animal acting with increased "vigilance".

This is the basic need conflict that occurs in almost all animals, but certainly in all mammals. Humans, however, have expanded their need repertoire beyond basic needs to include much higher-level needs than just safety and security. In fact, in 1943 Abraham Maslow developed his famous (and now seemingly a little controversial) hierarchy of needs. Maslow contended that as humans develop, their need requirements expand and become more psychological and social than simply physical. As we can see in his simple pyramid, the needs of humans move from simple basic needs like food and safety, to psychological needs and social needs, through to self-actualisation and existential needs. As one level is attained, the next level becomes important.

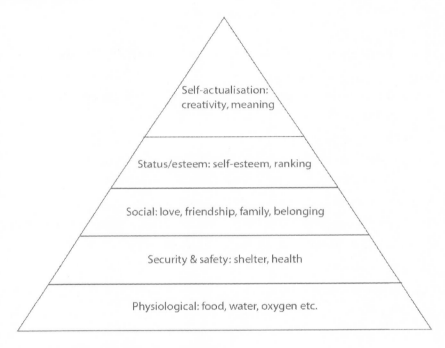

Maslow's Hierarchy of Needs

The needs that Maslow compiled have been expanded on over the years, and, although the concept of them being hierarchical has been questioned, what is certainly true is humans have many different needs that must be fulfilled for them to be happy, and these same needs can cause fear when threatened.

In 2010, a group of psychologists tried to update Maslow's hierarchy to include both biological and evolutionary needs of humans and placed them in a hierarchy that they felt better described our developmental stages through life. As we are not interested in any hierarchical order here and only care about the needs themselves, I have taken the liberty of combining the pyramids and paring their needs down to simplified groups to end up with the following list:

Basic Physiological Needs
Food, water, oxygen, sex, warmth, sleep etc.

Self-protection
Shelter, safety, security, good health, rest, order, stability

Social Connectedness
Love, belonging, intimacy, social acceptance, affection, affiliation, trust

Status/Esteem
Ranking, position, social status, respect, prestige, self-esteem, dignity, achievement, mastery, power, freedom

Cognitive
Beliefs, values, understanding, finding meaning, purpose, play, predictability, equality, fairness

Aesthetic
Beauty, creativity, form, balance, tranquillity, peace

Parenting
Reproduction, raising children to reproductive age

Self-actualisation
Realising potential, self-fulfilment, personal growth

For humans, a goal of achieving these needs triggers the BAS—through the motivating chemicals of dopamine, oxytocin, or serotonin—with the amount of activation depending on the importance of the need, and its novelty. When I say importance, I am talking about the perceived importance placed on the need by the individual, and this of course will change with urgency. Water is an important need for us all, but it is never going to spike the BAS unless we're dying of thirst.

Novelty is also important because once we become accustomed to achieving a goal, the approach drive (BAS) becomes diminished i.e., the motivation for each need is decreased as that need is met. For example, very few of us feel excited and filled with hope every time we buy food from the supermarket, or joyful that we have attained the need of security when we go home for the evening. This is because, for most of us, the needs of food and shelter have been met. And yet, we do feel excited when we buy a new house, or we go to an expensive restaurant, because these are novel occurrences, but also because they tap into the other needs of social acceptance and prestige. Even the novelty of going to fancy restaurants will fade if we do it too often, though. Novelty is often best described in today's world when we talk about "shiny objects"—things that spark our BAS to pursue them simply because they are new and novel, even if they have very little practical use or value.

For most of us, food, water, and shelter simply do not activate our approach drives much anymore, but they will certainly activate our FFFS if we suspect that they are under threat. Think how you would feel if an eviction notice landed on your doormat tomorrow morning rendering you homeless.

Now, while these may not be the best examples in the world, I hope they give you some idea of how the mind distinguishes between importance and novelty.

This goes for all the needs that humans attain, not just the basic needs. Psychological needs like self-esteem, and social needs like intimacy and ranking, make us who we are. We build ourselves around these needs and they drive the way we act and the way we approach life. If we suspect that one of these needs is under threat, then our bodies will act in the same way that it would for a predator, because if we lose any of these needs, or any one of these needs gets diminished, it could be disastrous for our psychological well-being, which is just as important to us as our physical well-being. This is why, as far as the

FFFS and BIS are concerned, a threat to our self-esteem is just as dangerous as a threat to our personal safety, and the anxiety will be just as real.

This means, then, that as well as gaps being formed from the usual rewards like hunger, thirst, or reproduction, gaps can also be formed with the more abstract rewards of social advancement, prestige, or social connection. Likewise, as well as gaps having the ancient threats of loss of security or safety, they might also be constructed with the loss of financial security, self-esteem, social ranking, or the fear of social isolation. These gaps are just as real to our minds as any physical threat gap might be, and just as severe.

We strive to achieve the needs that will make our lives more complete and more fulfilled, but once we have achieved them, we then fear losing them. This is why, the more we have, the more we fear losing. Most people attribute ideas like this to wealth and material things, but it just as easily applies to every need that humans attain from self-esteem to self-actualisation. Once we've got it, we are terrified of losing it, as it becomes part of who we are and there is nothing more terrifying than losing a part of oneself.

Let's take a brief look at each of the needs in the updated version of Maslow's pyramid to give us an idea of the things we strive for, and the things we might fear losing.

Basic Physiological Needs

The most fundamental needs that all living things must deal with are the basic physiological needs such as food to eat, water to drink, and oxygen to breathe, for without these things, we would surely die. It is clear why Maslow put these at the base of his pyramid, because if we are lacking any one of these basic physiological needs, then we will not care a great deal about the other needs. If we are dying of hunger, we will not care so much about our self-esteem, or social respect from those around us, we will just try to get food however we can.

We might never dream of looking for dinner in the garbage, but a homeless person who hasn't eaten for three days might not think twice about it. If we don't have these basic needs, then they will become our primary drives, and if we feel that these needs are under threat, they will quickly become our primary fears.

Self-Protection

Almost as fundamental as the physiological needs, are the needs that involve our safety and self-preservation. These include the drive to find proper shelter for ourselves and our families—homes that are safe and secure from physical dangers and devoid of leopard-print wallpaper. We strive to keep our bodies safe, intact, and healthy, and work towards making sure that this safety and security will be present in our futures as well. We plan for our financial futures because the fear of losing our safety, security, or health, now or in our later years, is a fear that terrifies us to the bone and is as deep rooted and as primeval as that of the physiological needs.

Starting a business is a simple example of building gaps from self-protection needs: The excitement and possibilities of freedom and fortune that come bundled with being a business owner would be set against the very real fears of failure and future financial, and by extension physical, security being under threat. New businesses hold big rewards and big risks, and therefore carry huge possibilities for anxiety. That is why most people don't start businesses.

Social Connectedness

Humans are, by our very nature, social animals, and so the need for social contact and connection plays an important role in our motivations and drives. The most obvious—and it could be argued the most important—need of all is love. The reason that love could be considered the most powerful of needs is because, however you view

43

it, the main drive of all living things is reproduction, and love is the emotion that humans use to bond to their mates in order to reproduce and bond to their families to help them survive long enough to reproduce. Some people have argued that all the needs above this group in the pyramid, like self-esteem, status, and prestige, are there to help us find the best mate possible and give our DNA the best chance of survival. Whether or not that is true is of no importance to us here, as all we are concerned about is the needs themselves and not why the needs are there. That is an argument for a different book.

Love is not the only player in the needs of our social world, though. Humans have evolved both biologically and socially to be part of a group, as this has many advantages over being alone, although sometimes I find it difficult to see this. This, of course, begins at the very moment we are born, as humans are one of the few animals that depend entirely on their caregivers for all their basic needs, and even after that, being part of an extended group will have helped our ancestors with the rearing of children as well as other activities like hunting, foraging, and protection.

This means that, as humans, we strive for social connectedness of all kinds, as being part of a group, and having family and friends and social circles, fulfils that ancient need. Of course, not everybody needs social connectedness in the same amount. Natural introverts tend to be much happier being alone, and they like their social connections to be made up of small groups or individuals that they feel very close to, whereas extroverts often tend to prefer the larger social groups and can thrive in groups where the connection may be tenuous.

Of course, the introvert-extrovert personality types are on a sliding scale, like most things, and so most people will find themselves somewhere in between fully introvert and fully extrovert and will therefore have differing degrees of need for social connection. One thing is for sure though, all of us, to one degree or another, need social connections and will feel anxiety when there is a possibility that a connection comes under threat. The hermits who live in seclusion may convince themselves that they do not need social connection, but it is simply their fear of social interaction overcoming their need for connection that leads them to isolation, and whether they admit it or not, anxiety is running their lives in a negative way.

Social connection is hard-wired in all of us, as it is for all primates. Years ago, scientists used to believe that all new-born primates (including humans) bonded with their mother because she was the one that they associated with the food that they needed. They suggested that the bond was formed through the association of seeing the mother as milk was given. The main point of this was that the milk was the driving force of the social bond with the mother as food was a known primal need. This was discredited, though, when Dr Harry Harlow performed his now classic (albeit rather cruel) experiment where he took several baby monkeys and created two analogue mothers for them[3]. The first mother was a wire model on which he placed a milk bottle. The second had no milk but was covered in soft cloth. What he found was, instead of the monkeys bonding with the simple analogue mother with the food as expected, they in fact spent over 18 hours of each day cuddling with the soft mother. This was the first step to realising that, although babies certainly need food, there is more to the primate social bond than the fulfilment of basic physiological needs. We need contact.

As we all have relationships of some description, we are all only too well acquainted with the anxiety created due to the threat of loss of social connection. The aching anxiety triggered in the aftermath of an argument with a loved one can testify to how the threat of a loss to our social connections can create havoc. Even though we may rationally know that the relationship is unlikely to end over such an argument, the gnaw of anxiety sets in as we feel the sudden loss of

---

[3] Affectional responses in the infant monkey - Harlow, H. F., & Zimmerman, R. R. [1959]

connection that was there only hours earlier, and the faint unconscious possibility that it could be gone completely tomorrow. The palpable relief when the problem is cleared, and we make up, is testament to how anxiety lets us know that something is wrong and there is something that needs to be done.

Our brain has evolved with a feature that leads us to seek social connection, and it does this by rewarding us with oxytocin when we experience a strong social bond, but it will also "punish" us with cortisol when we are socially disconnected or feel the threat of isolation. In fact, one of the most interesting things about social connection is what happens in the brain when we lose it. What happens when we are spurned by a lover, excluded from a social group, or rejected by a friend?

The English language has been rife throughout its history with descriptions of social rejection with lines such as "the pain of rejection", "hurt feelings", or a "painful memory", which equate the emotional pain of social exclusion with real physical pain. The most interesting thing, though, is that these are not simply metaphors: Science is showing that the emotional pain of rejection triggers the same areas of the brain as physical pain, which means that the brain cannot really tell the difference between physical and emotional pain[4]. Although physical pain may feel "physical" it is, like everything else, just a perception in the mind created from signals from the body that it has been damaged. We can see this more clearly when we remember that pain can be reduced through simple distraction, or placebos, and stopped completely through meditation or hypnosis. This can be seen in the photos of devotees in India who put needles through their tongues and swords through their cheeks during the festival of

---

[4] The common neural bases of experiencing physical pain and social rejection - Eisenberger, N. I., Lieberman, M. D., & Williams, K. D. [2003]
An fMRI-based neurologic signature of physical pain - Wager et al. [2013]
Social rejection shares somatosensory representations with physical pain - Kross, E. et al. [2011]

Thaipusam. They have stopped the pain that they should feel with meditation and trance.

It is no wonder, then, that the fear of possible rejection, exclusion, or abandonment, would trigger the FFFS, and therefore cause anxiety, just like the anticipation of real pain or bodily harm. Our brains really do not know the difference.

Status/Esteem

When Maslow developed his hierarchy of needs, he separated this category into two sections: (i) Acceptance from others (prestige, status etc.) and (ii) esteem for oneself (dignity, self-worth etc.). I have joined them together to keep things simpler and because I think they often play hand in hand with each other.

Status, ranking, and prestige are very important needs in the competitive society in which we live today and play a huge role in how we act and interact with other people. Whether we know it or not, we are constantly ranking ourselves against those around us trying to gauge our position in the social hierarchy and trying to improve it. Social position is undoubtedly important to us as humans as it is with most primates, because evolutionarily speaking, the individuals who rank higher on the social ladder get the best food, the prime spot, and of course the pick of the mates. This is hard-wired into us and is still not that different in our modern society. As money is the most common gauge of social success in most countries today, those higher up the ladder have more of it and therefore still get the best food, the best things, and often, the pick of their partner.

While ranking and the respect of others both play a huge role as needs required by humans, an arguably more important need is that of the respect and dignity we hold for ourselves. It doesn't really matter how much respect and adoration we receive from others, if our self-love, self-appreciation, and self-worth are low, then we will never feel we deserve it anyway.

Building a solid "sense-of-self", then is an important need for humans and one which we strive for often. The fear of losing it is also a trigger for the FFFS and a common builder of anxiety gaps. I will talk much more about this later.

Cognitive

Cognitive needs are the requirements that we have for intellectual stimulation and mental engagement. These needs include a desire for knowledge, understanding, learning, and problem-solving. The need to learn, to gain knowledge, and to understand the world around us drives us to expand our world and our lives beyond that of our homes and family group. It is true that some people have a more burning need than others to learn and understand, but the need is there in all of us and when it is stifled it can cause anxiety.

Along with the drive to learn, and the growth of knowledge, comes the building of new beliefs about ourselves and the world. These beliefs can also play a very powerful role as needs to be lost if they're threatened in any way. We will look more at this later as they can play a crucial role in anxiety and who we are.

Cognitive needs also encompass more moral ideals like fairness. Fairness is a much bigger need in humans than most people think both in the workplace and in social situations. Research has consistently shown that employees who perceive their workplace as fair and just are more engaged, satisfied, and committed to their jobs, and it is often a more important factor than money alone. They also found that perceptions of fairness were related to lower levels of absenteeism and turnover[5]. Social fairness is also important, and here research has

---

[5] Justice at the millennium: A meta-analytic review of 25 years of organizational justice research | Colquitt, J. A. et al., (2001)
The management of organizational justice | Cropanzano, R., Bowen, D. E., & Gilliland, S. W. (2007)

shown that people value fairness and justice in their interactions with others[6].

When people feel they are being unfairly treated, it can trigger the possible loss of that cognitive need and open a gap.

Aesthetic

Another need that people (some people more than others) strive towards is aesthetic pleasure. Many people need beauty and art in their lives, and there is no doubting that surroundings affect our moods[7]. We can all imagine how we would feel differently sitting at the beach watching the sea lap up against the white sandy beach compared to sitting in an office cubicle facing a plastic partition and a computer. Beauty does affect us, and although most of us may not be artists or creators of beautiful things, we can still appreciate them and strive towards having them in our lives. We like our living spaces to look a certain way and many of us enjoy music throughout the day. There are many aesthetic needs that we have that we may not think about, but we would notice if they were gone. How many of us take holidays to beautiful places to recharge our batteries?

Parenting

Parenting is one of the needs that has been added much more recently than the others, when scientists aimed to bring the aging pyramid up to date and in-line with current scientific thinking. They added finding and keeping a mate as two other important needs, but I have included those in the Social Connectedness grouping to keep things simple. I couldn't deny, though, that the need to be parents is

[6] Psychological perspectives on legitimacy and legitimation | Tyler, T. R. (2006)
[7] The cognitive benefits of interacting with nature | Berman, M. G., Jonides, J., & Kaplan, S. [2008]
The benefits of nature experience: Improved affect and cognition | Bratman, G. N., Daily, G. C., Levy, B. J., & Gross, J. J. [2015]

strong in most people, and even after offspring are born, the need to raise children well, and instil in them all the needs and values already discussed here, is a powerful drive. It also, of course, brings with it some of the biggest fears of all parents—losing or failing their children. There is no doubt that giving their offspring the best start and the best opportunity for the future is a powerful drive for all parents, but just like all the other needs before it, it can also become the biggest fear. The gaps created because of the hopes and fears of parenting can be immense. Not being a parent myself I can only imagine the anxiety that parents suffer because of their children. I am told there is huge joy to be had as well, but I'm still not convinced that the anxiety is worth it.

Self-Actualisation

At the very peak of Maslow's hierarchy lies the need for self-actualisation. This is a person's need for self-fulfilment and for them to realise the potential in their life. This could be a drive to be the best they possibly can be at a particular activity, sport, or role in life. As it is a higher order need, it is less common than the other needs in this list, but it can still act as a driver for the BAS and possibly even a threat for the FFFS if someone's goal of self-fulfilment is perceived to have been blocked for some reason.

The Personal Perception of Needs

These needs, then, give us the foundations of what we should approach and what we should avoid for us to survive. Needs that we want to gain will help form the BAS in our gaps and this will motivate us to try and achieve those needs, while needs that we fear losing will help form the FFFS and will motivate us to protect them. The problem is it can easily be seen that people don't all approach or avoid the same things with the same enthusiasm. We don't all want the same things in life and many of us fear things that others don't, so there must be more than just needs involved in the formation of gaps. We don't all place the same importance on the same needs. This is why we must also look at values.

Values

In many mammals, other than humans, it is easy to see the motivations that drive them, as they are mostly the inherent needs baked into them from birth in what we call "instincts", and although they may still have to be taught how to fulfil these needs, the drives for each need are clear cut. In humans in today's world, though, it is not always so clear. While we certainly have needs that are necessary for our survival and healthy development, not every human will view these needs the same. Upbringing, education, and social environment play a huge role in how we perceive not only the importance of each need, but the best ways for us to fulfil those needs. This is where values come in.

If someone considers something is good for their life and will help them to fulfil a need, then they value it. If they see something as bad for their life and might result in the loss of a need, or is of no benefit to them, then they disvalue it. While the needs are similar, if not the same, for every human, the values that we place around those needs certainly are not. In a crude example of the simplest of needs—food— we can see the difference in values between a meat eater and a vegan in the pursuit to fulfil the need to eat. One values meat as a food source, the other does not. The need to eat is the same, but the value surrounding the need to eat is not. Of course, if starvation or health issues were a real possibility, then I imagine both camps might re-evaluate their values to some degree. This is how needs differ from values.

Values become even more important as we move up through the levels of needs in Maslow's pyramid. The different beliefs and values we hold about higher-level needs like relationships and status and self-esteem determine our actions and what we move towards and away from. No two people hold the same beliefs, or the same values, and so in any situation, each person will build their own unique anxiety gap forged from the values that they hold dear. One person might value the need to reproduce extremely strongly, while another may decide that career is a more important need. It is these values around higher-level needs that most people think of when they hear the term "values".

It is also important to note that the values that form around needs can be different depending on where we are from. While humans might all require the same needs, people's values can be dependent on cultural background. Certain cultures value independence while others hold the collective good to be more valuable. Some cultures respect assertiveness and aggression, while others view it as a weakness. For every value held as important by a culture, there will be other cultures that deem it less valuable or even disvalue it completely. These differences in values mean that the anxiety gaps formed can differ wildly from culture to culture, but the result of each gap is the same: Anxiety.

Our beliefs and values play a huge role in making us who we are, and an even bigger role in how we respond to the world around us. We perceive the world and those around us through the tinted lenses of our values, and they govern what we choose as our goals and what we learn to fear. In many ways, then, the values we hold as humans (for those not living in poverty at least) are more important in the formation of our gaps and the production of our anxiety, than are our needs. Our needs tend to be innate and mostly the same as most primates and mammals, but as we have grown as a society, our values have changed, and it is these values that determine what we want to approach and what we want to avoid. It is these values that form our gaps. It is these values that make our anxiety.

Values are arguably more important than needs because they are the needs viewed through our belief systems, and throughout history beliefs have been shown to trump needs time and time again: There have been hunger strikes, self-immolations, suicide attacks and many other events that show that values and beliefs can be stronger motivators than the base needs of hunger and safety. Values are what point us to the needs that we hold personally important and help us form the gaps that drive our lives.

Values differ from needs in another, and much more important, way: They can change. Many of our values change over time as we grow, and even our deeper-rooted core values can be changed through "life-changing experiences" such as sickness, near-death experiences or even by becoming a parent for the first time. At these times we might feel we need to re-evaluate our values in-light of an experience that makes us question what we hold important.

One of the most famous examples (albeit fictional) is Ebeneezer Scrooge, where a single night of traumatic revelations forced him to change his own values from the importance of wealth to the importance of people. Of course, it could also be argued, with good reason when we consider his backstory, that people and social connection were always Scrooge's true values, but over time he suppressed these values in favour of success and wealth, and as a result became deeply unhappy and very anxious. If his true values were wealth and success, he should have been immensely happy with everything he had, but the name Scrooge is most certainly not synonymous with joy. We will look at suppressing values and the consequences of not living to our true values later.

No matter what our own values are, whether we value success, prestige, wealth, family, honesty, kindness, integrity, or all the above, the values are built around ways to attain the needs from Maslow's list, and it is these values that help form our gaps. It is the thought of attaining or losing these values (and the needs that they represent), in every situation, that causes anxiety.

Simple Gaps in Life

We have already looked at the simple approach-avoidance gaps but have so far focused on the standard gap created by the fundamental physiological needs of food vs predator, and how anxiety (or vigilance) can be triggered in such a situation. As we have seen, though, there are far more needs that can be gained or lost by humans than just physiological ones, and even more values associated with these needs, and any two needs or values can create an approach-avoidance gap, and therefore trigger anxiety. If we are looking to gain a specific need or value, then our BAS will be activated, and if by approaching that need there is a chance that we may lose a different need or value, then our FFFS will also be activated. This is then an anxiety gap.

We can literally pick and choose any two needs or values and form an anxiety gap, and I can guarantee that every two combinations of needs/values have caused a gap, and therefore anxiety, in someone, somewhere, at some time, but I do think it will be useful to look at a few specific examples to show how they might work and offer a taste of different types of anxiety gap.

Public Speaking

There are few things in life that summon as much fear and anxiety in life as public speaking. In fact, it consistently tops the list of most common phobias, and that is why I thought it a good place to begin my examples. Most people can at least appreciate the anxiety associated with speaking publicly, and although if you are an anxious speaker your reasons may differ to mine here, I think you will be able to relate to it at least.

Let's use Phil as an example: Phil is a marketing executive for a medium sized company, and he has been asked to give a presentation about his marketing plan for the next quarter of the year. This is the first time he will have given a presentation to so many people as the usual presentation guy is off sick. Phil knows he is good at his job, and he is sure that he knows and understands his presentation material better than anyone else, and he is certain the slides he has put together are of a high quality. So why is he so anxious? Why does he feel sick and sweaty palmed before the presentation starts? The answer is, of course, because he has created an anxiety gap. How do we know there is a gap and not just pure fear? Because Phil is not running away. There is a conflict in Phil's mind that is causing anxiety, but also making him go ahead with the presentation. As we are only looking at simple approach-avoidance gaps here (I will discuss more complex decision gaps later), we will presume the conflict is caused by a need/value gain (BAS) vs a need/value loss (FFFS). Phil's approach need/value-gain trigger of the BAS could be his ambition to impress the boss and gain respect and further his career, thereby enhancing his financial security. Phil may not consciously think about these things, but they are there, under the surface of his consciousness. The FFFS of course is also triggered by the fear that he will mess up the presentation and the audience will laugh at him. He fears his hands will shake and he will forget what he has to say, and his colleagues will think he is weak and ineffectual, and he will lose their respect, and subsequently a good measure of self-esteem. This is a real fear for Phil, and even though he rationally doesn't believe it will happen, his unconscious is taking no chances and takes the precautionary step of cranking up the threat response. A gap is created. Once the BIS is activated to manage the gap Phil will experience anxiety and the risk assessment will kick into gear and lead him nervously into the presentation.

While the exact reasons and needs may vary, this is basically the same story for everyone who has ever been anxious about public speaking. Occasionally the FFFS may win, and the speaker will decide to pull out of the presentation. The problem with doing this, and the problem with all avoidant behaviour, is that the speaker will never get to see that their fears are unfounded. Public speaking gets easier over time because we get to see that the things we were scared about never happen. Phil sees that, although he didn't believe he did a great job with the presentation, nobody laughed, and everybody clapped at the end. So not only will Phil feel slightly less anxious next time, but he will also be a bit more comfortable, and be a little better at presenting. Most people in an audience can empathise with the speaker and so are less judgemental than we might think. Over time Phil will become a much better speaker and be able to perform with much less anxiety.

Asking for a Date

Every introverted teenage boy's nightmare is asking someone out on a date. Everybody knows the outcome will not be life threatening—nobody is going to beat you to death with a Barbie playhouse for having the gall to ask them out—so why is asking someone out on a date so paralyzingly terrifying? First, the BAS drive in asking for a date is consistent in most young people: They find someone attractive and are looking for love, sex, respect from their friends, or all the above. The drive to seek a partner or mate is strong in all animals and so is to be expected in humans as well. The fear on the other hand could have several different causes and depends heavily on the personality and beliefs of the person involved. Most people fear rejection, and this is the most common form of fear when asking someone for a date, as well as possible ridicule for having the audacity to ask. After all, we all know how cruel teenagers can be (usually through their own anxiety issues). Rejection is a loss of social connection, but it also brings with it a loss in self-esteem, as of course does ridicule, and so we try our best to avoid or at least minimise rejection and ridicule as best we can. If the fear of rejection and/or ridicule trumps the need for a date, then the BIS will suggest that it is better to avoid than approach. Welcome to my teenage years.

The Job Interview

Job hunting is a stressful affair, and the heated cauldron that is the job interview certainly doesn't make it any easier. We dive into that pit of vipers due to the need for more financial security or higher social status and ranking. Of course, the fear of saying the wrong thing, making a fool of ourselves and losing self-esteem, or getting rejected, creates a gap for the interview which inevitably cranks up the anxiety present as we talk. The more important the interview, often the more riding on it, and therefore the greater the fear of it going wrong.

Of course, not too many people will avoid an interview that they have arranged just because of the anxiety that they experience. Anxiety is much more likely to prevent us from arranging the interview altogether.

The Simple Status Quo Gap

Sometimes, there are times when anxiety is triggered without an obvious reward, goal, need, or value, to be approached. Sometimes it can be very difficult to see what the BIS could possibly be getting worked up about in situations where everything seems to be negative. One example of this in animal terms is if an animal is lying down trying to sleep and it senses a predator. Another example in modern day human terms might be if we get a phone call telling us that our boss is unhappy and wants to see us the next morning in his office. Neither of these seems to have anything to approach—nothing that could possibly spark the BAS into action—and yet there is without doubt a threat to fire up the FFFS. So why would the BIS trigger anxiety if there was not a gap in place? Should it not be a simple case of pure fear?

The answer boils down to a single factor that makes these examples different to the run-of-the-mill fight or flight response—uncertainty. In each of these cases the threat is unclear. The sleeping animal only senses a predator but is unsure if it is in danger or not. Likewise, even though it doesn't sound good, we cannot be sure how bad the meeting with our boss will be. It might, after all, be about somebody else. This means that, although there is a threat, it is an uncertain threat, and therefore provides some hope that the threat does not materialise, and a small amount of hope is enough for a small activation of the BAS. I call this small activation of the BAS the "Status Quo Gap" because it is a BAS gap activated through the hope that the threat does not occur and that the status quo is maintained. In other words, we remain the same, but more importantly, we remain safe. Of course, as the status quo is, by definition, not novel, the activation will be small, but it will still be a gap. If there is a gap, then the BIS will be activated and trigger anxiety to solve the problem, squash the threat, and maintain the status quo.

Very often in these cases, such as in the case of the meeting with an angry boss, there is not much for the BIS to work with, and it will be left running through memories, scenarios, and possible outcomes trying to find a solution. Occasionally it might turn up something useful that makes us feel better—maybe we remember something our boss said or something someone else did that suggests we won't be in the firing line—but more times than not it will simply leave us with anxiety, rumination, and worry until we attend the meeting and find out for sure.

It is the possibility of avoiding threats that is the main job of the BIS and therefore also the main job of anxiety. If a threat exists but there is the slightest chance that the threat will not manifest itself, then hope will also exist. When we have hope and fear together, we will also have an anxiety gap.

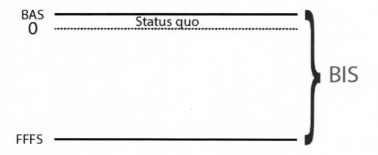

The status quo gap

You may have noticed that the above status quo gap is heavily weighted in favour of the FFFS, and as we have seen, in simple situations this usually means an avoidance strategy.

The reason we don't usually avoid the meeting with the boss when the threat seems to overwhelmingly outweigh the status quo is because there is usually more to each decision than meets the eye. The gaps created are never as simple as they might first appear and the simple approach-avoidance gap is insufficient for most situations, and therefore, in the next section I will expand the simple gaps to more complicated, but much more useful, decision gaps.

Decision Gaps

The conflict between approach and avoidance, as it stands, is a simple scenario and is one discussed in most literature on the subject. However, very few situations are as simple as they first appear, and once the BIS is activated, and it starts to perform risk assessment and analysis, then the decision automatically becomes more complicated. Even simple approach-avoidance situations are not as simple as we might believe. There are very often much more nuanced decisions determining our actions. This is not only true for humans but also animals. let me give an example with an animal like the previous zebra situation:

Let us imagine that a warthog has found a watering hole and its BAS is activated to urge the animal to drink. The warthog also smells a predator, and so its FFFs has also been activated as it senses a threat to its safety. As we have seen, this results in a conflict that causes the BIS to butt in and decide the outcome. However, if we break it down, the decision for the BIS is not as simple as it might first seem: There are more variables involved than might appear on the surface, and although each of these variables may well just lead to altering the size of the approach or avoidance portions of the gap, I find it useful to look at them separately.

For example, the warthog's decision is between drink and not drink, but if we think about it carefully, we can see that each of these choices has its own needs to be met and needs to be lost. To approach for a drink, the warthog must deal with the reality that if it goes, it may well fulfil its need for a refreshing drink, but it may also become a quick meat buffet for a predator, which is never a clever way to end the day, even for warthogs. These are both possible consequences of approaching (drink and possibly die). The other choice is to stay where it is, which, if it does so, would provide the need for security but could also result in it dying of thirst. These, then, are both the consequences of avoiding (security and possible death from dehydration).

This then, would result in double "decision" gaps with a gap for approach, and a separate gap for avoid, each with its own BAS need/value-gain and FFFS need/value-loss. The gap with the least negative net gap will be chosen by the BIS as the best course of action (I'll explain what I mean by that in a moment).

If the warthog was not too thirsty and a crocodile was floating nonchalantly under the surface at the water's edge, then the fear of loss of life through being eaten alive by a hungry croc would create the greater gap and the animal would not drink. If, however, the warthog had not had a drink for three days and was on the verge of dropping dead of dehydration, then the fear of this would increase the size of the FFFS of the avoid gap and so the warthog might well take the chance and run the crocodile gauntlet.

If this is a little confusing as to why the warthog makes the decision that he does, then please bear with me as I will try to explain in a moment.

Not Too Thirsty

Drink   Don't Drink

BAS ————————
            Need for water   ———————— BAS
0 ————————————————— Security ···········
                         Die of thirst
            Fear of predator   ———————— FFFS
FFFS ————————

Warthog will NOT drink

No Water for 3 Days

Drink   Don't Drink

BAS ————————
            Need for water   ———————— BAS
0 ————————————————— Security ···········
            Fear of predator
                              Die of thirst
FFFS ————————
                              ———————— FFFS

Warthog WILL drink

This can be very easily wrapped neatly into a single approach-avoidance gap (as I demonstrate below with a different example), with the fear of thirst simply making the BAS of the approach side of the gap greater, as the absence of a loss is considered as good for BAS activation as the presence of a gain (hope=relief). But, as I hope to show, the double decision gaps are good visual aids in more complicated decisions, and so I think visualising it like this is more useful in deciphering the needs involved than simply throwing it all together into a single gap.

If we take our previous example of hearing that our boss wants to talk to us tomorrow, we can see why most people wouldn't call in sick, even though they may be scared about the outcome, if we look at the decision gaps involved: The gap for going to work, as we have already seen, is easily in favour of the FFFS, as the status quo is no match for the possible negative outcomes of the meeting. The gap for not going to the meeting, though, also offers a small BAS motivation of safety, but a large FFFS motivation based around the fear of upsetting the boss, being fired, and being left financially vulnerable, as well as being seen as weak by all the people we work with.

Meet Boss   Avoid Boss

BAS		BAS
	Safety Status Quo	Safety
0	Fears of what might happen in meeting:	Fears of what will happen if don't go to meeting:
	Loss of ranking	Even more angry boss
	Loss of self-esteem	Loss of job and security
	Loss of security	Loss of respect from peers
FFFS		FFFS

Most people understand that the consequences of avoiding a meeting like this will usually be far more dire than the consequences of going. These fears would make the idea of avoiding the meeting a non-starter and push us into that meeting.

To look at these gaps in more detail, let's look at a different example—that of a man buying a new house. Now this, of course, is just an example, and there will be plenty of different reasons why people buy or do not buy new houses, but this is just one possible scenario.

Let's look at John, who is thinking of upgrading his house for a much larger version in a better part of town. Whatever John tells himself is the reason for buying the house, the real motivation he is feeling is a need for an increased social standing, a boost in his self-worth and prestige, along with the higher social circles that he might join by living in a more affluent area of town. John is excited about "moving up in the world". Of course, there are also fears that John has about buying the new house: It is expensive and will take a much bigger portion of his salary. John fears that if anything unexpected happens he won't be able to afford the payments and he will be evicted, effectively rendering him and his family homeless. It is a real fear and one that John must weigh up along with the positives that he feels may come with the house.

Now we might imagine that John's decision would be based on these two things alone, as he has a goal value and a fear value about buying the house, which would create a simple approach-avoidance gap. But, as we have seen, there are other things that will come into play that will affect the strength of both his motivation to buy the house and his motivation to forget the whole idea and stay where he is: On one hand, he has the gap formed from buying the house, created from the need of the social advancement pitted against the fear of financial ruin and bankruptcy, but he also has another gap to contend with—the one of not buying the house: The gap formed for not buying the house is created between the small gain of security and comfort of keeping the status quo, and the fears generated by missing out, getting left behind his peers, disappointing his wife, and ultimately losing his self-worth as a "provider" and a man. Psychologically these are some gruesome fears, and, if the BIS crunches the numbers and determines that the house is financially viable, they could well create a big enough negative gap to push the decision in favour of buying the house.

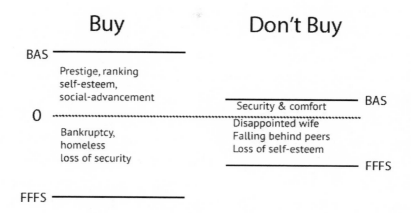

How Are the Decisions Made?

As mentioned earlier, when the BAS and FFFS have both been activated and laid out their stalls in a need/value conflict, the BIS then gets to work with rigorous research, and analysis of memory and environment, to determine what is in our best interest. The BIS generates each gap, populates them with needs and values, and determines the size of each gap. Later we will look at this process in more detail.

When making a decision, the BIS always errs on the side of caution and so will always opt for the decision that creates the least anxiety, which, in visual gap terms, means the one with the smallest net negative gap. To help understand this better, I will go through John's house-buying decision again, but this time using the gap model with arbitrary numbers out of 10 to make it easier to follow. I hope you will forgive the maths-like component, but I feel it important to help understand.

In the diagram below, then, we assign numbers to John's gaps so that he has a need/value-gain BAS score of 4/10 for buying the house, which relates to his excitement of moving up in the world, and a need/value-loss FFFS score of -5/-10, which is his fear of financial ruin and homelessness. If this were the only gap that John created, then he would not buy the house, as his fear is greater than his hope. But it is not the only gap, because John also has the second gap created around his feelings of NOT buying the house.

In this situation, John has a score of 1/10 for his gain for *not* buying the house, which demonstrates the comfortable, but certainly not novel, action of sticking with the status quo and remaining where he is, and a loss score of -3/-10 for all the fears he has of staying still and treading water in the same house. Not to mention a disappointed wife, which nobody wants.

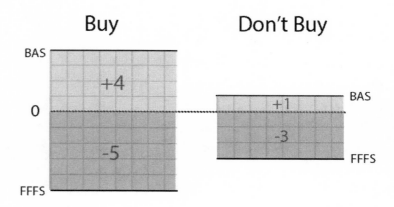

If we look at the net (or sum) of each gap (adding them together), we can see that the gap for buying the house has a net *loss* of -1 [4+(-5)] or [4-5], while the gap for not buying the house has a net *loss* of -2 [1+(-3)] or [1-3]. As -2 has a greater negative value than -1, the gap for *not buying* the house is considered to have a greater net negative than the gap for *buying* the house and therefore is the more dangerous choice and will have more anxiety associated with it. This means that with all things considered, and all of John's hopes and dreams and fears counted, his unconscious BIS will ultimately choose to buy the house, as the BIS always chooses the decision gap that has the least anxiety associated with it. The gap with the least anxiety, as far as the unconscious mind is concerned, is the least threatening to our survival, and therefore always the best choice.

This, I believe, is the main role of anxiety, and although we may think that we buy our houses and make other major decisions based on careful conscious deliberation of the pros and cons, most of the time, we really do not. The pros and cons might well help us to form our gaps, but ultimately, we go for the option that we need the most, or more likely, fear the least and the one that makes us feel less anxious, as that is the choice considered less threatening to our survival. We then rationalise it later.

Public speaking Revisited

Let's face it, most of us hate public speaking, and if it were left to a simple approach-avoidance gap, chances are the fears would win. The benefits of making a single speech rarely outweigh the perceived fears of losing our self-esteem, and if that were all there was, most of us would never walk on a stage in our lives. Luckily, though, that is not all there is. The double decision gap is in play in every situation, and therefore there are also fears related to not giving a speech.

In our previous example, Phil was terrified of giving his sales presentation, and the fear of losing his self-esteem would have outweighed his perceived benefits of that single act of bravery. But of course, Phil also knew that if he refused to do the speech, his boss would be angry, and it could affect his job and his future. Not only that, but his colleagues would think him weak, which would also negatively affect his self-esteem and his social connections. It is these perceived fears that would compel Phil to make the speech and override the fears of the speech itself. It would not, of course, diminish his anxiety.

	Speak	Don't Speak	
BAS			
	Impress boss, career boost, respect	Status Quo - safety	BAS
0			
	Mess it up - lose respect, lose self-esteem	Unhappy boss - career jeopardy lose respect, self esteem	
FFFS			FFFS

Peer Group Pressure - Asking for a Date Revisited

Much like in the public speaking example, most young boys would never get a partner if they relied on their own simple anxiety gaps to push them into asking for a date. Luckily, there is always peer group pressure to help. Peer group pressure is the pressure from friends or peers to try and push us into taking some form of action. This pressure can create its own anxiety gap based on the fear of disappointing these friends, losing their respect, and being ostracised from the group. The humiliation of being ridiculed for not acting is often enough to tilt the decision gaps in favour of asking for the date. This is the basis of peer group pressure in any given situation.

My Fairground Fear Revisited

When I was talking about my fear of fairgrounds in my younger years earlier, I said that it wasn't as simple as an approach-avoidance gap as there was more to it. Unfortunately, this is true. If I'm honest, the BAS for going to the fair was never particularly strong and it was more the fear of missing out and the peer group pressure from my friends that kept me going. Strangely enough, these days I find that I like theme park rides themselves, but I still hate going to fairs that are packed full of people and noise, and I can feel my anxiety rise when I go anywhere that vaguely resembles a fair.

Combining Decision Gaps

As I mentioned before, the idea of double decision gaps is simply a model to help visualise and simplify the conflict process in any decision, but to show why and how the BIS gets involved it is important (and useful) to show how the dual decision gaps can be combined to create a regular good old-fashioned approach-avoidance gap.

If we take the previous example of John buying his house, we can use the two decision gaps he created and combine them to form a single approach-avoidance gap made up of an approach of "buy the house" and an avoid of "don't buy the house". With the knowledge that the brain views an absent threat to be a gain, and an absent gain to be a loss, we can see that the fears that John has over not buying the house can easily become motivations for him to BUY the house. Conversely, any positive gains that he feels could be made by not buying the house, will then be added to the fears of loss that he already feels about buying the house.

In gap model form then, it results in adding the "buy the house" gap to the inverse of the "don't buy" gap (the don't buy gap turned upside down).

The Original Decision Gap

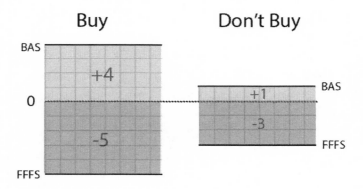

Decision Gap with Inverted "Don't Buy" Gap

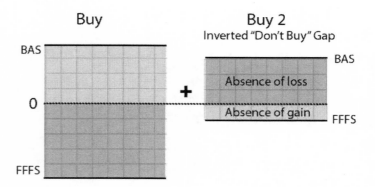

This means that the inverted "Don't buy" gap now offers an added BAS of +3 and an added FFFS of -1 to the overall approach – avoidance gap of buying the house.

As you can see in the image below, adding them together results in an overall gain score of 7 (4+3) and an overall loss score of -6 (-5 + -3), which gives John the overall net motivation score of +1 in favour of buying the house, which we have already seen he will do.

Combined Buy Gap

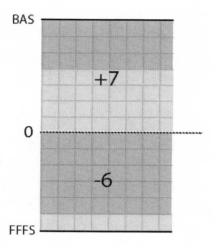

This can be done with all double decision gaps and shows how most decisions can be formed into simpler BAS-FFFS gaps, or at least gain-loss decisions.

Separating the decision gaps still has a role to play though, as it is much easier to construct them, easier to visualise the choices, and clearer to see the needs involved. It also allows us to see that both choices are primarily rooted in fear and so will generate feelings of anxiety based on the individual gaps, not the combined gap. As well as that, it also allows us to construct decision gaps with more than two choices without having to have a PhD in statistics. It also allows us to deal with approach-approach and avoid-avoid decisions much more easily, as we will see later.

Missed Needs

Combining gaps in this way, also allows us to explain why anxiety is felt when important needs are not met. As I have already mentioned, missing out on an expected and wanted need can be just as painful as losing a need that has already been gained (fear=frustration). Likewise, the avoidance of a painful loss can be just as joyful as the gaining of a positive need (hope=relief). This might seem a little hard to believe, but we can see it clearly in these two examples: How would you feel if you believed that you were about to lose your job through redundancy along with 50% of your company only to find out that you were being kept on? Nothing would have changed for you, your job is the same, but you would feel fantastic because you avoided the loss (unless you hate your job of course). Conversely, how would you feel if your lottery numbers came up and you thought you had won ten million dollars, only to find out that the ticket hadn't been bought this week? Again, nothing would have changed, but the loss of something you never had in the first place would make you feel terrible.

This doesn't just apply to major life upheavals like in these examples though. Small, everyday needs that are not met can cause anxiety, and can often be difficult to spot.

Taking Risks

If a decision is made by choosing the smallest net negative anxiety gap, then how is it that some people are natural thrill seekers, and enjoy putting their lives on the line for fun? Why do some people thrive on taking unnecessary risks? Are they breaking the rules and purposefully opting for the largest anxiety gap? Do they enjoy anxiety? The simple answer to both questions is no. Their personality and mindset naturally reduce the fear of the dangers they face and amplify the positives of the action as a need to push themselves and possibly compete, and they fear a life of boredom or being seen as a failure much more, thereby still making the smallest net negative gap the one in favour of the activity. It is still the result of combining their gaps to form large, but net positive, gaps that thrill-seekers perceive as excitement, that keeps them coming back for more.

If we look at a possible decision gap of a base jumper, we can see that the anxiety gaps are still in play as usual, and their decision process is the same as the rest of us. They just have different values and needs and therefore arrange their gaps differently to most people. I presume that they get more anxiety from doing nothing than during their thrill-seeking activities.

Jump	Don't Jump
BAS ————————	
Excitement & adrenaline	
	———————— BAS
0 ···	Security status quo ·············
	Fear of being boring
Fear of dying	Loss of self
	Loss of values
	Loss of respect
FFFS ————————	———————— FFFS

I must admit, this a total guess, as I am as far from a thrill-seeker as you can possibly get, unless you count the thrill of opening a bottle of wine on a Saturday night just before the football starts, but it is just an example to demonstrate how gaps and anxiety can make us do dangerous things as well as keep us away from them. What we fear most is the important thing, and not everybody fears the same things equally as we have already seen.

Chapter Three: Building the Gap

The Value Process

As we have already seen, the needs we want to gain or the needs we fear losing, along with the values we place on those needs, populate the gaps that are created for our decision making. But exactly how do our values of specific needs determine the size of those gaps, and how are we, as anxiety suffering individuals, supposed to consciously recognise the size of the gaps when much of the process goes on unconsciously?

For this we must look at the process that goes on within all of us between any given event in our lives and the emotion or action that seems to result from it. Many of us believe that any feeling, emotion, action, or response that we experience is directly caused by an external trigger. We say things like "you made me angry", or "that movie made me sad" or "this situation is making me anxious" as though events outside us have direct access to the way we feel. It certainly does feel like that at times, but it is not true, and although subtle, the difference between this idea and reality is an important distinction to make.

Our emotions, feelings, and responses are governed solely by the way we perceive the world around us; not by the world itself. We are solely responsible for how we feel in every situation (although very often it does not feel like it) and therefore solely responsible for the gaps that cause anxiety. We make ourselves angry, we make ourselves sad, and we make ourselves anxious. We do this with a very rapid three-step process that occurs between every stimulus and every response, that I like to call the *value process*, and while bodily *affect* (which I will talk about later) can influence this process, the resultant emotions are dependent on this value process alone. The three steps of this value process, that I have borrowed from Cognitive Behavioural Therapy (CBT), can be called *thought*, *inference*, and *evaluation* and they determine the needs and values within a gap and how big the gap is. They therefore determine, by themselves, how much anxiety we suffer.

Thought

Our minds are constantly filled with thoughts, some good and some bad, and every event, interaction, or situation conjures up a multitude of thoughts that run through possible scenarios, outcomes, or consequences of the situation at hand. These thoughts can range from the sublime to the ridiculous and most are dismissed out of hand without ever reaching conscious level, as the unconscious mind runs each thought[8] through the entire value process for validity and possible impact. The thoughts themselves carry no emotional value. They are just thoughts and will not elicit any kind of response until they have gone through the rest of the value process.

For example: Tom's partner was due home at 6:00 pm after work but still hasn't arrived home by 7:30 pm. A multitude of thoughts begin to race through Tom's mind. A few possible thoughts might be:

Something bad has happened (accident, abduction etc)
She has been caught up at work again.
She is having an affair.
She has probably gone for a drink with friends.
Maybe she has hired someone to kill me while she's out.

Each of these thoughts (and many more) might fleetingly cross Tom's mind, whether he notices them or not, but they will not elicit any kind of emotional response in Tom until they have been run through the entire value process. After all, they would all require quite different responses, and while his mind must make sure that all bases

---

[8] On making the right choice: the deliberation-without-attention effect | Dijksterhuis (2006)

are covered for Tom's own protection and survival, it doesn't want to unnecessarily waste resources, or risk unwanted action, on an unlikely or unimportant outcome.

As there are often too many thoughts running through the mind about any given situation for the conscious to deal with, the unconscious mind must use the value process to choose the thoughts that are most likely to result in gaining or losing needs. It must choose the thoughts that are most likely to impact our chances of survival, both physically and mentally. One of the ways that the mind will choose the most important thought is through the likelihood that it will happen. A thought that is likely to come true could be an important one to pay attention to. However, the mind does not base the choice of thoughts on likelihood alone. It must also take in to account the possible impact that the thought might have on survival. After all, the chances of Tom's wife having him murdered are quite slim, but if it is a possibility, then Tom can't afford to dismiss the notion out of hand as his life might depend on it. Therefore, the full value process must be completed before an overall winner, or winners, can be chosen, and the thought is only the first step.

Inference/Meaning

For each thought that is conjured up, the mind must generate a list of inferences. This is a list of things that could happen if the thought were true. It is the meaning associated with each thought. In other words, what does that mean to me? Each inference represents a consequence of the possible scenario shown in each thought, and each inference will often produce secondary inferences creating a knock-on effect of inferences. This is often done by the mind asking the question "what if that were true?" to the initial thought and each subsequent inference.

e.g., As one of Tom's thoughts might be "She's having an affair" his mind would then ask *what would happen then?* It might come up with the inference of "she will leave me". This might then prompt the inference of "I will be alone" followed by "I will lose the house" and finally "I'll never find anyone else" and possibly "I'll be alone and homeless".

This kind of inference chaining is done all the time by our minds but is different for each person and for every situation. The unconscious mind runs through lists of consequences to every possible scenario before we even realise that we're thinking about them. Why does the mind do this? Well, it's a survival mechanism. The brain's main objective is to try and see that our needs are met and that none of our needs are lost. This is the very core of survival and running through each possible scenario in a situation, both good and bad, like a computer programme, makes sure that we don't miss out on a possible threat or opportunity.

Of course, each inference on its own still holds no emotional value and therefore holds no weight in decision making until the mind decides on the impact of each scenario. To do this, the mind runs through the final step of the value process—evaluation.

Evaluation

The evaluation is where the unconscious mind puts weightings to each inference to determine how much impact each inference could have on our survival. The evaluation does this with a two-step weighting system: The first step is to determine how likely a thought or inference is to occur, and the second step is to determine what impact the said thought or inference would have on survival if it were to occur. For simplicities sake, we can think of this weighting system as being on a scale out of 10 (although of course the brain does not think of it like this) with the first step being between 0 and 10, and the second step between -10 and +10.

For the first weighting step, +10 would mean that we perceive the inference to be certain to occur, while 0 would indicate a perception that it will certainly not occur. This is the probability that our mind calculates for each thought or inference to occur. In Tom's example then, his mind might calculate that the chance of his wife having stopped for drinks is 9/10, while the probability of her having him murdered is only 0.01/10. If the first weighting were the only criteria, then of course the brain would always choose the most likely outcome and act accordingly, but this would mean that we would never be prepared for less likely but possibly much more damaging outcomes and would more than likely never survive as a species. Therefore, the second weighting step is also needed.

The second step is the mind calculating the impact of each inference on our survival on a scale between -10 to +10. At the very bottom of the scale, -10 would be seen as a catastrophic life-ending situation, and as we increase towards 0 the consequence is lessened. At 0 the situation would be deemed as causing no concern at all and would be neutral, neither good nor bad. The evaluation then rises again up to a possible maximum of +10, which would be the greatest thing that could possibly ever happen.

The mind quickly runs through each inference and weights it, as if with one of these scores, depending on the perceived impact on survival. The impact really stems from how much our unconscious minds value the needs that we might attain or lose, which is, of course, based on our own personal values. The higher the value of the need, the greater the impact evaluation. This is different for every person and for each specific situation and can change depending on current circumstances and current values. For example, a man who is head over heels in love with his wife and depends on her emotionally might be devastated by the thought of her leaving, while another who had become disillusioned in his marriage and was looking for a way out, might not really care that much at the thought of his wife leaving and may even feel a sense of relief or hope. This means, then, that no outcome has an intrinsic value, but is, instead, subjectively viewed as either good or bad through our own perception.

How is This Applied to Gaps?

So far, in our hypothetical situation of Tom's missing partner, his mind has generated a list of thoughts about things that might have happened, extrapolated those thoughts into inferences of what the consequences might be if the thoughts were true, and evaluated each inference for its likelihood of happening and how heavily it will impact his life. All of this is done, pretty much, without Tom even knowing about it. But how would this apply to gaps and anxiety? How does the brain determine which thoughts are the most important ones to pay attention to and which ones it can safely ignore? For this we must steal a little bit of simplified mathematics from economics class. I apologise in advance if you don't like maths.

As we have seen, for every inference generated, the mind creates a double-weighted evaluation comprising a likelihood score, or "perceived odds of happening", and an impact score, or "perceived value if happened". The two together can then help the mind determine which thoughts need to be paid attention to, and which can be ignored.

We can roughly follow the mind's process if we apply a simplified economics/decision theory equation for expected outcome (Bernoulli's equation[9]) and tweak the wording a little to account for the mind's subjective guesswork:

[9] Exposition of a New Theory on the Measurement of Risk (translation) | Bernoulli, Daniel (1954 orig.: 1738)

$$\text{Perceived Outocome} = \text{Perceived Odds of Happening} \quad x \quad \text{Perceived Value if Happened}$$

The relative size of the perceived outcome will determine how much attention needs to be paid to each thought and inference. A high positive perceived outcome means that a scenario could result in needs being met, while a "high" negative perceived outcome means that a scenario could represent a viable threat to needs and values. Once the mind has run through the process for each thought, performed its calculations and built a list of perceived outcomes, it will pick the inferences (with the associated needs/values to be gained or lost) with the greatest perceived outcomes, both positive and negative, and it will form a gap.

I should point out that the way the brain works, is of course much more complicated than this, but the above equation does allow us to model and follow the process and assign values for ease of understanding.

Example

Let's take a run through Tom's thoughts and a few example inferences that he might make to get a better idea of how this might work with both the odds and value being out of 10. Note that in this example the "Odds" is the "perceived odds of happening" and is scored between 0 and 10, while the "value" is the "perceived value if happened" and is scored between -10 and 10. This means that the "Outcome" or "perceived outcome", will result in a percentage score between -100% and +100%.

Thought/inference	Values/needs	Odds	Value	Outcome
Something bad has happened		1		
1. *I will lose my wife*	Love, connection	1	-9	-9%
2. *I can't cope without her*	Self-efficacy	0.5	-8	-4%
She's busy at work		8		
-*She's fine, she'll be home soon*	Social, love	8	1	8%
She's having an affair		0.5		
3. *I will lose her*	Love, social	0.5	-8	-4%
4. *Everyone will laugh*	Prestige, esteem	0.2	-7	-1.4%
5. *I will lose my home*	Security	0.3	-8	-2.4%
6. *I will be alone forever*	Social	0.1	-9	-0.9%
She's having drinks		9		
7. *She's fine and back soon*	Social, love	9	1	9%
Hired someone to kill me		0.001		
8. *I could die*	Safety	0.001	-10	-0.01%

These are just some examples to give you an idea of the process that the mind might go through to make sense of a situation and to ensure that Tom has the best possible chance to get his needs met and to avoid losing valuable needs. This is how the mind protects us.

You may have noticed that the perceived values of happening for the positive outcomes are quite low (1/10) and you may be thinking that the value should be higher for the safety of Tom's wife, but if you remember the brain's BAS system favours novel situations and the safety of Tom's wife is just the continuation of the status quo. This doesn't mean that Tom doesn't value his wife—in fact his fear of losing her shows that he obviously does—it just means that he doesn't get excited at the thought of her returning safely, he just hopes that she does. Her safety is not an approach drive and does not have to be when there is anxiety. In fact, the value I have assigned to her returning is probably too high, but as this is just an example, we will go with it.

Once Tom's brain has run through the value process for all of Tom's possible thoughts, it will choose the ones with the greatest perceived outcome and form a gap. In a survival scenario (which our minds consider is almost every scenario) this would make sure that Tom is concentrating on the most positive and most negative outcomes which puts him in a prime place to get his needs fulfilled and prevent him from losing valuable needs.

Tom's gap would be between the thought (hope) that his wife is just having drinks, and the thought (fear) that something bad has happened and he could lose her. Both thoughts have their highest absolute outcome at 9% which isn't particularly high, so although Tom might feel a little bit of anxiety, he will not be unduly stressed at this time. To simplify the gaps, and to be consistent with our gaps from before, it makes more sense to build the gaps with these percentage scores as values out of 10 and -10 instead. To do this we just divide the overall "outcome" percentage by 10, making 9% equal to 0.9.

His gap at this time can be seen below:

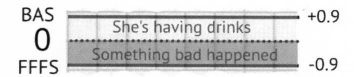

Of course, in real life it is possible to have more than one gap formed, and more than two thoughts chosen, but our unconscious minds usually offer our conscious minds only the simplest of options, and of course it makes it simpler for us here.

A Change in Time

As we know, anxiety can change with time as the likelihood of an outcome changes. If Tom was only feeling a little bit anxious at 7:30 pm, he would be feeling a lot more at 11:30 pm. At 11:30 pm, while the value of each outcome remains the same, the odds of his wife being out for a drink have reduced to 4, while the odds that something bad has happened have *increased* (in Tom's mind at least) to 5. This means that the perceived outcome for drinks has become 4% (4x1) and the perceived outcome for something bad happening has become -45% (5x-9). This would result in Tom being "frantic" as his anxiety levels soar due to the increase of activity in his FFFS.

Something bad has happened		5		
1. *I will lose my wife*	Love, connection	5	-9	-45%
She's having drinks		4		
2. *She's fine and back soon*	Social, love	4	1	4%

You can see Tom's gap at 11:30 pm below:

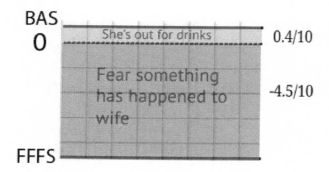

It is important to note that in situations like this where anxiety is present without a decision to make, a simple gap is in play, and anxiety is generated. Unfortunately, as there is no decision to make, there is not much control to be had over the situation or the anxiety, and so the BIS goes into overdrive to try and find a thought, a memory, anything, that might ease the anxiety. This results in worry, as no action can be found to solve or escape the situation.

Tom will find himself unable to think about much else as the worry takes hold and the anxiety gap about his wife grows by the hour.

Anxiety and Anger

This is also the reason that when Tom's wife finally comes home at midnight, he feels an overwhelming sense of relief as the anxiety gap is closed upwards. Of course, the release of the bottled frustration and anxiety could quickly get channelled into anger towards his wife for coming home late, and Tom will undoubtedly have a few chosen words with her on her arrival. It should be noted, though, that the anger in this case is not being caused directly by the original anxiety gap itself, as the anxiety is dissipated upon his wife's return, but instead the anger stems from Tom redirecting his thoughts to blaming his wife for his previous feelings of anxiety and channelling the remnants of chemicals such as adrenaline in his body to fuel his newfound rage.

Not every case works this way, though, as it *is* certainly possible for anger to stem directly from the anxiety created by an open gap, as many people cover their anxiety with anger during the anxious episode itself. They find the feelings of anxiety to be so uncomfortable that they cover them with the feelings of anger by creating thoughts of blame alongside the thoughts of possible loss, thereby hiding their anxiety under a blanket of rage. This is often the case with people who are considered angry people, as they assign blame whenever anxiety appears, to prevent them from feeling vulnerable or appearing weak to themselves, although we all do it to some degree when blame helps ease the anxiety a little by turning it into anger. Tom could have smothered his anxiety with anger before his wife returned with thoughts such as: "Why hasn't she called, she knows I will be worried", or "She's doing this on purpose", or "I knew she had someone else".

There would be no reason for Tom to get angry if anxiety was not present. In most situations of anger (if not all), if you look hard enough, you will find underlying anxiety. You will find gaps with blame.

Anxiety itself, then, is not an external threat or an emotional disorder, it is caused by the thought processes between stimulus and emotion. If my partner is angry and says she hates me, my emotional levels will be very different if I think "Oh she is just angry, she doesn't mean it" to if I think "she hates me, she is going to leave me, I will be left all alone". What person would not feel anxiety at the thought of being left alone? Anxiety is the rational and normal response to that situation. It is the thought and entire value process itself that is irrational and unhealthy, and it is this that is often behind anxiety disorders.

Association and Conditioned Learning

There are, of course, times when the reaction to a stimulus or situation seems to occur more automatically than the usual value process, and the gaps seem to be formed almost instantaneously. These are times when the brain uses association to relate the current situation to something that happened in the past. This is called conditioned learning and can be either positive or negative. The most famous conditioned learning experiment is Pavlov's dogs[10]. This is an example of positive association, as when Pavlov fed his dogs, he also rang a bell. Eventually the dogs associated the bell with food and would begin to salivate upon hearing it even if no food was present.

---

[10] The Work of the Digestive Glands | Pavlov, I. P. [1902]
Conditioned Reflexes: An Investigation of the Physiological
Activity of the Cerebral Cortex | Pavlov, I. P. [1927]

On the negative association side, sadly, we have poor Little Albert[11]. In an experiment that would hopefully never get past the approval stage today, John B Watson at Johns Hopkins University, at the beginning of the twentieth century, took a healthy nine-month-old baby with no phobias, whom they called Albert, and subjected him to an experiment like Pavlov's. They initially introduced Little Albert to a white rat and observed no fear from the infant, but whenever the boy touched the rat, they would hit a steel pipe with a hammer producing a loud jarring sound which made the boy cry. Over many trials Albert began to associate the white rat with the loud noise and eventually reached the point where he would cry as soon as he saw the rat and try to crawl away. The saddest part is that the research team claimed they didn't have time to undo the conditioning, and Albert left the University with an intense fear of rats and mice, which apparently grew to include rabbits and dogs and anything furry as he grew up.

Little Albert's ordeal is a cruel but profound example of negative conditioned learning and shows how easily the brain can learn to associate situations or objects to generate fear or anxiety without the subject understanding why. This is how most phobias are created, but it can also play a role in anxiety, as the brain makes quick associations in the memory and activates the FFFS. It is not that the value process is absent in these situations, it is just that this value process has been run through so many times to make it almost automatic. The brain needs no conscious help for this and can run through the value process instantly. It uses memory to help simplify and speed up the process to make it more efficient.

Associations like these can range from the severe to the seemingly more innocuous. An example of a severe association might be the case of a child who is abused by her father every time he is drunk. She may learn to associate the smell of alcohol on her father's breath with the

---

[11] Conditioned emotional reactions | Watson, J. B., & Rayner, R [1920]

86

abuse, and this may lead later in life to intense anxiety whenever she smells alcohol on someone else's breath. It may be someone she loves who has never hurt her, and she may not even know the cause, but intense anxiety will erupt and cause her serious social and mental distress.

A less traumatic example could be a student who takes very stressful exams who might begin to associate the large exam hall with their stress and will become anxious every time they enter an exam hall.

There are many possibilities for people to make negative associations with places and for these places to evoke anxiety. A child who is bullied at school may begin to get anxiety every time they see a school. A child who was always punished for fidgeting in church may experience anxiety in future churches.

There is an unlimited number of things, people, or places that the brain can use to make associations. Anything that was perceived as a threat in an earlier time and activated the FFFS will be stored in memory with all the associated sights, smells, sounds and feelings that accompanied it. Anything that crops up later in life with a sight, sound, smell or feeling that the brain thinks is sufficiently close to the ones in memory to be a possible threat will provoke an FFFS threat response, generate a gap, and trigger fear or anxiety.

Habits

One of the biggest drivers of our actions and therefore one of the biggest causes of anxiety is habit. Habits are caused by conditioning, like we saw above with association, but can be discussed separately as they are a specific form of association that we all experience in everyday life. After all, we all have habits, be they good or bad, but not all our associations will lead to habits[12].

A simplified reason for habit conditioning is what is called "Hebb's law"[13]. Hebb's law has been described with the statement "neurons that fire together, wire together", which means that whenever two sets of neurons are activated at the same time consistently, they "fuse" together, and will continue to act together in the future. As habits are a specific form of association, this is how both habits and associations are made. In the case of Pavlov's dogs, the arrival of dinner resulted in the firing of one set of neurons, while hearing the bell resulted in the firing of a different set of neurons. Because these two sets of neurons were made to fire together many times, they ended up "fusing together" and so every time the dogs heard the bell, both sets of neurons would fire. This is the basics of conditioning, and conditioning is the basis of our habits.

Smoking is the easiest demonstration of Hebb's law and habits, because as well as the obvious physical addiction, there is also a mental habit component, as all smokers will have their "triggers" that cause them to light up. Whether it be after a meal, drinking coffee, or reading a newspaper, certain places or activities have had their associated neurons fused with those for smoking a cigarette and so the two actions are forever intertwined. In fact, beating the mental habit can be the most difficult part of quitting smoking. Even now, after quitting smoking for years, certain activities or places will trigger a small twinge of desire for a cigarette within my brain. This mental habit is true for all addictions.

Smoking, and addiction in general, is, of course, not the only habit that we can acquire. Anything done enough times can be turned into a habit. Automating repetitive actions reduces brain power and is

---

[12] The role of the basal ganglia in habit formation| Yin, H. H., Knowlton, B. J (2006)
[13] The organization of behavior: A neuropsychological theory | Hebb, D. O. [1949]

therefore made into a habit by our unconscious to make our lives easier and enable us to concentrate on other things. Things as simple as brushing our teeth become habits so we don't have to waste mental energy on reminding ourselves to do it.

The reason habits are important here, though, is because, much like association, they can play a significant role in affecting anxiety. The simplest way that habits affect anxiety is through avoidance. If certain situations cause anxiety, but avoidance of those situations results in the relief of that anxiety, then our brains will form a habit of avoidance, because it will be considered a positive outcome by our unconscious mind. We will begin to avoid situations that cause anxiety without really thinking about it. It will be the default action and can mean we miss out on a lot of the good things in life. I have certainly been guilty of this throughout my life.

Another way that habit can result in anxiety is through prolonged and frequent negative mental thoughts. If a negative mental thought process leads to a positive outcome of reduced anxiety, whether that be through finding an answer to an anxiety-inducing problem or instigating avoidance, it can lead the brain to believe that the negative mental thought was a good thing, as it resulted in a positive outcome. If this happens enough times, the brain will learn to automatically throw up this same negative thought process in the future, as it believes it is good for relieving anxiety. The problem is, of course, that this leads to a habit of negative thinking which has only a tiny success rate of relieving anxiety but fills the mind with constant negative thoughts in the vain hope that "this time it will work". This is the kind of habit that typifies anxiety sufferers.

Both habits and association can also be formed through learned conditioning as we grow up. If our caregivers are overprotective and fearful of us making our way in the world, forbidding us to do things because they are deemed dangerous, or doing everything for us to keep us safe, then we can grow up seeing threats where there are none.

Through association and habit, our brains become overly sensitive and perceive the everyday world as a threat to be avoided. We would see needs that could be lost in the most mundane situations, and gaps formed everywhere we looked.

The Conscious Role in Decision Making

Most of us like to believe that all the decisions that we make are consciously deliberated on and purposefully made; we like to believe that we are in control, but if you really think about it, it is easy to see that most decisions are made without our knowing. We only need to consider how many people consistently make the wrong decisions to see this, and by wrong decisions I mean decisions that are detrimental to themselves and make no sense to anyone else. The people who stay in damaging relationships, stay in jobs they hate, or buy things that they know they do not need. These, and many decisions like them, are certainly not logically made decisions, but are made because of the anxiety and fear that is rooted in faulty beliefs and values but are then justified by the conscious mind.

This justifying of decisions by the conscious mind was cleverly demonstrated by the neuroscientist Joseph Ledoux in his ground-breaking studies of split-brain patients[14]. Split-brain patients are those individuals that have had their left and right brain hemispheres surgically separated, usually because of severe epilepsy, leaving the two hemispheres unable to communicate between themselves as they do in the rest of us.

This has some interesting consequences as Ledoux demonstrated when he gave the right side of the brain the command to wave (the right side of the brain is connected to the left eye so can be communicated with separately). When the person waved, he then asked the left side of the brain (via the right eye) why the person was waving. As the left side of the brain is the centre of language, it allowed the person to speak, but as it had no idea about the command given to the right side, it also had no idea why the person had waved, but

---

[14] A divided mind: Observations on the conscious properties of the separated hemispheres | Joseph E. Ledoux PhD, Donald H. Wilson MD, Dr. Michael S. Gazzaniga PhD (1977)
Emotions and the dual brain - G Gainotti, C Caltagirone [1989]

instead of saying "I don't know", the conscious mind invented a reason, and the person said that he had seen someone that he knew outside the window. This is astonishing and demonstrates that the conscious mind is more than happy to invent reasons for decisions that have been made without its knowledge. LeDoux repeated this many times with different actions, and every time the conscious mind created an explanation. It seems that the conscious mind does not like to be without an explanation and has no problem fabricating one at any time.

Does this mean, then, that the conscious mind has no part to play in decision making at all? Well, nobody yet can say for certain, but it does seem that it plays a much smaller role than most people would like to believe, but it appears that, at the very least, the conscious mind can be used critically to think about the thoughts and decisions that are being made unconsciously and change them. This kind of critical thinking is called metacognition and is the way that humans can overcome our natural decision making and behaviour and change them to be more in line with what is more logical and really in our best interests. As you will see in the next section, I am of the belief that metacognition is simply a mental, conscious, tool for manipulating the gaps in our favour.

In real life, when we are experiencing anxiety, we never think of the values/needs that we might gain or lose, they never cross our mind at all, and in fact, in many cases, we might wonder if values or needs are present at all. What is important to remember is that the value/need gaps are constructed entirely by the unconscious, and very often the unconscious does not allow us access to that information. Sometimes we can have anxiety without even realising why, but other times the values/needs will manifest themselves in our conscious brains as thoughts, and the conscious will generate a meaning, be it right or wrong.

Decision Complexity and the Unconscious

The decisions that we make can lie anywhere on a linear scale from simple to complex depending mainly on the number of factors to be considered in the decision-making process. The simplest decisions consisting of a couple of variables, such as which of two men is taller, or would you prefer $10 or $5, can be made by the conscious mind (or at least appear to be) as it can easily decide between a few things, but as the decision begins to get more complex and involve more variables, such as which employee we should hire, then the vast bulk of the number crunching is done by the unconscious mind. It is worth remembering that the conscious mind has been estimated to be able to deal with around 50 bits of information per second, while the unconscious mind is thought to be able to crunch around 11 million bits per second. Now, while these exact numbers might be a little questionable, are way too confusing to understand, and certainly not without controversy, the huge difference between the two highlights that the unconscious mind does the bulk of the heavy lifting.

Of course, sometimes we may think that the conscious mind makes the decision because we may believe the decision is easier than it is, but as we have already seen, very often the conscious is simply giving the rubber stamp and taking credit for the hard work of the unconscious. A simple example might be the seemingly easy decision of when to cross the road. We may think that it is a straightforward decision that the conscious mind is making, but the unconscious mind is making a multitude of calculations that quickly weigh up the speed and direction of the cars, the perceived aggressiveness of each driver, and our expected walking speed in current footwear. Eventually it will throw up a result and probably instigate the crossing before the conscious mind has even had time to applaud itself on such a smart decision.

Of course, just because most choices are made by the unconscious, does not necessarily mean that they all involve anxiety.

This would be extremely implausible as the human mind is a complicated machine, and not all decisions will involve a threat mechanism of some kind. I think it is fair to say, though, that many of the decisions we make on a day-to-day basis, do involve anxiety, especially those that rely on values and incorporate social expectations. For our purposes here, though, it does not really matter how many of our decisions are directed by anxiety, because we are not looking at decisions in general, we are looking at anxiety. This means that although not all our decision will be anxiety-led decisions, we can say with certainty that all the decisions that cause our anxiety are anxiety-led decisions, and as we are specifically looking at what causes anxiety, these are the only decisions we care about.

For our purposes here, then, we will be looking at only those decisions that are mediated by, and cause, anxiety.

Free Will

As mentioned earlier, the conscious mind can and does play a part in the decision-making process on occasion, and this is what is commonly, and popularly, known as free will. The concept and discussion of free will is beyond the scope of this book, but I understand that it is a very important concept for many people, and some may struggle to get past this point without a brief clarification, so I will discuss it here a little more.

I certainly don't want to get into a deep philosophical debate about the meaning and existence of free-will, but all I will say is that just because your conscious mind may not be aware that a decision is being made, does not mean that you are not making the decision. People seem to believe that their conscious mind makes them who they are, but it can certainly be argued that our unconscious minds play a much bigger role in making us who we are than our conscious, and therefore when our unconscious makes decisions, it is still we who make those decisions even if we aren't consciously aware that we are doing so. After all, our unconscious is the seat of all our beliefs, values, and memories, so could there really be a better part of us that makes us who we are?

A simple analogy to this might be a large multinational company like Amazon. The head of Amazon and chief decision maker is currently Jeff Bezos, but Jeff Bezos is not Amazon. Amazon is made up of over half a million employees, each involved in a management structure with supervisors that make decisions every day. For most decisions made in Amazon, Jeff Bezos will have no knowledge of them being made. He won't even care. Amazon will continue to operate on a day-to-day level with no input from Bezos. Sure, he will get feedback from each of the departments, and the big decisions that he makes will be based on the feedback from each of these departments that has been gleaned from millions upon millions of individual decisions that have been made throughout the year.

Does Jeff Bezos have free reign to make all decisions for Amazon's future? Probably not. Board members and shareholders will no doubt make sure that any decision that is made is done so with the feedback of the company, the success of the shareholders, and a predefined mission in mind. Within those constraints he probably has a good deal of room to manoeuvre, but I doubt he could do anything crazy that would put the company in jeopardy. Calculated risk, yes; all out suicide mission? Probably no t.

In this analogy, then, we are Amazon, and our conscious minds are Jeff Bezos. This is how we act as humans. Much of our day-to-day running is done without any conscious knowledge. Even most of the decisions we make are made without conscious knowledge. The ones that are made (or at least known about) consciously are made based on evidence gathered, and risk assessments performed, by our unconscious. Whether we make that final decision consciously or are just simply putting the rubber stamp to it is certainly hotly debated, but for our purposes, it doesn't really matter. Either way, we are still making the decision, and most of the legwork is being done by the unconscious, especially when those decisions are based on the protection and self-preservation of ourselves and our mental well-being.

Of course, on occasion, as already stated, our unconscious might be leading us down a detrimental path, and our conscious mind must step in. This can be done through a logically reasoned decision, or, more commonly, with what we know as "willpower".

Willpower

One of the ways that the conscious mind can be used to make a decision and override (or at least aid) the unconscious mind is through what is sometimes called willpower.

Willpower is used whenever an instantly gratifying impulse is set against a possibly negative future consequence—like refusing that last piece of pie (the instant gratification) because it will make you fat (the unwanted future consequence)—or when a current hardship is endured through the promise of future gains—like going to the gym every day (a daily hardship) to turn a flabby belly into a set of washboard abs (the future gain). Basically, whenever an approach-avoidance decision gap is formed between the present and the future, willpower can come into play. Willpower seems to be conscious in so far as it brings our attention to the future consequences and helps the unconscious mind alter the gaps accordingly. Our conscious mind can help concentrate on a specific consequence and therefore artificially, but only temporarily, change the gap.

A simple example is the cake or no cake decision when the dessert trolley is wheeled round at the end of a meal. If we are full, then the decision is much easier, but if we have a little bit of room left, have a sweet tooth, and that mound of oozing chocolate is pulled up next to us, the decision can be much harder. In fact, with the instant gratification of a chocolatey glucose hit looming large, and the real-world consequence of dessert being relatively minor, the easy decision is to throw caution to the wind and tuck in and go for the all-you-can-eat dessert platter. After all, our instinct is to get as many calories as we can to survive. With a little bit of attention though, we might feel the bulge of our belly against our already overstrained belt and realise that we might have to expand to a new notch yet again, or we imagine the shame we will feel when we tell our friends that we ate half a pound of cheesecake, or we feel the guilt of breaking the promise we made to ourselves only yesterday lunchtime. The attention brought to these possible consequences (that could negatively affect other needs), and the added importance that it brings to them, can change the decision gap in favour of leaving the cake tray unmolested and opting for a consolation coffee instead.

One problem with the whole concept of willpower, though, is that like many things it is very controversial now. Baumeister and his colleagues did lots of studies that showed that willpower was a depletable energy source that could be used up when used too much, but recent studies seem to have come to very different conclusions and show that willpower can remain intact[15].

In situations where willpower is being used to favour future outcomes, I am of the belief that willpower is solely bringing attention to consequences, and therefore altering the decision gaps in favour of our future selves. This means that willpower is not a mysterious energy within us, but it is simply directed attention which, of course, cannot be used up, but it can be affected by mental fatigue when overused. Mental fatigue doesn't mean that you can no longer bring attention to

---

[15] Ego depletion and the strength model of self-control: a meta-analysis | Hagger, M. S., Wood, C., Stiff, C., & Chatzisarantis, N. L. [2010]
No evidence of the ego-depletion effect across task characteristics and individual differences: A pre-registered study | Dang, J. et. al., [2018]

your gaps, but it might mean that the consequences seem less important than they otherwise might, and so you might decide not to bother bringing your attention. For example, if we have had a tough day at work, or an argument with our partner, we may well say "What the hell, I deserve some hot fudge sundae". It is also why ice cream seems like such a good idea when we are upset, even when we are dieting. The consequences just seem a little less important than they did before. This is also the reason there is always chocolate near the checkout in supermarkets—they know we are tired after shopping and no longer have the mental energy to resist. The consequences of a single chocolate bar seem trivial when we are worn out and hungry.

We can use this idea of mental fatigue to explain the results of Baumeister's famous experiment where students were broken into two groups and taken individually into a room filled with the smell of freshly baked cookies in the air and a bowl of cookies sitting on the table. One group of students was allowed to indulge themselves with the cookies while the other group was told to eat radishes and had to resist the temptation to eat the cookies. Once this part of the study had finished, the students were given puzzles to complete, that were impossible to solve, and timed how long they tried to solve them before they gave up. The cookie eaters, and a control group that had not been in the cookie room, lasted over twice as long on the puzzles as the radish eaters. Baumeister and his colleagues took this result to show that using their willpower to resist eating the cookies left the radish eaters with less willpower for the puzzles, and so they gave up earlier.

This was a landmark study on willpower and was accepted as fact for years until more and more studies began to dispute the idea that willpower can be used up. In fact, studies seem to show that when people believed that willpower could be used up, they gave up on things quicker than those that did not.

If we think of willpower as simply the application of attention to consequences, though, we can see that while the cookie eaters could relax and chomp on their cookies, the radish eaters had to concentrate on the idea that they were part of a study and convince themselves of the negative consequences if they ate the cookies. This mental exercise would have resulted in a little bit of mental fatigue, and probably not a small amount of irritability, which they would have carried into the puzzle room. Now, while the radish eaters could have continued with the puzzles for as long as the cookie eaters if they had wanted to, their slight mental fatigue (and probable bad mood for the unfairness of having to forego the cookies) would have affected the attention they brought to the consequences of not doing the puzzles. The positives of persevering with the puzzles would have seemed lessened, and the negative consequences of quitting would also have seemed reduced. I can almost hear the students thinking "screw this puzzle, I want cookies, what are they going to do anyway?". This would have made the quitting gap the more favourable outcome way before it would have for the cookie eaters (who might also have felt a little indebted to the scientists for the free cookies). But they could easily have continued if they had perceived the consequences more damaging.

Non-Approach-Avoidance Gaps

Avoidance-Avoidance Decisions

Imagine a young boy who has a choice to make between doing his chores as dictated by his mother or doing his homework that is due tomorrow, and he only has time for one. Neither of these is particularly appealing, yet the decision of which one to do will certainly cause him anxiety, and neither is going to fill him with excitement to complete. Of course, he may get a sense of satisfaction at the end of completing either, but as a reward, satisfaction certainly seems a little feeble.

This is what psychologists would call an avoidance-avoidance decision—two things that we would rather avoid doing altogether but must choose one. How does that work? How does this kind of choice tie into our model of using gaps?

Well, we would again have to construct two gaps for a decision to be made between them, only this time the approach line would probably not reach far above the reference line as satisfaction tends not to rank highly on a young boy's things-he-wants-to-do scale, and pleasing his parent or teacher often lags far behind the fear of annoying them.

The first gap, then, would be the "do homework" gap. The approach for doing homework would be low as it is not generally considered to be a fun activity and would consist of solely the possible satisfaction of completion or possibly the feel-good notion of pleasing the teacher and getting a metaphorical pat on the back the next morning. The FFFS line, however, would be based on the fear that if he did the homework, he could not do the chores. This would make for a possibly angry mother and conjure up all the negative consequences that are related to having an unhappy mother when all her anger is directed at the young boy.

Likewise, doing the chores would have an FFFS line linked to not doing the homework and possibly provoking unsavoury repercussions from the teacher the next day.

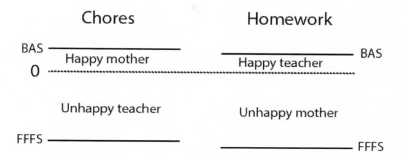

Now remembering that a dual decision gap can be converted into a single gap, since an absence of a loss is considered a gain to our brains, this dual gap would trigger anxiety and the BIS would go through its risk assessment routine and consider the winner to be that with the least negative outcome (which in the above example would be to do chores). It would weigh up all the times he had disappointed his mother, and what the consequences were, against previously encountered situations where he had disobeyed the teacher. Whichever seemed the "lesser of the two evils" would be the outright winner. Of course, whichever he chose, there would still be the fear and anxiety of repercussions from whichever authority figure he disobeyed, but the anxiety from the decision would be gone, and once the next day rolled around and the punishment determined, all fear and anxiety would be gone. If, however, the decision was not made, and neither chores nor homework were done, then fear and anxiety for both would remain.

The main thing to note here, though, is that even though the decision may be considered an avoidance-avoidance decision, it is still, in fact, an approach-avoidance decision, but with extremely limited approach motivations. (If there is no approach motivation at all, then there is no uncertainty, and we are left only with fear or despair)

Approach - Approach Decisions

In late 1996, just over a year after I finished university, I decided that I was going to postpone the decision of choosing an appropriate career and do the old "solo traveller" thing for a few months. I decided that I would work my socks off for 6 months or so, save every penny that I could, and then jet off for 6 months of backpacking. The only thing left to do, was to decide where to go. After some time, I had narrowed the possible options down to two—Europe or Southeast Asia. Both had huge positives going for them, and both had places that I had always wanted to visit, so how would I choose between them? How does anyone choose between two things that both look awesome?

This is what psychologists would call an Approach-Approach decision. A decision between two things, both of which we want. After doing enough research on each decision, it can often boil down to two things—finding something that we want more or finding something that we fear happening or missing out on, or might regret, more. My choices, for example, threw up the positives of better, more consistent, weather, different cultural experiences, and quality Asian food for Southeast Asia, while Europe was what I perceived to be easier to travel through alone and had historical sites that I had learned about in history class, not to mention quality beer. I ultimately chose Southeast Asia, but not for any of the positive reasons that I researched or mentioned before. Oddly enough, it was the fact that I considered Europe easier to travel around that swung the balance. I'm not sure if it was a fear of giving into my own fears that made me not want to choose Europe, or a fear of other people thinking I had taken the easy option, but my main reason for choosing Southeast Asia in the end was because I perceived it to be more difficult, not because it had something better. Of course, as I am still living in Southeast Asia to this day, it appears that I made the correct decision even if the reasoning may have been a little suspect.

This demonstrated—to me at least—that even approach-approach decisions, are double approach-avoidance decision gaps, as very often the fear of missing out on something, or the possible social repercussions of our choice, can play as much a part in our decision making as the good stuff, and as much as it might seem like a choice is between two almost perfect options, there is always a downside to every decision, and therein lies the fear. Looking for possible regret can often be more enlightening than looking for the joy. It is not a very heartening thought, but that doesn't make it untrue.

This is why I believe the double decision gaps are more useful than the traditional approach-avoidance, avoidance-avoidance, or approach-approach gaps, as they allow us to see the good and bad, or the hope and fear, behind all decisions, but also allow us to build gaps with more than two choices. For example, if I had also had South America in my sights (which I did for a while), then I could have built decision gaps for all three choices with ease. Something that is a lot more difficult with the traditional view.

Unfinished Bell-Ringers

Most people have many things that they need to do. Some of those things are important; some not so much. For most people, though, there are a bunch of things that need doing in their life, but they have put them off until an unspecified later date. These things can be as major as expressing love to an unaware sweetheart or writing a book, or as simple as changing the batteries in the TV remote. The only thing that these things have in common, is that they are not done. They are unfinished business. The problem with any kind of "unfinished business" is that it becomes a "bell ringer" for anxiety. I call it a bell ringer, because, like Pavlov's dogs, it produces anxiety in a person without that person fully understanding why or even being aware of the trigger. They may feel that something is missing but can't quite put their finger on it.

The problem with these to-do things that are never done is that, although we may feel that we forget about them, our unconscious never does, and unfortunately for us, our anxiety is built from our unconscious. We can basically look at any possible undone act, any unfinished task, or any unaccomplished goal that we feel we should have done, and we can construct a gap—and we do. All the time. In scientific terms, this is called the Zeigarnik Effect, named after psychologist Bluma Zeigarnik who noticed that waiters could remember hugely complex orders, but only while the orders were still open. As soon as the order was complete and paid for, it was also forgotten. This led her to conduct many behavioural experiments[16] around this effect and how it could affect motivation and memory, and she found that unfinished tasks created what she termed a "tension field" that kept the task in unconscious memory until the task was completed. The tension field is certainly a good name for anxiety.

Baumeister and Tierney continued this research and wrote about it in their book "Willpower: Rediscovering the Greatest Human strength" where they determined that the Zeigarnik effect will in fact keep an unfinished task in unconscious memory until such time that the conscious mind makes a concrete plan of how to complete the task. They discovered that the unconscious mind is not trying to solve the problem, or even make a plan itself, but is simply trying to remind the conscious mind to make a plan. Once a plan is in place, the unconscious mind can strike that problem off the list. Of course, a plan needs to be a detailed one, and cannot simply be "I must do that one

---

[16] Das Behalten erledigter und unerledigter Handlungen [Memory for completed and uncompleted actions] | Zeigarnik, B. (1927).
On finished and unfinished tasks | Zeigarnik, B. (1938)
Über das Behalten von erledigten und unerledigten Handlungen [On the retention of completed and uncompleted actions] | Zeigarnik, B., & Bäuml, K. H. (1980).

day" because that is not a plan and is just what we do to every single unfinished task on our lists. But if we write in our diaries "complete that task tomorrow at 10:00 am"—that is a plan. Of course, if we then fail to follow through on that plan, it will be thrown back in the mixer of undone things and pop up again as a bellringer later.

So why don't we just do these things? Why do we leave these things unfinished if they cause us anxiety? Well, the main reason we leave simple things undone is because they are often avoid-avoid decisions and so the incentive is based more on fear than reward. We don't change the batteries in the remote because it is inconvenient to go the shops to buy more, (and of course the unconscious mind would never remind us to buy more when we are at the store, but only when we need the remote) but we also worry that if we don't, we will one day be unable to change the channel. Anxiety is in-built, and when we leave the things undone, we leave anxiety to run rampant.

But how can going to the shops to buy batteries be considered a fear? Surely there is nothing in expending a bit of energy that might trigger the FFFS. Well, firstly there is the fear of missing out on doing something more interesting than the job at hand. Never underestimate the fear of missing out—it plays a powerful role in our lives and has certainly not been overlooked by the creators of social media apps. Secondly, what to us might appear laziness, or an aversion to exercise, could well have been considered a life-or-death decision by our ancestors. For our ancestors, wasting energy on a meaningless task could have been deadly. If a predator attacks while exhausted, then our ancestor's chances of survival would have been drastically reduced, and so energy was used extremely judiciously. A waste of energy would have been putting the body, or family, or home, in jeopardy, and would have been frowned upon by the unconscious mind and could have been deterred with a brief splash of FFFS[17].

[17] Neuroendocrine Circuits Governing Energy Balance and Stress Regulation: Functional Overlap and Therapeutic Implications | Yvonne M. Ulrich-Lai 1, Karen K. Ryan [2014]

Risking all of this over a couple of batteries? Not worth it.

This would come as no real surprise to neuroscientists, as it has long been known that there is a large overlap of neural circuits between those that govern energy balance in the body and those that trigger the stress response, and they have been shown to affect each other in many situations[18]. It has also been shown that it requires more brain power to avoid being lazy than it does to avoid exercise[19]. The brain is all about efficient use of energy to aid survival. To be honest, the idea that energy intake and expenditure is linked to stress levels, probably shouldn't come as too big a shock to anyone, because who doesn't like a big old tub of ice cream when they're stressed?

It should be noted though, that a hardwired instinct to conserve energy should not be used as an excuse to become a couch potato. That brings with it far more problems with the Self and anxiety than it solves and is going to make the problem worse not better.

These fears of missing out and wasting energy can lead to the formation of gaps for unfinished chores: Here is a simple example of a gap for an unpleasant chore—mowing the lawn. Does Dave mow or not mow?

This is basically a decision gap between mowing the lawn, and not mowing the lawn. The gain side for mowing the lawn is not too impressive and is based solely on the aesthetic need of having a nice-looking lawn at the end of it and the pride of doing a good job. The losses, though, are the inconvenience of doing it in the first place and the primeval fear of wasting energy on a meaningless task that has no survival benefit. In other words, Dave can't be bothered. On the no-

---

[18]upreregulation: Functional overlap and therapeutic implications | Ulrich-Lai, Y. M., & Ryan, K. K. (2014)
Neurocircuitry of stress: Central control of the hypothalamo-pituitary-adrenocortical axis | Herman, J. P., & Cullinan, W. E. (1997)
Central nervous system control of metabolism | Myers, M. G., Jr., & Olson, D. P. (2012)
[19] Avoiding sedentary behaviors requires more cortical resources than avoiding physical activity | Cheval et. al., (2018)

mow side, the gain is simply the satisfaction of doing something significantly more enjoyable than mowing the lawn, which, of course, is absolutely anything at all. The loss on the other hand would be based around the fear of an unhappy spouse, or more likely, sneering, and judgemental neighbours, which could cause all kinds of havoc with self-esteem, prestige, and social ranking.

Mow   Don't Mow

BAS _____   _____ BAS

        Nice Lawn   Avengers Movie
        Pride
0   ....

                        Angry Wife
        Wasted Energy   Sneering neighbours
                        _____ FFFS

FFFS _____

As we can see in the above diagram, Dave decides not to mow because the grass is not too long, and therefore the neighbours not too sneering and the wife is not overly upset. Not to mention the new Avengers movie is on the TV, which he has been waiting weeks to watch. This makes the "don't mow" gap less negative overall than the "mow" gap and therefore the obvious choice.

But these two gaps are not fixed. As the grass grows, so too will Dave's fear of being judged by the neighbours, and so will his anxiety for the unfinished task. Whenever he least expects it, his unconscious will fling the lawn into his conscious mind and ask for an update, and the longer he ignores it, the more the anxiety will grow and fester. Eventually, though, he will reach a day where he is feeling bored with nothing on TV, his need for a beautiful garden will be at an all-time high, he feels particularly sensitive about his neighbours, or the grass reaches an intolerable length. Or, more likely, his wife has finally had enough. If all those things somehow happened at the same time, then the gaps would look like this:

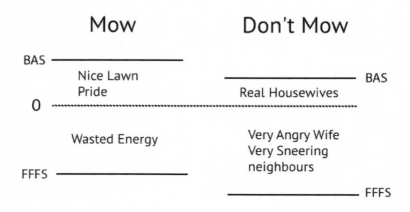

And Dave would finally mow the lawn.

Loss Aversion

When I was in high school, I was the second fastest runner in my year. Not at long distance of course, my short legs were never designed to run anything with bends, but at the 70 m sprint I was king. Well second anyway. I had come second in virtually every 70m race there had been during my years at high school, but I could never beat K (name abbreviated obviously). That kid ran like a coked-up cheetah. The problem was I never really believed I could beat him and, although I tried every time and would have loved to have snapped that imaginary tape before him, I knew inside that it was probably never going to happen.

When sports day of my final year rolled around, I was in the final of the 70 metres again, facing K. This would be the last race I ever ran at high school, in fact, as it turns out, it would be the last competitive race I would ever run again. The stakes were high. The problem with the 70 metres is it's not very long. This is great for people like me with short legs and the stamina of a potato, but it is not so great if you get a bad start—there's not a lot of time to make up for lost ground. And boy did I have a bad start. The start was so bad in fact, that by the time I had reached the halfway stage I had only managed to claw my way back to third. I was behind K in first place, and D in second. D was fast, I knew that, but I couldn't come in third in my last race.

I still to this day don't know how I did what I did, but for the next few seconds of that race, I know I have never run so fast, or physically exerted myself so much, in my life before or since. My legs burned and my lungs screamed, but I pushed myself beyond my limit. I pushed myself to a physical speed I didn't know I had. And I came second. I managed to beat D with a Herculean effort I had never displayed before, all because of the threat of losing my second place standing.

I honestly believe if I could have had a good start, and run like that, I would have had a chance of beating K. But I could never summon that kind of effort to win. Maybe it's because I didn't believe I could, or maybe I didn't want it enough, but I know I never felt that much pain when I ran before, and never went as fast. The fear of losing and coming third was greater than the drive of winning the race and forced me to find physical reserves I didn't know I had. I can still feel what I felt during that race to this day. And most of it came from blind stubbornness not to come third.

I'm not an oddball here though, this is true for most people—the fear of losing something outweighs the pleasure of gaining something. This is called "loss aversion" and it has been estimated that the pain of losing is psychologically about twice as powerful as the pleasure of gaining[20]. This is one of the reasons that the FFFS is such a powerful

---

[20] Loss aversion in riskless choice: A reference-dependent model | Tversky, A., & Kahneman, D. (1991).
Beyond valence: Toward a model of emotion-specific influences on judgement and choice | Lerner, J. S., & Keltner, D. (2000)

motivator, why gaps are easily influenced by the thought of loss, and why anxiety is so prevalent.

Closing a Gap

As we already know by now, anxiety is caused by a conflict between approach and avoidance motivations −the drive to fulfil a positive need vs the fear of losing a different need. While the conflict exists, so too does the anxiety. The only real way to stop the anxiety in any given situation is to collapse the gap. There is of course, the second option of passive avoidance, which means that we avoid the anxious situations altogether and never experience the gap in the first place. We avoid going to the party or call in sick on the day of the big meeting. The problem with passive avoidance is that we never get to experience the anxious situation, which, while it may sound like a positive, can have very negative effects on the quality of life, not to mention the sense-of-self. I mean, if we avoid everything that makes us anxious, we end up never doing anything that will cause a conflict—which is most things.

Collapsing the gap, then, is the only real option to stopping the anxiety. There are two ways to collapse a gap—collapse up or collapse down—but both require action. Collapsing down means basically to remove all approach motivation and any hopes of a positive need being fulfilled, and leave ourselves with only avoidance motivation i.e., fear, and therefore active avoidance. A quick example might be someone who has a fear of dogs. If that person were to see his friend in the street, but also see that his friend had a dog, he may quickly become conflicted and anxious. On one hand, he wants to meet his friend and enjoy the social interaction that that would bring, but on the other hand his fear of dogs has activated his FFFS. His anxiety is high, but he cautiously approaches his friend and his dog. On his friend's reassurances that his dog is friendly, he approaches the dog. Upon sensing the fear, though, the dog starts barking. Immediately, the benefits of meeting his friend are outweighed by the fear of the dog, and his gap collapses downwards. Fear is now the only motivation present, and he makes his apologies and quickly escapes from the situation. This is not a great scenario, as now he is more than likely to use passive avoidance whenever he encounters situations that involve dogs.

Collapsing the gap upwards, on the other hand, is the result of a positive action that pushes through the anxiety and ends in a result that shows that the fear was misplaced. In the same situation, the man who is anxious around dogs might decide that being with his friend outweighs the anxiety he feels so he sticks around and spends time with the friend and the dog regardless of the barking. Over time he sees that the dog is indeed friendly and grows fond of the dog, and all his fear is removed. The gap collapses upwards, and he enjoys the time he spends with his friend and the dog. Of course, this doesn't mean that he won't get anxious around other dogs in the future, but with this dog he will be fine, and it will have demonstrated to him that some dogs, at least, are safe, which will also have a positive effect on his future canine interactions. Collapsing the gap upwards is the best way to remove the anxiety and reduce it in the future.

Values in Gaps

Gaining and losing needs is the basic driving force for anxiety, but as we have already touched on, how we value those needs is often more important than the needs themselves in how our individual anxieties are formed. If two men of the same age, socioeconomic background, and lifestyles, are due to retire, will they both view impending retirement the same way? Probably not. While one man may look forward to retirement because he values time spent with his family, opportunities for self-growth, and the time to relax that retirement affords, the other man may dread retirement because he fears being bored, having no goals, losing the social contact that work provides, and losing the identity that came with his position. Our values, and the lenses we build from them through which we perceive life, play a critical role in the formation of our gaps and therefore our anxiety. This means they also play a major part in our decision making.

Cognitive Dissonance

Values play a major role in more complex decision gaps. These can sometimes be difficult to see and can cause unforeseen anxiety when these values come into conflict with incongruous actions, thoughts, or behaviours. This is known as cognitive dissonance and was first investigated by Leon Festinger[21] in 1957. In his theory, he proposed that humans strive for psychological consistency, and any time there is a conflict of values, beliefs, actions, or thoughts in a person, that person will become psychologically uncomfortable and will take steps to reduce the inconsistency (and the discomfort). As you might expect, more recent studies[22] have shown that this cognitive dissonance (and psychological discomfort) is highly correlated to anxiety and could mean that the steps taken to reduce the inconsistency is driven by the need to reduce anxiety and close a gap.

Festinger first discovered this idea of cognitive dissonance while studying a cult that believed that the Earth was about to be destroyed by a flood. Some of the more committed members had given up their homes and lives to follow the cult in anticipation of the end days. When the flood did not happen as expected, many of those that had gone all-in chose to believe that the Earth had been saved through the

---

[21] A theory of cognitive dissonance - Festinger, L [1957]
Cognitive dissonance - Festinger, L [1962]
Cognitive consequences of forced compliance - Festinger, L., & Carlsmith, J. M [1959]
[22] Menasco & Hawkins (1978) | R M Suinn (1965)

faith of the cult members themselves rather than accept the fact that the cult leader was plain wrong. They could not live with the cognitive dissonance between their belief and the reality, so they changed their version of the reality.

Leon Festinger also gave the example of smokers who continue to smoke even though they know that it is bad for them. This causes cognitive dissonance in their minds as they balance the competing thoughts of wanting to smoke but knowing that it is killing them slowly.

Festinger suggested that there are three ways that people can resolve the dissonance, and these are the same for all cases of cognitive dissonance:

1. *They can change one of the beliefs/behaviours/values to bring the two conflicting things closer together.*
For the smokers, this would probably mean quitting smoking.

2. *Get new information that would overcome the unwanted belief.*
Smokers could find new research that throws into doubt the link between cigarettes and health issues, thereby relieving them of the fear of dying.

3. *Change the importance of the cognition.*
Smokers will often tell themselves that life is short, and everyone will die eventually, so why not live doing something you enjoy doing. Thoughts like this tone down the fear of the health impact of cigarettes and shift the focus to a more care-free lifestyle. Most smokers that don't quit will use something along these lines to reduce their anxiety from smoking.

Cognitive dissonance is a fancy name for what we might call a value gap and can be called into play when we must make value decisions. If a decision is made that means someone's actions are not in line with their values, a gap can remain open. And the only way to close it is by choosing one of the three cognitive dissonance resolutions from above.

Example:

Trevor has made an error at work. He lost a customer receipt and could lose the company a lot of money. Trevor has an opportunity to lie about the whole thing and claim that he never received the receipt and there is very little chance that anyone will find out, but he has always considered himself to be an honest and trustworthy person and takes great pride in this value. Trevor has a decision to make: On one hand he could lie and continue as normal, but if he did, he would fear a massive hit to his value of honesty and therefore to his self-image. His second choice, of course, would be to come clean and tell the truth. If he did this, he would feel good about maintaining his honesty and trustworthiness and even building upon it, but he would also fear the consequences to his job. He would feel the fear of a risk to his job security and his future success and the possible loss of respect from colleagues. Ultimately Trevor would choose the option with the smallest net negative gap and the least risk i.e., the one with the least anxiety. His BIS would make this decision through risk assessment automatically and Trevor would implement the result. The decision would ultimately rest on two things: how much does he value his honesty, and how dire does he deem the possible consequences of telling the truth?

If Trevor chooses to lie and cover up his error, a value gap might remain open even though there is no longer a decision to be made. This is because the cognitive dissonance between his action and his value will still create anxiety. After all, just because he decided to save his job doesn't suddenly mean that the fear of losing his value disappears too. The value of honesty is part of who he is, and so by acting in contrast to this value, he is risking losing a small part of himself, which will damage his self-worth (see later). While this gap remains open, Trevor will continue to walk around with a nagging anxiety, and probably not an insignificant helping of guilt and shame which are a direct result of diverting the anxiety to blame himself, so to minimise the discomfort of the anxiety he may well utilise one of the 3 options to reduce the cognitive dissonance.

The first option would force him to admit to his mistake and his deceitfulness and come clean to his boss, thereby closing the gap, but opening himself up to the same risk to his career as he feared earlier. Before he did this, another decision gap would open similar to the first, but with confessing as the least net negative gap.

The second option might see him tell himself that everyone in business lies. It's a dog-eat-dog world and you must lie to get ahead. Everyone would have done the same. The money will still be lost even if he loses his job, so what's the point of confessing? He may even talk to friends who he thinks might agree with him to elicit reinforcing opinions of his actions.

The third option might see him tell himself that nobody can be honest all the time and lying one time doesn't make him a bad person. It's just a one off and won't happen again. He is still basically an honest person, there was just no real choice in this situation.

Each of these options would help Trevor close, or reduce, the gap involved in his anxiety, but while the first option would close the gap completely once the consequences were known and leave his values intact, the second and third options could only reduce the gap between his actions and his values by reducing the importance of his values. This would certainly reduce the anxiety, but at what cost? He might believe that this is a one off, but doing it once makes repeating this dishonesty in the future easier, as his values are not as strong as they once were. Over time this could lead to a deterioration of the values that he once held dear, and Trevor could no longer consider himself an honest person.

If Trevor wants to relieve the anxiety and keep his values intact, then the only way to close the gap completely is to own up to his dishonesty and choose option 1.

Just like anger, earlier, I am slowly coming to the belief that shame and guilt are direct consequences of turning blame inwards as a result of value-based anxiety gaps.

Other Beliefs

Of course, values aren't the only beliefs that can cause anxiety gaps. General beliefs that we feel are under threat can be just as serious. An extreme example might be if we had great respect for an important religious leader who we admired to be a pious and good man, but we then read news that the leader that we admired so much had been accused of sexual assault. This would place our belief in jeopardy. Even though the situation has little to do with us directly, the fact that the accusations question a belief that we hold dear would result in an anxiety gap, and of course anxiety.

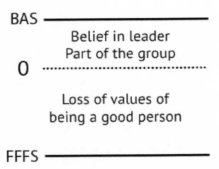

As with most gaps—and all cases of cognitive dissonance—we can choose to ignore the problem and experience anxiety every time we are reminded of the person or the news about him, or we can opt for reducing the anxiety through one of Festinger's choices: 1. Believe the news and change our belief and decide that we will no longer respect the accused person. 2. Look for "evidence" that will allow us to continue believing the leader and label the accusations as false, such as the trustworthiness of the accusers, the veracity of the claim, or any biased motivation that might be fuelling a "witch hunt". 3. Decide that we never really cared that much for the man anyway, and it won't affect our life either way, or decide that sexual assault really isn't that big a deal and shouldn't affect how we view someone. The easiest, and most common option, at least to begin with, is the second one, as very often the fear of losing a strongly held belief is considered much more damaging than simply calling strangers liars, especially if you have been a vocal supporter in the past.

If we went with the most common response to cognitive dissonance—Festinger's second choice—it would result in decreasing the size of the FFFS and the loss of values as we would have rationalised this fear and told ourselves that we can continue to believe in the leader because "it's all lies" and we could discount the evidence against him. This could remove the FFFS and the anxiety completely leaving us with a robust BAS and therefore an overall positive gap.

BAS ————————————————
    Belief in leader
    Part of the group
0 ·····································

Of course, if we don't believe our own discounting completely, we could still be left with a residual gap that will keep springing anxiety on us every time we think of it.

This situation could also be made into a double decision gap between believing the leader and not believing the leader, and all the choices in Festinger's list will consciously change the FFFS of one side of the gap. For choice 1, the fears of not believing the leader are reduced and lead to this becoming the obvious winner. For people who choose the second choice, the reduction is seen in the FFFS of the 'believing the leader' gap as we can see above, and this becomes the overall winner and the automatic choice. If the third option is chosen, then either of the decision gaps could have their FFFS reduced and become the default winner depending on the thought process involved. They might even both be reduced as the third option involves a degree of "caring less" or trivialising the problem. Either way, anxiety is reduced. For now.

We should not underestimate the importance and influence that our beliefs hold over our decisions and how much anxiety they cause in our lives. One of the many reasons that the world seems such an anxious place today, is that with the advent of the internet, news and opinions are so easily accessible. The anxiety caused through the fear of losing a belief is also one of the reasons why many areas of life are becoming so partisan. People now have the choice to read and watch the news they want, and of course they choose the news, and choose to mix with the people, that agree with their world view. This way there is much less chance of their belief systems being under threat, and their anxiety is lessened. They feel safe, but more importantly, feel that their beliefs are safe. But, as we know, this has far more serious repercussions on society.

Incongruous Values

Very often the beliefs or values we hold are not of our own making but were thrust upon us by our parents or caregivers during our upbringing. These beliefs and values can be very deeply rooted, so deeply in fact that we may not even know we have them, and yet they can still play an important role in forming anxiety-triggering value gaps if parts of our lives are incongruous with these values. And this doesn't mean that either the value or our actions are morally bad, it just means that they are opposite and incompatible.

Let's take Alice for example: Alice was brought up in a family of little means, and with puritan values, and she was taught to believe that the only way to get rich was to walk all over other people, which was obviously bad. She was taught that to be wealthy was to be evil. The problem is, now that Alice is a business owner and trying to expand her business, she is caught between the conflict of trying to be successful and the belief that all rich people are evil. If Alice becomes rich, will that mean she is evil? The conflict between these two values will cause Alice tremendous anxiety, and the only way out is to either give up her belief or give up her business. If she does neither then she will never be free of the anxiety caused by this belief gap. Unfortunately, there is a good chance that the underlying belief could lead to self-sabotage if she does not recognise it, and it could lead to her business failing anyway.

Instant vs Latent Decisions

As we saw in the earlier example of Trevor and his decision to lie or tell the truth, even when a decision is made a gap sometimes remains open. Making a decision does not always mean that all gaps are collapsed, and anxiety levels are reduced to zero, and, in fact, in some decisions anxiety can linger for a substantial amount of time after a decision has been made. I call these decisions "latent decisions" as they incur latent anxiety.

There are two main kinds of decision gap that encompass all others—the instant decision, and the latent decision. These names are not based on when the decision is made, as any decision that is not made instantly is simply being avoided or deferred and is not actually a decision at all. They are, instead, based on when the anxiety associated with the decision will completely end.

In an instant decision, once the decision has been made, i.e., once the gap with the least anxiety associated with it has been selected, then the issue will be fully resolved, both decision gaps will collapse, and all anxiety will be removed. Acting on any instant decision will collapse all gaps and null all anxiety associated with that decision. Of course, you may still wonder what would have happened if you had chosen the other option—buyer's remorse is a thing—but it will not cause anxiety.

Whether or not to go to a party is an example of an instant decision gap. Once the party is over, the anxiety gap of going to the party completely collapses, and you can lie in bed the same night anxiety-free. Of course, there could be other gaps created when you remember the drunken karaoke rendition of My Way you did standing on the bar, and you think of what your co-workers will say on Monday, but this is a separate gap altogether. Another example of an instant decision is the public speaker: His anxiety before and during the speech might be very high, but as soon as the speech is over, a sense of relief will wash over him as all speech related gaps are collapsed.

Latent decisions, on the other hand, are those decisions that might be made now, but the consequences of such will not be fully known until a later date. With these latent decisions, there will be latent anxiety present even after the decision has been made. In other words, the anxiety caused by the selected choice (the least negative gap) will remain until such time as the result and consequences are known, although the level of anxiety may well change over time.

Using our previous example of John buying a new house, we can see that even when John chooses to buy the house, and therefore collapses the non-buying gap, the gap formed for buying the house will remain, and will not fully collapse until the house is paid for. The gap will of course diminish over time, as will the anxiety, and it will generally be dealt with unconsciously rather than consciously, but until John is 100% certain that buying the house is not going to

bankrupt him—and that's not going to happen until it is fully paid for—
then his anxiety will remain.

So why does the anxiety change over time? Well, firstly, soon after
John has bought the house, the initial gain needs will be reduced as
the new house loses its novelty (so his worries may seem a little more
negative to start with), and secondly, as the months roll by, and the
payments are made and the total balance outstanding is reduced, the
chances of bankruptcy lessen—and so does the anxiety. Time is a great
healer of latent anxiety and although the levels of anxiety for John may
never hit zero until he experiences the relief of a fully paid mortgage,
they will diminish to background levels that will simply slot in with the
low hum of anxiety noise that the unconscious deals with every day.
Too many unresolved latent anxiety gaps, though, can result in a
background hum of anxiety that can be overwhelming. If you've ever
felt the load-lightening feeling of relief, you know what it feels like to
collapse a gap.

Another example of a gap that is a latent decision gap is starting
a business: The anxieties inherent in starting a new business stay in
place for a long time, especially in the business's fledgling years, but
they pale in comparison—to the entrepreneur at least—to the original
anxiety of NOT starting a business.

This brings us to an important point, however: Deciding if a
decision is instant or latent is an important first step in beating
excessive anxiety. You should make a conscious point of acting on all
instant decisions and not putting them off, because, by their very
nature, the result and consequences of instant decisions are
immediate, and are never as bad as you think they will be. Putting off
these decisions, just pushes the full anxiety associated with the
decision to the back of your mind where it sits and pollutes your
unconscious. Making the decision and acting upon it, collapses all

gaps, and nulls all anxiety, and leaves only the consequences to deal with.

An important question to ask yourself, then, is "Is this decision an instant or a latent decision?". Will taking action in this situation collapse all gaps and leave only the consequences? If so, then you should make the decision and take action. It's that simple. Not easy, but simple.

Latent Worry

Imagine you go into work one day and your boss makes a negative off-hand comment about your work, nothing too obvious, but enough to make you question the stability of your job. As you're busy, you put it out of your mind and get on with the rest of your work and think nothing about it for the rest of the day.

When you get home, though, you feel a gnawing sense of anxiety in your stomach; you're irritable and crabby with your family, and you can't shake that feeling of dread. The fear of the loss of security in your job has opened an anxiety gap which you had ignored for most of the day. You may not even realise the cause of the gap to start with as you pushed it from your mind so early on, but your unconscious creates the gap anyway and the anxiety that you feel is very real.

This kind of gap is quite common and too many of them can build up to gnaw away at your sanity. Looking for the worry in these latent anxiety gaps and addressing them wherever possible can achieve wonders in reducing overall anxiety levels.

One example of this that I can remember, is the time I said something to my boss that at the time I considered innocuous but later realised could be taken the wrong way, especially by a non-native English speaker. The more I thought about it, the more I worried, and as I tend to largely overthink things, this filled me with huge anxiety. As I didn't want to go home and stew on this all evening, which I knew I would, I went to my boss to explain my meaning and apologise if there was any misunderstanding. Luckily, she hadn't taken it the wrong way and was surprised to hear me say that there might have been any offence taken. My anxiety gap immediately closed, and I could relax. I even think my boss appreciated the thought.

There are two lessons here: The first is that very often the anxiety and worry that we feel about other people only reside in our own minds, and second, this can be confirmed and/or solved by just talking to people.

As we will see later, journaling and writing about feelings in general, can be a good way to pick up on these latent worry gaps and let us know what needs to be solved to ease our anxiety.

Chapter Four: Emotions

"When a man is prey to his emotions, he is not his own master."
Benedict de Spinoza

Anxiety as an Emotion

As discussed throughout this book, the drives and resulting actions of moving towards or away from things that could be beneficial or harmful to us are innate and automatic and baked into our survival circuits requiring no conscious cognitive process for them to happen. In fact, because we know that approach and avoidance behaviour is displayed by all living things, including single-celled organisms, such as bacteria, it is plainly clear that no brain or nervous system at all is necessary for the survival of a species through approach and avoidance behaviours. All the development of the nervous system has really done, is allowed species to develop more novel and effective ways to approach or avoid things and offer more varied things to approach and avoid.

This is important when we come to differentiate between the brain circuits that result in behavioural responses, such as the body's reaction to fear, and the feeling that we associate with them. The problems mainly arise when scientists use words such as "the fear circuit" to describe the FFFS because this leads us to believe that it is this circuit that causes the sensations that we experience as the feeling of fear, when in fact science suggests that the circuits that prompt us to approach or avoid things are completely different circuits in the brain to those that give us the subjective feelings of fear, excitement, hope, and anxiety.

This shouldn't come as too much of a surprise when we look at other living things. We may imagine that animals experience subjective feelings of fear (although there is very little evidence of this), but I doubt many of us would imagine a bacterium fleeing a predator in abject terror. There must be a distinction, then, between the systems that trigger avoidance and the processes that cause the feelings of fear.

The subjective feelings of fear and anxiety are bi-products of our conscious mind—which is rather a latecomer to the party in evolutionary terms—and are not necessary for behaviour to be displayed based on approach-avoidance circuits. It has been shown in laboratory studies,[23] that survival approach and avoidance motivations can produce reactions and behaviours in humans with no conscious cognitive effect of fear or anxiety. In other words, humans can act scared without feeling scared. This obviously makes it extremely difficult to test if any animal ever feels the emotions of fear and anxiety—I mean we can't ask them, can we?

We do know for a fact, however, that humans can feel emotions, and we also know that we can experience the emotions of fear and anxiety, because we have all experienced them for ourselves. The first thing we need to do then, is determine what exactly an emotion and a feeling is and make sure that we treat them separately to the survival circuits that trigger them. This certainly isn't helped by the fact that the terminology of emotions and feelings doesn't always seem to be universally agreed upon, and different people will publish different definitions making the whole thing incredibly confusing for everyone, including scientists. Therefore, I am going to choose the system that seems to make the most sense to me. It is important to note, though, that there is no right or wrong in this, as it really all boils down to

---

[23] Unconscious emotion – Winkielman, Berridge [2004] | Anxiety – a book by Le Doux

semantics, and if neuroscientists can't agree amongst themselves, then what hope do we have?

The system of classification that I will use is that emotions are unconscious, and feelings, or the experience of emotions, are conscious. I will use the term emotions to describe the physiological *results* of the survival circuits in our brains. In other words, the emotion of fear is the physiological response, or how our body reacts physically, to the FFFS being triggered alone by threatening stimuli such as those that we have already been looking at. The physiological response of fear is the routine of neurochemicals and physical reactions in the body that are triggered by a threat to enable the individual to respond with fighting or fleeing or freezing. This includes the cortisol in the brain, the heart pumping quickly from adrenaline to get the blood quickly to the limbs, the breathing fast and shallow, the tunnelled vision, and the sweaty palms. These make up the emotion of fear. Freezing, fleeing, or fighting are possible behavioural expressions of the emotion of fear.

One of the reasons I like this naming system is because it allows us to have emotions that we never know are there because we don't "feel" anything, but by our usual language usage are still called emotions. So, from here on in, I will be using the term emotion to describe the physiological responses to a survival circuit including all the chemicals, hormones, and neurotransmitters that such a response would create.

Feelings, on the other hand, are our cognitive perception of those emotions. When the survival circuits in our brains instigate a fight or flight reaction, which means that our bodies are undergoing the emotion of fear, our bodies are filled with the results of that emotional response (the hormones and chemicals related to fear), but it does not necessarily mean that we will feel scared, and if not, it would mean that we have no feelings of fear. This happens all the time when the body runs its emotional programmes, but they never impact on our feelings in a meaningful way. Or at least in a recognisable way.

The problem is that fear is an easy one, and hence the one most often used to discuss emotions and feelings. For years, the fear response has been reasonably well understood, although it has turned out to be a lot more complicated than the amygdala-centred emotion that was previously thought, as entire brain regions are involved, but what about happiness or sadness? Do these have specific programs run by fixed networks of the brain? Does the same happiness emotion program run for everyone? Are all feelings of happiness the same?

For centuries, since the writings of Darwin, scientists believed that emotions were fixed and universal, and that everybody had the same emotional response for fear, sadness, happiness and anger, and everyone experienced their associated feelings the same, and this could be shown by the "universal" facial and bodily expressions that were shown. After all, everyone smiles when they are happy, and frowns when they are angry, right? Well, everyone thought so, but it turns out that it might not be the case after all, as recent studies have shown that it is far from as simple as that[24].

The original study to support Darwin's theory, conducted in far-off tribes, showed the people all smiled when happy, but this was later shown to be tainted with bad methodology, and you don't have to go to lost tribes to see that not everyone shows the same facial expression to the same emotion. Thailand, for example, a place I called home for twenty years, is often known as the Land of Smiles, but the smiles do not always mean that the people are happy. In fact, there have been 13 clearly identified smiles that are commonly used by the Thai people,[25] and I am sure there are probably even more, covering everything from

[24] Emotion and autonomic nervous system activity in the Minangkabau of West Sumatra - Levenson, R. W et al. [1992]
On the universality and cultural specificity of emotion recognition: A meta-analysis - Elfenbein, H. A., & Ambady, N [2002]
[25] Working with the Thais - Henry Homes, Suchada Tangtongtavy

embarrassment to sadness, to horror. Even after the 2004 tsunami, many people witnessed the Thai people reacting to the horror with smiles. It is not only Thai people, of course, many of us may also find ourselves smiling when embarrassed, unsure of a situation, or to soothe tension. These smiles are not triggered by happiness, but they do show that expressions of emotion can be guided by culture. It is also true, as most people will know, that we don't only cry when we are sad or shout when we are angry. Most people have cried when they are happy, frightened, relieved, or angry and shout when they are excited, happy, or scared. You will see both behaviours when someone wins an important sporting tournament.

Why am I telling you this? Well for years now a huge debate has been raging whether emotions and the feelings they produce are fixed and universal, but the most recent compelling scientific evidence suggests that they are not[26]. The most recent studies seem to suggest that there are no fixed emotions or feelings, as such, that are passed down genetically from our ancestors, and lots of the top scientists in the field are beginning to agree with this point (although not all by a long shot). This means that not only does everybody not smile when they are happy or shout when they are angry, but that your experience of happiness might be completely different to mine. Not even the physiological responses are the same for everyone: The chemicals and neurotransmitters in my body when I feel happy might be very different to yours.

If there are no fixed emotions or feelings, then, what does that leave us with? Well, we certainly do have many physiological responses to external and internal stimuli, and many of them can be grouped together due to their common underlying circuits, their physiological and behavioural objectives, and the way they are experienced consciously. Fear, for example, may not always be

---

[26] How Emotions Are Made: The Secret Life of the Brain – Lisa Feldman Barrett

triggered by the exact same system every time (although fear, being one of the simpler emotions, seems to be fairly consistent), but because it results in some measure of a fight or flight response, then it could be deemed to be an emotion of fear. So, however it is generated, a response that results in a physiological reaction that leads to a fight, flight or freeze response, would be deemed a fear emotion and a response that results in the formation of a gap is an emotion of anxiety. The fact that the neural circuits involved in any emotion have not been found to be consistent[27] is why it is much more elegant to use our conceptual systems of the BAS, FFFS, and BIS to form our gaps and generate the emotion of anxiety.

These emotions, of course, are completely unconscious and may or may not register as conscious feelings. You can certainly have an anxiety response without consciously registering it as anxiety, and many people do all the time. The questions must be asked, though, how do we, as people, feel and recognise the feelings of emotions as they happen? Why do we sometimes not consciously feel anything? If happiness is not a fixed, genetically inherited emotion then how do we know when we feel it? How do we know the difference between the feelings of anxiety and fear? Well to answer these questions, we must delve a little deeper into how the brain monitors the body.

How do we Feel Feelings?

Interoception

If we are to understand the way that our brain conjures conscious feelings of emotions, we first must understand some of the other jobs of the brain. We all know that the brain controls the body—managing the beat of the heart, or the rhythm of the breathing—without our being consciously aware of it. But what we might not know is just how

---

[27] Neural correlates of individual differences in fear learning | MacNamara et. al. (2015)
An fMRI study of personality influences on brain reactivity to emotional stimuli - Canli, T. et al. [2001]

the brain decides on how quickly the heart should beat, or the lungs breathe. To do this, and to regulate everything that the body does, the brain keeps mental maps of the entire body where it simulates and predicts what the body will need.

To keep the predictions as accurate as possible, the body receives massive amounts of information from all over the body telling it everything from the temperature, the oxygen levels, glucose levels, vitamin and mineral levels, the presence of foreign invaders and so on. If something is essential for the body to survive, the brain will receive constant updates on the status of it so it can keep tabs on what is needed.

This information from the body that allows total body-mapping by the brain is called *interoception* and allows the brain to regulate the energy of the body and keep us, as living organisms, ticking along. Interoception plays such a big role in how our bodies are run, that it could easily be called the sixth sense, and is arguably just as (if not more) important to us for our survival as our other five senses of sight, sound, smell, taste, and touch.

Affect

With all these signals bombarding our brains from not only our five senses but all parts of our body at the same time, our brains are constantly changing the allocation of resources to the body to try and maintain equilibrium and overall body health. This means that our brains are constantly churning out different mixes of chemicals, hormones, and neurotransmitters to cope with whatever the current situation is. If our body tells our brain that water levels are getting low (or sodium levels too high), then our brain will release chemicals that will instigate a feeling of thirst and motivate us to find water to drink. This means that our brains and bodies are constantly filled with ever changing "soups" of chemicals that will change the ways in which our brains and bodies behave. The state of our bodies and brains at any given time because of this "soup" of ingredients and the resulting effects that it has on our bodies is called the **Affect**. The *affect* is what we might think of as an unconscious mood. It is how our bodies "feel" and can affect our brains accordingly. If you've ever felt grumpy because of hunger, or irritable because you're hot, then you have experienced the results of *affect* on your state of mind. Every person alive has experienced the *affect* caused by lack of water, and we all recognise it as a feeling of thirst.

Of course, areas and systems of the brain like the BAS, FFFS, and BIS also play a part in determining the *affect* within our bodies as they release chemicals that add to the overall ingredients of the chemical "soup". So, the overall *affect* and mood that we feel at any given time, is determined by the state of chemicals in our brains, which is heavily influenced by both the interoception from our bodies[28] and the neural systems of the BAS, BIS, and FFFS.

Arousal and Valence

As most of us know from experience, sometimes we feel like we're in a good mood, and sometimes we might feel in a bad mood, often seemingly without reason. This is due to the chemicals in the brain that generate the *affect* at any given time, but in the language of *affect* we term them as positive **valence** for an *affect* that makes us feel good, and negative **valence** for an *affect* that makes us feel bad. A good mood is simply the brain's interpretation of a positively-valenced *affect*, while a bad mood is the opposite. But of course, not all good or bad moods are created equally. Some days we may just find that we feel a bit low, whereas others we find ourselves enraged about something our co-worker said. Conversely, one day we could be

---

[28] How does interoceptive awareness interact with the subjective experience of emotion? An fMRI Study | Terasawa et. al. (2011) Neural systems supporting interoceptive awareness | Critchley, H. D. [2004]
How do you feel? Interoception: the sense of the physiological condition of the body | Craig, A. D. [2002]

happily sitting watching TV with our family, while the next we are filled with excitement as we await friends at our birthday party. How strongly the *affect* changes our mood is called the **arousal**.

With *affect* consisting of valence and arousal, then, we can plot the *affect*, and therefore the mood as interpreted by the brain, on a graph of valence vs arousal.

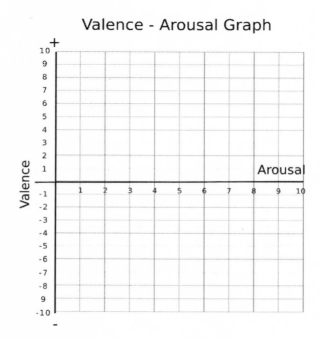

This means that at any given time, our *affect,* and hence our mood, can be plotted somewhere on this graph. We may not always be able to pinpoint how we are feeling as maybe our brains have not consciously interpreted our *affect* into a specific mood, but our *affect* will always be somewhere on the graph.

Categories and Patterns

If we think of *affect* as being created from a soup of chemicals, hormones, neurotransmitters, and different electrical signals, it is easy to see that there is a near infinite number of combinations of *affect*. In fact, the number of different combinations means that most of the time all we know is that we feel good or bad, and how good or bad we feel. In other words, most of the time, we only feel the *affect* and the overall mood it puts us in, we never actually notice anything consciously, except that we feel "bad" or good". Occasionally, though, our brains will recognise a pattern. A combination of signals will trigger a memory in the brain, a memory of a time when that exact *affect* was felt before. A time when that *affect* was given a name. The name that characterises a specific combination and pattern of *affect* is called a feeling of emotion.

This is what is known as the construction theory of emotions, whereby the emotions that we feel are not inscribed within us from birth but are rather learned and then constructed as we grow. This happens slowly over time as we go through childhood, without our realising it. From days when we feel good and our parents say "you look happy" we begin to associate the *affect* that we feel, and the behavioural response like smiling to the emotion that has been named as happiness. Likewise, when we are feeling down, and we are asked "are you okay? You look sad" we begin to associate that particular *affect* with the name of sadness. The construction theory of emotions argues that this is how all emotional feelings are formed and is why emotions seem to be culturally specific and not universal as previously thought. This means that feelings of emotions are in fact just a recognition of the feeling of *affect* and not anything more innate.

As a questionable analogy, if you throw some meat, onions, herbs, a bit of sauce and some pasta into a dish, the result will generally be some generic homemade pasta dish. I know this because I make some of the weirdest pasta dishes you have ever seen and will never find in

133

any respectable cookbook. Occasionally though, if the pasta I use is flat and layered, I will call the dish lasagne. If the pasta is long and thin and the sauce is meat and tomato based, I might call it spaghetti Bolognese. If I decide to use the same pasta but throw in some bacon and make the sauce from eggs and cheese, then I would proudly proclaim a spaghetti carbonara (albeit rightly open to derision from Italians).

The point of this gratuitous pasta metaphor is that emotional feelings are very much like this: Most of the time, *affect* is like a meal made by randomly throwing together ingredients, but occasionally those ingredients will come together to form an *affect* that is recognised and labelled and could be put on a menu—this is an emotional feeling. I know this sounds odd, and maybe even a little disconcerting as it goes against everything we have been told for the past few decades, but it is a theory espoused by Lisa Feldman Barrett and her colleagues, and is slowly gaining popularity amongst neuroscientists, even among some of the heavy hitters. If you want to read more on this subject, I highly recommend the book *How Emotions Are Made: The Secret Life of the Brain, by Lisa Feldman Barrett*. It is an excellent book and one which resonates strongly with me.

It is important to note that circumstance and learned memory will also often play a role in the categorising of our affect as feelings. If we have a negative *affect* before giving a speech to a room full of strangers, we usually know what to call the feeling even if we have never felt it before, due to our knowledge of the circumstance and what we have learned of others giving speeches. Learned memory can be just as powerful as experienced memory.

How is the Affect Linked to Gaps?

Up until this point, I have been discussing the use of gaps, and the approach-avoidance systems that they represent, solely as a mechanism for self-protection and decision-making. We have already seen that decisions are made by choosing the gap with the smallest net negative (or biggest net positive) and that what we call anxiety is created as a risk assessment and conflict resolution program by the BIS. This is all very mechanical and lifeless, though, and we know that anxiety is anything but lifeless. Anxiety is felt. This means that the gaps must be related to our feelings in some way, so let's look at how the gaps themselves can lead to how we feel (at least partly).

Plotting the *Affect* to Form Emotional Feeling

We can see how gaps lead to differing *affect* and moods and how this can then lead to the feelings of emotion by plotting the valence and arousal of each gap on a valence-arousal graph like the one we made earlier. I will try hard to make this not too nerdy and not make you feel like you're in maths class again (presuming you don't already), but I do feel that this is a useful way to visualise how our feelings are created. I will use a few examples and plot them on a typical valence-arousal graph. Of course, this is an overly simplified way of looking at it compared to what really goes on in our bodies, but sometimes simplification helps.

To do this we must assign numbers to our gaps. In this case the reasons behind the gaps are unimportant, but the size and structure of the gaps are very important. To do this, and to keep it as simple as possible, we will grade the strength of the gain motivation on a scale between 0 and 10, and the threat motivation on a scale between 0 and -10 as we did before. As mentioned earlier, this makes the valence of the *affect* simply the sum (or net) of these two motivation values. The arousal of the *affect* will be determined by the size of the largest gap, i.e., the BAS or FFFS. We can then plot these "moods" or *affect* levels on a valence-arousal graph as shown below. Please remember that this is just a simplified model and in real life any *affect* produced by a gap will be added to the baseline *affect* generated through interoception and other bodily and mental processes. In other words, if you are already feeling in a bad mood, then this can make the gaps more negative.

It is also clear that the gap model has clear limitations when it comes to generating values for the arousal of an anxious episode. Arousal in real life will depend on many factors, and therefore it is not possible to make a simple model that generates an accurate valuation of both valence and arousal. As we will see later, though, when it comes to determining your own valence and arousal values during anxious episodes, this is not an issue, as you can learn to "feel" the relative values of both valence and arousal and therefore do not need to rely on basic gap mathematics. The gap model is intended solely as a device to help you view your anxiety differently.

When decision gaps are in play, there are two possible scenarios that can generate feelings: The first is the anxiety felt during the decision-making process, due to the two gaps. The second is after the decision has been made and a latent decision gap remains to still generate anxiety. In the following examples, I will use simple approach-avoidance gaps only to make things simpler, as using both gaps together will overcomplicate things (see appendix for more information).

Here I will look at a few different kinds of gaps for differing levels of valence of arousal and plot them all on the same graph at the end.

Positive Valence Gaps

Gap 1. Small Gap, Larger BAS

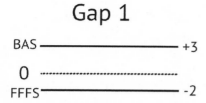

This gap has a slightly larger BAS than FFFS, but the overall gap is quite small. The net gap will be +1 (+3-2) and so this will lead to a very slight positive feeling as it has a positive valence of +1. The largest gap here is the BAS gap with a value of +3, so the arousal value will be 3. This is not a very high value as it is out of 10 altogether. This will mean the overall feeling will not be very strong. In real life, this kind of small positive feeling might be something as simple as sitting with a loved one watching TV together and might be called "contentment".

Gap 1: valence +1, arousal 3

Gap 2. Medium Gap, Larger BAS

This is a gap that has a reasonably large BAS and a smaller FFFS making it a positive emotion but also one with a fairly larger arousal. It is still not a massive gap but big enough to produce a noticeable *affect*. The valence for this feeling would be + 3 (5-2) and the arousal 5 (BAS largest gap). This gap might represent a person waiting for friends at a dinner party and could be called "anticipation" or "expectation".

Gap 2

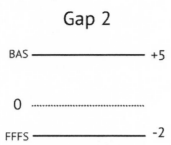

BAS ———————— +5

0 ······························

FFFS ———————— -2

Gap 3. Large Gap, Large BAS

This gap has a sizeable BAS and a rather small FFFS denoting a relatively large valence as well as a large arousal giving the person a strong and very positive emotional *affect*. The valence of this emotion will be +7 (+8 − 1) and the arousal 8 (BAS gap). This will result in an *affect* that has a high positive valence as well as a lot of arousal. An example of this might be someone that is waiting to go on the holiday of a lifetime and might be called "excitement".

Gap 3

BAS ———————— +8

0 ······························
FFFS———————— -1

Negative Valence Gaps
Gap 4. Small Gap, Small FFFS

This gap is almost the inverse of gap 1 and has a small FFFS but an even smaller BAS offering a slightly negative valence and a relatively small arousal. The valence is -1 (+1 − 2) denoting a slightly negative valence and the arousal 2 (the FFFS gap). This kind of affect might be caused by someone waiting for their new mother-in-law to arrive at a dinner (I guess it depends on the mother-in-law) and might be called "concern" or "apprehension".

Gap 4

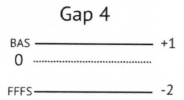

Gap 5. Medium Gap, Much Larger FFFS

This gap has quite a large FFFS and a smaller, but not insignificant, BAS activation. This results in a medium valence of -4, but a rather large arousal of 7. This might commonly be known as "anxiety" or "agitation". This might be caused by a waiting for an important interview.

●

Gap 5

```
BAS  ─────────────────── +3


0     ...............................


FFFS ─────────────────── -7
```

Gap 6: Large Gap, Large FFFS

Here we have a gap with a huge FFFS of -10 and only a small, probably status quo, BAS gap of +1 resulting in a large overall valence of -9 (-10 + 1) and arousal of 10 (FFFS gap). This would probably be a case of anticipatory fear, meaning the person is terrified, but there is still a hope that the bad thing does not happen, and the status quo is preserved, which, of course, makes it distinct from pure fear. This could be a case of anyone expecting a life-threatening situation e.g., soldiers waiting for an attack.

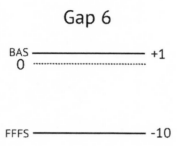

It is important to note that the above examples are just that— examples. They are standard situations that anyone might experience. This does not mean of course that someone with anxiety won't feel different arousal or valence levels in any of these situations.

It should also be noted that this gap model has only been created as a visual model for anxiety and does not work for other emotions such as sadness and depression. Depression is synonymous with very high negative valence but low arousal, which is not possible with this model of anxiety gaps. The model is not meant to be a description of all emotions just an aid to help people visualise their anxiety.

We can now add these gaps and their associated valence and arousal values to the same graph that we saw before:

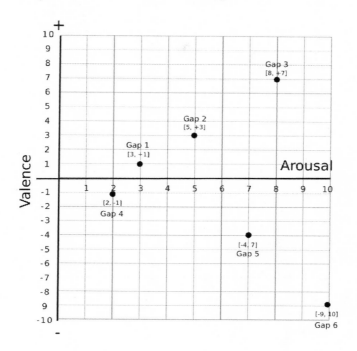

Every one of us, provided we are not in a coma or a vegetative state, will experience these *affect*s, and they will generate moods within us that we may or may not consciously interpret. Occasionally, though, we will recognise a specific *affect* state and we will remember that specific *affect* has a name. This will then be a conscious feeling. Each person may well have a different name for each *affect* state, depending on their upbringing and early introduction to emotions, but for most people (at least those from within the same society), the emotions that we feel usually fall into standard areas on the graph with only subtle differences.

This means that we can fill in the valence-arousal graph with the areas that most people will feel their general emotions. Not everyone will be the same, but it will give us an idea of how the brain constructs its feelings of emotions from the overall *affect*. As we will see later, though, some anxiety sufferers may be playing with a wildly different graph.

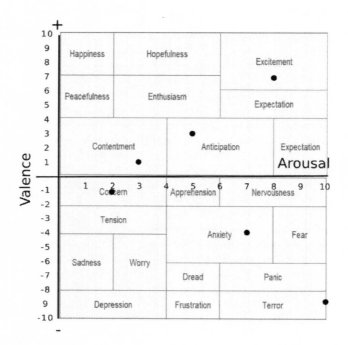

What is important to understand is that these feelings are just perceptions of the *affect* that have been assigned names, and we have learned to associate these names with the *affect* as we grow. This means that, as mentioned earlier, the names may differ slightly from person to person, and it also means that we can assign feelings like fear and terror even though there is uncertainty and not a lone activated FFFS. This graph is what I would consider a standard graph, but as we will see later, when we look at emotional granularity, this graph can be changed.

I created this valence-arousal graph based on feelings that are associated with the *affect* caused by anxiety gaps. This makes it different to the valence-arousal graphs that are used in most scientific work. In most valence-arousal graphs, we find a full range of emotions that include emotions such as anger, jealousy, shame, and guilt as well as the ones that I have used here. The problem with this, in my view at least, is that each of these emotions can have varying valence and arousal depending on the situation. For example, anger can range from a simmering contempt to a full-blown rage. They could all be classed as anger but obviously have very different valence and arousal levels. The same could be said for jealousy, shame, and guilt. These are not emotions that are easy to plot with specific valence and arousal values. Another issue, of course, is my belief that most of these emotions are simply caused by anxiety with blame aimed at either someone else or oneself. Even jealousy could be directed anxiety from a gap forged through the fear of a possible loss of something we deem important that someone else has.

This means that emotions like anxiety, anger, shame, and guilt should not be placed on the same valence-arousal graph as each other, in my opinion, as they could all produce very wide-ranging values of both valence and arousal. Instead, they should each have their own valence-arousal charts in a 3D matrix.

That is why, I have restricted my valence-arousal graphs to only those emotional feelings that are associated with anxiety and generated through the anxiety gap. That is of course, except for sadness and its associated feelings, as these are areas of the graph that are not accessible to the anxiety gap anyway.

My valence-arousal graph, then, is just a tool to help visualise our affect in terms of emotional feelings and try to demonstrate how the construction of emotions works, and it is not intended to mirror any scientific use.

It is also important to note, that the valence and arousal are not the cause of the *affect* but the result. By this I mean that we do not consciously label an emotional feeling from the combination of valence and arousal in real life, there is much more to it than that. The valence and arousal values themselves are only our own cognitive perceptions and rationalisations of the *affect* that we can consciously experience. They are just cognitive constructs that allow us to consciously evaluate the *affect* that we are feeling and assign numbers. We have already seen that emotions like anger, as well as shame and guilt, need an element of blame for them to be differentiated from other negative feelings. This blame does not show up in any perception of valence and arousal and so would not really be indistinguishable from anxiety and fear if we were to base our feelings on valence and arousal alone. That subtle cognitive cue of blame, though, would give us a third dimension and allow us to recognise that the emotion is not simply anxiety, but anger, or shame, or guilt. We need to experience the whole *affect* to recognise the emotional feeling. It is very much like trying to experience a pasta dish from its list of ingredients rather than experiencing the dish first-hand with our smell, sight, touch, and taste. It just doesn't work.

That's the last time I will talk about pasta I promise.

The *Affect* Heuristic

As well as forming our overall mood and allowing us to feel our emotions, the *affect* plays a significant role in the actual formation of the gaps that cause anxiety and, therefore, in the decisions we make, meaning that just like many actions of the body and mind, *affect* can feed into a feedback loop with anxiety.

Affect plays a part in how we perceive the benefits or risks of things, with benefits and risks tending to be inversely correlated to each other. In other words, if we think something has a lot of benefits, we will also think that it has low risk and vice versa. This is an unconscious *affect* process and is not due to any conscious risk assessment. This was demonstrated in a study[29] that showed that by changing students' perceptions of the benefits of nuclear power by giving them positive information, it also made their perception of the risks of nuclear power drop. Another group was given information on the risks of nuclear power and how dangerous it could be, and this also reduced their perception of how beneficial they thought nuclear power to be. When benefits are increased, risks are decreased, and vice versa. As no extra information was given to support this added outcome, it was clear that these were "emotional" processes and could only be down to positive and negative changes in *affect* and not conscious number crunching. Learning about the risks created a more negative *affect* in the body, which in turn led to a perception that the benefits were less, while learning about the benefits first produced a more positive *affect* and lessened the perception of the risks.

This effect on benefit and risk also means that the *affect* can drastically alter the value processes that our mind runs through and therefore the gaps that are ultimately produced. If the general *affect* in the body is negative, then more weight will be given to negative inferences, and to the evaluations assigned to them, as the risk is exemplified, while a positive *affect* will do the opposite. I am sure you have experienced this yourself when you have been sick or in a bad mood, or maybe hungover, and you can't help thinking the worst about everything, while if you are happy and in a good mood everything just seems a little more likely to turn out for the best. This is the effect that *affect* has on the value process and therefore the anxiety gaps formed.

This also means, of course, that *affect* plays a role in decision making. If a negative *affect* increases the likelihood of negative inferences and evaluations, and reduces the likelihood of positive inferences and evaluations, then, as well as increasing anxiety, it is also more likely to lead to avoidance decisions. This will also lead to a

---

[29] The affect heuristic in judgments of risks and benefits – Finucane et al [2000]

feedback loop whereby negative *affect* creates more negative gaps, which create more anxiety, which creates negative *affect*...and so on.

Decisions influenced by *affect* are often said to be using the "*affect* heuristic" and the *affect* can play such a crucial role that Robert Zajonc, a well-known social psychologist, once said that "we do not see just a house, we see a handsome house, or an ugly house", and that "quite often 'I decided in favour of X' is no more than 'I liked X'". He also said that we buy the cars we 'like', choose the jobs and houses we find 'attractive', and then justify these choices by various reasons. These are all unconscious decisions based on gaps that are strongly influenced by *affect*.

Part 2: Anxiety Becoming a Problem

"Man is not worried by real problems so much as by his imagined anxieties about real problems."
Epictetus

Chapter Five: The Causes

Do we Really need Anxiety?

Over the past few chapters, I have been describing how people get anxiety and how we experience that anxiety as a physiological response (an *affect),* a behavioural response, and a conscious emotional feeling. One thing that you may have noticed I have not mentioned is anxiety disorders. This was done very purposefully though, as I wanted to show that not only does everybody get anxiety, which they do, but that the anxiety we experience—up to a certain level at least—is essential for our survival. Anxiety is not an obsolete vestige of our ancient "lizard brains" going haywire in this modern world, as many would have you believe (in fact the idea of a lizard brain has been disproven many times[30]), it is as important now as it has ever been. Sure, there are times when our brains make mistakes and anxiety flares up inappropriately, but that would have happened to our ancient ancestors also. It is true that there are probably more opportunities for our brains to make mistakes now as there is less mortal danger to most of us than there was in the past, but it is inherent in the system to err on the side of caution, as keeping us safe is the whole point of anxiety.

As we have already seen, anxiety plays an essential role in our decision-making process, and the drive to relieve ourselves of anxiety forces us to move towards our goals, or away from possible threats. Without anxiety, crucial decisions would often never get made, and this would be detrimental to our survival, and we may not have made it this far as a species.

---

[30] Affective neuroscience: The foundations of human and animal emotions | Panksepp, J [1998]
Close-up view of the "triune" brain. In A. Diamond (Ed.), The development and neural bases of higher cognitive functions | Diamond, J. [2000]

Let's, for an example, look back at a hypothetical stone-age ancestor (although this could quite easily be made more contemporary) who, with his family, lived happily in his cave. There was fresh water nearby and plenty of food in the forms of fruit trees and small animals to hunt, and our ancestor was very content. One day when he was hunting far from his cave he saw the tracks of a predator—a predator that could be a danger to his family. He had not seen these tracks in this area before, but as there was just one set and they were sufficiently far away from his cave, he didn't give them much thought. Over the next few weeks, though, our stone age friend began to see more and more predator tracks, and they were slowly getting closer and closer to his home—and to his family. His anxiety levels began to rise as his positive need for a secure home began to form a bigger and bigger gap from the fear of possible harm—and loss—to his family.

Eventually the tracks got so close, and the fear side of the gap became so large, and his anxiety so unbearable, that he had to act: Our ancestor's action could be to create better security and defences to keep the predators out, hunt the predator, or simply to move to a new area, but whatever his chosen course of action, the anxiety he felt would compel him to do something to keep his family safe. Without anxiety, the man would have only fear to protect him. That would, of course, mean he would have to wait until the predators showed up at his door before he acted, and by then it may well be too late. Anxiety, then, is an important defence mechanism that is in-built to keep us safe. Of course, it doesn't always feel like that, and we'll get to that shortly.

Even with anxiety in modern life, with its gaps built around non-life-threatening fears, it still has an important role to play. If we consider the very simple situation of Shelley from accounting being given a deadline for her presentation to the boss, it is easy to see the problems that would be caused if anxiety did not exist. If Shelley never felt anxiety, then the idea of a looming deadline would hold very little sway over her actions and she would probably leave the work until the very last minute, if she did it at all. With anxiety though, her main goal would be to do a good job and impress the boss, but as the deadline got closer, her fear of losing her job, or losing the respect of her boss for doing a bad job, would widen an ever-increasing gap generating ever increasing anxiety. Eventually the anxiety would get sufficient to compel Shelley to start her work. There is a good chance that her work would be of a higher quality because of the anxiety than without it.

I am sure that this makes sense to most people, as people only get anxiety when they care about something, and only people that care will do a good job. People that don't care, don't try. It is the anxiety brought about through caring and worrying about consequences to something that we care about that compels us to do a good job at something.

This is now a well-known phenomenon called the Yerkes-Dodson Law. Too little or too much anxiety arousal on difficult tasks and performance declines. Just enough anxiety arousal and we reach a sweet spot of motivation and performance. This can be seen in the Yerkes-Dodson curve below:

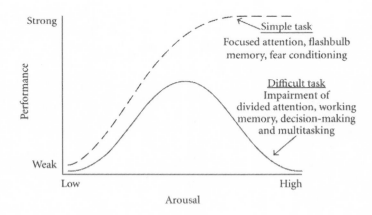

The Yerkes-Dodson Curve

Descartes said:

"When hope is so strong that it altogether drives out fear, its nature changes and it becomes complacency or confidence. And when we are certain that what we desire will come to pass, even though we go on wanting it to come to pass, we nonetheless cease to be agitated by the passion of desire which caused us to look forward to the outcome with anxiety. Likewise, when fear is so extreme that it leaves no room at all for hope, it is transformed into despair; and this despair, representing the thing as impossible, extinguishes desire altogether, for desire bears only on possible things."

So what Descartes is telling us, is without a gap between hope and fear, without anxiety, there is no motivation, and there is no life.

How Anxiety Begins

Anxiety is a major player in shaping who we are from the moment we are born. When we are born, all we have as far as threat responses go, is the startle pattern, which is what makes us jump if we hear a loud noise or there is a sudden movement. It is the very basic security software that comes bundled with our nervous systems. After a few months, though, babies start to recognise people, particularly their primary caregivers, and so small motivations start to develop around the caregivers and what they provide—the hope of a cuddle, or some food, as well as the fear of being abandoned by the caregiver and all food and security being lost. This is the very beginnings of anxiety. When babies wake up and their mother is not present, they get separation anxiety, as they become conflicted with uncertainty between the hope for food and cuddles, and the fear of being left to die. They have their first anxiety gap—so they cry.

As babies grow, they collect more things that they need, and more things to fear, and the opportunities to build anxiety gaps increase. Of course, many of the things to fear are learnt from those around them, so many of the gaps they form are like those in their family. This is often where irrational fears are formed that can cause anxiety later in life, but it can also be used, for better or worse, by parents in the training of their children:

Whether we like it or not, anxiety gaps are used throughout the upbringing of children to teach them and help them learn how to act and how to behave. Raising children and teaching them right from wrong usually follows either positive reinforcement or punishment, in other words offering a reward or promising a negative loss. Why does a child pick up their toys after playing with them? Because they know they will either get praised if they do or admonished if they don't. But why is a child fearful of being admonished by a parent, even when there is no physical violence? It is not the admonishment that the child fears, but what the admonishment represents and the possible consequences of it. If boundaries set by parents are strong, the child already knows the consequences, and, of course, the fear of abandonment lies deep and has done from very early days.

The anxiety caused by decision gaps is used to keep children acting in line with the wishes of the authority, and to teach them the preferred way of acting. Of course, the way that these forms of teaching and control of young minds is used will also shape the young mind into what it will later become, and if care is not taken, it can cause issues later in life. If a child is only ever "rewarded" with love, affection, and positive attention when they are successful, and they are punished whenever they make mistakes, the child might grow to always be looking for perfection and will fear making mistakes and disappointing other people. This kind of "perfectionism" is obviously impossible to maintain and will cause massive amounts of anxiety in most tasks. It is this judicial use of teaching techniques that makes parenting such an important, and stressful, job. It also emphasises the importance of anxiety in our lives from the very moment we are born.

We have learnt from anxiety all our lives, and we still do, and always will. Anxiety is a teacher, a protector, a guide, a mentor, and a motivator. It keeps us alive; it keeps us fed; it drives us and makes us successful; and it keeps us on the right path. But sometimes, as with most things, it can go a little too far. Sometimes, in its drive to help us, it locks us in our own prison for our safety. Much like the supercomputer VIKI in the movie iRobot that subjugates humans to "protect them from themselves", anxiety can sometimes go a little too far in its efforts to help. This is, of course, when we are venturing into the world of anxiety disorders.

Anxiety Disorders

We have already seen that everybody suffers from anxiety, but the chances are, if you are reading this book, then you already know that your anxiety does not come under the heading of "normal" anxiety and doesn't play by the normal rules. Just like we have some people that are optimists, and others that are pessimists, and it easy to see that some people are more naturally "emotional" than others, it is safe to say that different people experience differing amounts of anxiety.

Some people never even register the anxiety generated by their BIS, while others may find themselves completely immobilised by theirs. The amount of anxiety experienced by people is on a sliding scale between the two extremes. Everybody experiences anxiety differently, but everyone is somewhere on the scale. An important line to draw on the scale, though, is where exactly anxiety starts to negatively impact everyday life. When excessive anxiety begins to negatively impact life for an extended period, we start to venture into possible anxiety disorder territory. But the amount of anxiety experienced and the impact it has on life, on its own, is not enough to determine an anxiety disorder. After all, if we imagine a soldier in the trenches on the front line of battle waiting for the order to attack, we can say with reasonable confidence that his anxiety levels will be extremely high and will occur every day that he must wait. This does not mean to say, however, that he has an anxiety disorder. His anxiety is certainly severe, and it is certainly prolonged, but it is also perfectly reasonable for the situation that he is in.

This is an important distinction between healthy anxiety and unhealthy anxiety disorders: As well as being excessive in both severity and frequency, and having a major impact on life, the anxiety associated with a disorder is also disproportionate to the situations that trigger the anxiety. This means that whatever seems to have caused the anxiety is not as serious as the level of anxiety would suggest.

When a person suffers from an anxiety disorder, their life is significantly affected because of the decisions they make and the limitations they put on themselves. The difference between anxiety disorder sufferers and those with standard levels of anxiety comes down to the formation of the gaps. Anxiety disorder sufferers will form gaps where non-sufferers will not, and even when both form a gap, the anxiety disorder sufferer's gap will likely be much more negative, and therefore produce much more anxiety.

The very existence of anxiety disorders relies on the frequent formation of overly negative gaps: If someone's gaps are more negative than usual on a regular basis, they tend to experience more anxiety, more often, and will also choose to avoid situations more often as the anxiety inherent in the gaps becomes too much to tolerate. This avoidance and the self-imposed limitations on life due to the anxiety are what are often used as the diagnostic indicators for anxiety disorders.

Anxiety disorders and negatively distorted gaps, it seems, go hand-in-hand. But what causes these gaps?

What Can Cause Too Much Anxiety?

If we want to see what causes anxiety disorders, we need to find out what can cause some people to have more frequently negative anxiety gaps than most other people. What is it that increases the probability that any gaps produced will be largely net negative and largely in favour of avoidance?

The most obvious place to start is the three major systems that lead to the formation of the anxiety gap—the BAS, FFFS, and BIS. There is a lot of evidence to suggest that people have differing amounts of sensitivity to each of these. Some people might have an overly sensitive BAS, while others might have an overly sensitive BIS or FFFS. It is of course, possible to be overly sensitive in more than one system. The sensitivity of a system is mostly thought to be genetic, but this has not been determined with any certainty at this time.

The problem is that the sensitivity of each system is not directly linked to the presumed behavioural output of that system. In other words, an overly sensitive BAS does not necessarily mean that the person will be a thrill seeker, even though the system might suggest that. Likewise, an overly sensitive BIS does not mean that the person must have an anxiety disorder, although it certainly increases the likelihood that anxiety is increased. In fact, studies done on the system sensitivities have found that the final behavioural outcome of the BAS and BIS systems are dependent on the sensitivities of all three systems. Put another way, the activity of the BIS depends on how sensitive each of the BIS, BAS and FFFS systems are. It is a combination of all of them. Only the output of the FFFS is dependent solely on the sensitivity of its own system[31].

For this reason, and the reason that sensitivity is usually considered genetic, we can consider system sensitivity to be meaningless to us. Firstly, if the behaviour of the BIS is dependent on

---

[31] J.A. Gray's Reinforcement Sensitivity Theory (RST) of Personality | Pickering/Corr

the sensitivity of all three systems, then there is little use in targeting one for change when we do not know how it will affect the overall outcome. We could, of course, look at the sensitivity of the FFFS (sometimes known as amygdala sensitivity), but the next point makes that idea less appealing.

Secondly, if the sensitivities are genetically inherited, it suggests they are "hard-wired" making them extremely difficult to overcome or change. This is unhelpful because we know that the effects of the FFFS and BIS *can* be changed, and we know that fear and anxiety can be curbed because it has been shown in studies of therapies like CBT, and it can be clearly seen in people that experience life-changing events. After all, if values can be changed throughout life, and values and beliefs play a major role in the production of anxiety, then it must be true that anxiety levels can be changed without directly targeting any systems within the brain. This, at least in my view, makes thinking in terms of system sensitivity unhelpful, because it can lead to feelings of helplessness and powerlessness when, in fact, we know that anxiety levels can be changed, with or without knowledge of any kind of sensitivity.

So instead of looking at the sensitivity itself, I will be looking at some intermediary causes that have been shown to influence anxiety (which could, of course, themselves be results of the sensitivity or could be learned through the environment; either way these causes can be modified).

First, though, we need to look at the general things that make anxiety disorders different from regular anxiety and what specifically characterises and causes excessive anxiety, and then we can break them down.

Characteristics and Causes of Excessive Anxiety

These characteristics have mostly been taken from CBT anxiety disorder literature with a few added through the research of this book and from more up-to-date scientific literature:

1. **See threats where there are none and unable to distinguish easily between threat and safety.**
   This means that the person will see need/value losses in situations that do not warrant it, and form gaps where none should be. This is based on issues at the "thought" and "inference" level of threat assessment whereby negative inferences are made about negative thoughts regarding the possible loss of a need, and this leads to gaps being formed.

2. **Increased Avoidance Habits**
   As we have seen, passive avoidance and active avoidance can be powerful and useful safety features and keep us out of danger, but if the avoidance becomes a habit and passive avoidance plays out to prevent every situation that might cause a threat, then this is a problem. This can have a major impact on the quality of life as it can prevent any actions that involve even the possibility of threats.

3. **Intolerance of Uncertainty**
   Uncertainty is inherent in anxiety, as the very definition of anxiety requires a level of uncertainty to distinguish it from fear or despair. The unknown outcome of the conflict between hope and fear—approach and avoidance—provides the uncertainty that epitomises anxiety.
   Some people deal better with this uncertainty than others. Some people, and of course I am talking about anxiety disorder sufferers, can hate the idea of uncertainty so much

that they will do anything to prevent it. This can lead to avoidance behaviours and sticking to things that have a sure outcome.

In terms of gaps, intolerance of uncertainty generates its own values to lose, as the sufferer fears losing control of the situation and themselves, which brings about fears of the loss of esteem and sense of self, all adding to the negative FFFS side of their gaps.

4. Catastrophising Threats

The term, catastrophising, is often used when discussing anxiety disorders, because it is so common, and describes when a threat is made to seem much worse than it really is. Very often anxiety disorder sufferers will automatically opt for the worst-case scenario in a situation and make the threat side of the gap much bigger than it otherwise should be while minimising the possible positive side. There are other forms of extending the threat line, like catastrophising, that I will talk about later, but they could, at a push, all be filed under the catastrophe umbrella.

Catastrophising is based on the inference and evaluation level of threat assessment and value process, whereby the inferences are often determined to be the most negative possible and are evaluated to have the most catastrophic impact on the sufferer's life.

5. Perceived Inability to Cope

Very often, when the evaluation of a possible threat has been catastrophised and the worst-case scenario imagined, people can begin to believe that they will not cope with such a profoundly negative outcome, and they will fall apart or have a breakdown. This creates a new reason to be anxious, because now they fear that their whole world will fall apart, and they will not be able to cope with life.

In gap terms, the perception of not coping, just like the intolerance of uncertainty, creates new values to lose and therefore adds weight to the negative loss side of the gap. If a person feels they will not cope, then newfound fears of losing their entire sense of self can be brought into play.

6. Emotional Granularity

We have already looked at the new model of emotions called "constructed emotions", where the conscious emotional feelings that we "feel" are simply the recognition of certain patterns of *affect*, and we now know that this recognition of patterns is determined by our learning to link an emotional tag to our bodily states at any given time. This means, of course, that not everyone will assign the same emotional tag to the same *affect*. It also means that some people have a bigger emotional vocabulary than others. While some people might only recognise *sadness,* others might be able to differentiate the feelings of *melancholy, regret, grief,* and *despair.* This greater emotional vocabulary is called emotional granularity, and low emotional granularity has been shown to be linked with social anxiety disorders[32] and other affective disorders, while high emotional granularity has been shown to reduce anxiety in people who are stressed[33] and lead to people visiting the doctor less frequently, using medication less frequently, and spending fewer days in hospital for illness[34].

---

[32] Differentiating emotions across contexts | Kashdan et al [2014/2020]
[33] High Emotion Differentiation Buffers Against Internalizing Symptoms Following Exposure to   Stressful Life Events in Adolescence | Nook et al [2021]
[34] Emodiversity and the emotional ecosystem | Quiodback et al [2014]

7. Negative *Affect* due to unhealthy Interoception

As we have already seen, the feelings that we experience are based on emotional responses and the overall *affect* that we experience. The *affect* is partly based on the brain's mapping of the body to manage energy resources, check for damage or threats to the body, and to ensure its survival. The mapping of the body uses the signals that the body sends to the brain as constant updates, and forms the overall *affect* based on the current state of the body and the mind along with a prediction of what it believes will be needed. The mapping of the body is called **interoception**.

If something is not quite right with the body, signals will be sent to the brain which might result in a negative *affect* for a time while the brain tries to fix the problem. If our body needs food, we often feel a negative *affect* and become irritable. Many people's mood changes drastically when they are hungry. I have seen this firsthand.

Most interoception like this is perfectly normal, but sometimes issues with the body can cause interoception that leads to abnormally negative *affect* and therefore to bad moods and anxiety. When I talk about issues with the body, I am not talking about unseen serious health risks like cancer or heart disease (although these will most certainly negatively impact *affect*), I am, instead, talking about simpler issues like problems with the gut, inflammation, and allergic sensitivities. These are all things that can negatively impact *affect* but are also things that can be changed and made better. I will talk more about the things that can influence *affect* later, and we will look at things that you can do to ensure that interoception isn't worsening your anxiety.

Grouping the Problems

The above list is useful for looking through and seeing possible reasons for anxiety being more severe than the normal, but I understand that this list is not particularly helpful when it comes to trying to make changes. Finding ways to increase the confidence of coping, or reduce the sensitivity to threats, or in fact to have any meaningful impact on the seven things above, is no easy task and can often seem impossibly out of reach. They just do not seem to be rooted in any parts of our daily lives. That is why I have grouped the seven things above into three main sections, or root causes, where each section can be worked on and improved in an overall sense and will then have a positive impact on the causes of anxiety.

I should point out, that while it is not practically possible that these seven things could be separated so cleanly in real life, and there definitely is a lot of overlap, I think it is a good way to simplify things and make it clear what you are working towards. An improvement in these three areas will bring automatic improvements in anxiety, and although I will discuss some things you can do to improve some of the above seven points specifically, most of the discussion will be about improving one or more of the following three areas.

Here I will list the three areas with a brief description, and then I will go into more detail for each one.

1. The Mind

It should not come as too much of a surprise that the mind has a lot to answer for when it comes to anxiety. All kinds of wrong thinking, limiting or harmful beliefs, and overly pessimistic evaluations, can lead to gaps showing up where they shouldn't and gaps being much larger than is needed, but it is important to realise that, contrary to popular opinion, it is not the only anxiety player in town.

2. The Self

When I talk about the self, I am referring most of all to the idea of an overall sense-of-self, which can include the concepts of self-image, self-worth, and self-efficacy. Although there are other aspects of the self that can also be important, it is beyond the scope of this book to go into that much fine detail. Improving these can change the way we view threats and build confidence in coping with the anxiety that most certainly will appear. It may be a bit of a controversial subject right now, but plenty of studies have shown its powerful relationship with anxiety.

3. The Body

A huge, often unsung, villain in the story of anxiety and the way we feel in general is interoception. Interoception, just to remind you, is where the brain senses, interprets, and integrates signals from the body and uses them to form a complete minute-by-minute map of the body. This map then helps to form the *affect* that we feel as mood and can use to construct our emotional feelings. If something is wrong with the body, the signals to the brain will say so, and the interoception may construct an overall negative map of the body and provide us with a rather dour *affect*. Negative *affect* can widen gaps and lead to anxiety. And this is just the beginning.

As mentioned earlier, there is a lot of overlap in these three things, and while it could be argued that the self and the mind are the same thing because the self is simply a construction of the mind, I think it is more useful to separate them like this in order to change them. While the self may well be a construction of the mind, it is a deep construction—one that is based on deep-seated beliefs and values—and while the mind does what it does on the foundation of this self, it is usually not aware that it is doing so. I will discuss this more in the next chapter.

Think of working on the mind and self separately as working on the same issue from opposite sides—the self at the bottom and the mind at the top. As the Self influences the mind and the mind influences the Self, working on them both has an exponential effect on the outcome.

The Mind

*"Stressful life situations, per se, are less
important in the production of
anxiety...than the way in which situations
are perceived by the individual."*

Aaron Beck

The mind is the first to blame when people think they are
suffering from an anxiety disorder. It is, after all, the seat of all our
thinking and pondering; worry and rumination. The difficulty is that
problems with the mind are often buried deep and are more issues
with the self than with the mind itself. It has even been said that CBT
is so successful because it improves people's sense of self more than it
changes the mind. That said, there is no doubt that the way the mind
works does influence and even trigger anxiety episodes, and even
though many of these triggers are based on beliefs and values
stemming from the self, addressing the problems with the mind offers
another way to address the inherent issues within that are causing
increased anxiety levels.

In this section, then, I am going to look at some ways in which the
mind itself can influence the anxiety gap and produce anxiety through
the way it processes information, the way it uses memory, and the way
its workings can be influenced by external stimuli.

In Part 1, we looked at how the mind assesses every situation for
goals or threats to survival through the value process of thought-
inference-evaluation. This process can be hijacked at every point along
the way by cognitive biases, brought about through limiting beliefs and
a low sense of self, and can result in an exaggeratedly negative gap
through overly catastrophic inferences and evaluations. It is these
cognitive biases and their effect on the value process that are major

contributors to anxiety disorders, and no matter how we cut it, it is the mind that creates them.

Cognitive Biases

Cognitive biases are errors in unconscious thinking that make us misinterpret information that we receive from the world around us. In other words, we create our own reality in our minds that does not accurately reflect the reality outside us. There are many cognitive biases that affect every one of us to some degree or another, some more seriously than others.

Many of these biases you may have heard of already, like confirmation bias, which is the tendency for people to look for and interpret information to support their own beliefs and disregard information that does not, no matter how factual. This is a common bias in the world today, especially with the political partisanship and partisan news networks that exist and the ease at which people can choose their information sources. Another famous one is the Dunning-Kruger effect, whereby people with little knowledge or ability in something will often drastically overestimate their own knowledge and ability in that same thing. A little bit of knowledge is a dangerous thing. We have all met people like that and they are plain to see on social media.

Here though, we are talking about anxiety, and there are several cognitive biases that have been scientifically linked with anxiety disorders[35]: These biases are known as attention bias, interpretation bias, memory bias, and judgement bias.

---

[35] Cognitive biases in anxiety disorders and their effect on cognitive-behavioral treatment | Craske, Pontillo [2001]
Social Anxiety (Third Edition) | Kuckertz, Amir
Cognitive Biases in Emotional Disorders: Information Processing and Social-Cognitive Perspectives | Mineka, Rafaeli, Yovel

Attention Bias

Attention bias, in its general form, is where a person tends to unconsciously give more attention to certain stimuli over others. In anxiety disorders, these stimuli are usually threats. This means that people with anxiety disorders will be more likely to focus on something that they perceive to be a threat than to something that is not.

Interpretation Bias

Interpretation bias in anxiety sufferers leads people to perceive something that is neutral or ambiguous as threatening, or something that is mildly negative as catastrophic. Any neutral information that is received will be interpreted with a negative bias and is more likely to be seen as a threat. This will, of course, result in more threats been perceived than are present, and, combined with the attention bias, more attention given overall.

Memory Bias

Memory bias, as the name suggests, occurs when a person's memories are selectively remembered as more threatening than they really were, or only negative memories are recalled during an anxious episode. Unfortunately, while memory bias is included in many theories of anxiety disorders, the scientific evidence for the link between memory bias and anxiety disorders, other than PTSD, is still rather slim compared to the other biases mentioned here, so I will not discuss memory bias too much, even though I feel that it does play a part. It might still be a good idea to check your recall of memories is not overly negative in any given situation though.

Judgement Bias

Once a threat has been perceived, a negative judgement bias will lead a person to perceive the magnitude of the threat to be much greater than it really should. People with judgement biases often perceive the effect of a threat on themselves will be much worse than the threat itself warrants. This bias plays a major role in skewing the evaluation part of the value process in a negative direction.

There can be many different reasons for someone having cognitive biases, from conditioned learning, deep rooted beliefs, or a low sense of self, but as these are *cognitive* biases, there is no doubt that it is the mind that pulls the strings. The mind has somehow been trained to believe that using these biases will keep us safe, but what it does, of course, is lead us into anxiety.

This can be seen if we recall two entries on our list of what constitutes an anxiety disorder and compare them to our cognitive biases:

1. **See threats where there are none and unable to distinguish easily between threat and safety.**

4. **Catastrophizing Threats**

Seeing threats where there are none and being unable to distinguish between threat and safety is a combination of the interpretation and attention biases, while catastrophizing threats is use of the judgement bias.

Seeing threats where there are none also begins with the first part of the value process— Automatic thoughts. The catastrophizing of threats is done within the inference and evaluation portion of the value process and leads to even more negative threats within the gap. We will look at each of these a little more now.

Negative Automatic Thoughts

As we have already seen, in every situation that we, as humans, find ourselves in, our minds try to come up with an explanation as to why it is happening and the consequences that it might bring for us. This results in a string of possibilities that the mind throws up that could explain the situation or what might happen next as we saw in Tom's thought process earlier when his wife was late coming home. These possible explanations thrown up for a given situation are often called automatic thoughts and happen to everyone. There are several different ways, though, in which our minds can distort our perception of a situation and make these thoughts more negative than they should be, and we call these *negative* automatic thoughts. Everyone will have negative automatic thoughts, and there can be many reasons for someone to have *overly* negative automatic thoughts. These are usually caused by a negative *affect* brought about through illness, allergy, stress, hunger, tiredness, or just having a bad day. For some people, though, negative automatic thoughts can often be the default setting. Chronic negative *affect* from issues within the body, a low sense of self, or simply a learned habit of negativity and cognitive biases can make negative automatic thoughts the default. When negative is your go-to setting for automatic thoughts, you will see threats where none should be and be unable to easily distinguish threat from safety. This is the first characteristic that is the calling card of anxiety disorders.

I will discuss the different kinds of faulty thinking that cause negative automatic thoughts in part 3 when we look at trying to change them.

Negative Inferences & Evaluations

As we already know, after the thoughts have been processed and the winners with the highest perceived expected outcomes chosen (often called the HOT thoughts), the mind will continue through the process of inference chaining and evaluating the resulting inferences to build gaps. The problem is that if a person is suffering from a low sense of self, limiting beliefs, has a generally negative *affect*, or has developed a habit of being negative through conditioned learning, then the inferences and evaluations will also be overly negative. Not only will they have originated from a negative automatic thought, but they will also be skewed on the negative side themselves due to judgement bias.

This compounds the problem two-fold: First the 'perceived odds of happening' are increased for the negative inferences and decreased for the positive ones (remember risk vs benefit)—a result of the interpretation bias—and second, the 'perceived value if happened' is evaluated much higher for the negative impacts than positive—an unfortunate result of the judgement bias.

When these two things are combined—an increase in "perceived odds of happening" and an increase in negative "perceived value if happened"— we end up with much higher levels of "perceived outcome" for negative inferences than for positive ones, because if you remember:

$$\text{Perceived Outocome} = \text{Perceived Odds of Happening} \times \text{Perceived Value if Happened}$$

This will, of course, result in more frequent negative gaps, generally more net negativity to each individual gap, and therefore more severe anxiety.

It should be noted that attentional biases of some description are present in all people during anxious episodes, but there is a disproportionate level of attentional bias in anxious individuals, as well as the other forms of cognitive bias. It is also evident that these biases can influence our value processes negatively and therefore skew our anxiety gaps in favour of more frequent, and more extreme, anxiety leading to anxiety disorders.

We will look at tackling these cognitive biases in part 3, along with the negative thoughts and inferences that they produce, but more importantly we look at fixing the negative affect, limiting beliefs, and low sense-of-self that cause them.

Emotional Granularity

Number 6 on the list of things that can lead to anxiety disorders is emotional granularity.

6. Emotional Granularity

As a quick recap, emotional granularity refers to the broadness of the vocabulary used to describe emotions. If we use the same handful of words to describe everything i.e., happy, sad, angry, anxious, scared etc., then we would be described as having a low emotional granularity. This can cause two problems: First, we might end up not having labels for much of the *affect* we experience and therefore miss out on feelings that others might experience, instead experiencing only *affect* and moods. Second, we might assign the same label to a broad spectrum of affects, thus condemning ourselves to experience every form of irritation as anger, or every form of agitation as anxiety.

In the first problem, not having a name attached to an affect pattern, we would just feel affect and mood and not recognise any specific feeling. For example, you may have heard of the word schadenfreude, which according to the Oxford English Dictionary means the "malicious enjoyment of the misfortune of others". Most of us now recognise when we are feeling a bit of schadenfreude, as it has become such a popular online phenomenon, but the word itself did not enter the Oxford English Dictionary until 1982. This means that before 1982 people (outside of Germany) who took pleasure in the misfortunes of others had no name for their feeling. They may have thought "I'm enjoying seeing the misfortune of that other person", but it's highly doubtful. It is much more likely that they just had a strangely good feeling about something and couldn't quite explain why, and maybe even felt a little bad about it. Schadenfreude has allowed us to consciously feel that enjoyment and know what it is we are feeling. The word has added to our emotional granularity.

The second problem is the one that is more likely to lead to excessive anxiety and possibly anxiety disorders, because if our emotional granularity is low, and we only have a few different and distinct feelings that we recognise and can consciously experience, then we might label many things as anxiety that should not be. We might see nervousness, apprehension, trepidation, concern, anticipation, or even excitement as anxiety and therefore feel it in the situations where these arise. Now, while the automatic emotional response of anxiety might well be responsible for many of these types of feelings (nervousness etc.) as they can all be products of an anxiety gap, recognising, and therefore feeling, them all consciously as anxiety is destructive. If every small gap is interpreted and felt as "anxiety" and there is no differentiation, then anxiety will obviously be seen as an overwhelming problem and avoidance will seep into every aspect of everyday life. A lack of emotional granularity can lead people to view perfectly normal anxiety as something more insidious.

As you can see in the diagrams below, when we add numbers to the valence and arousal of our gaps, as we did before, and then apply them to valence-arousal graphs, we can see very different results between a person with high emotional granularity, and a person with low emotional granularity.

Low Granularity

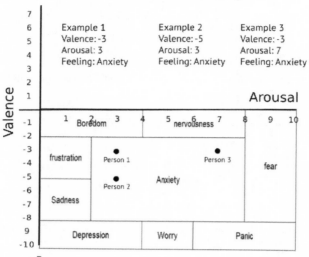

High Granularity

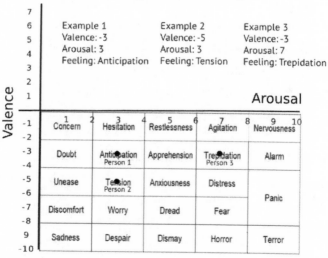

As you can see in the three examples above, the person with low emotional granularity only experiences anxiety in each scenario, whereas the person with high granularity experiences 3 different emotional feelings i.e., anticipation, tension, and trepidation. While these are all created via the same gaps, and are all possible synonyms for anxiety, the experiencing of different feelings allows the person with higher granularity to see that not everything is anxiety. It is a subtle, yet profound, distinction to make, and one that we will take advantage of later.

Emotional Construction Bias

As I mentioned earlier, some neurotransmitters or hormones, such as adrenaline (epinephrine), have no bearing on the valence of the emotions that we construct but will impact the arousal. In fact, it has been well documented that high levels of adrenaline in a person will elicit a high state of arousal but not a specific emotion until that emotion has been triggered by experience. This is one reason why the arousal is difficult to model with simple gaps.

This was demonstrated in 1962 when Stanley Schachter and Jerome Singer injected 184 male volunteers with adrenaline but told them they were trialling a new drug called "Suproxin" to test their eyesight[36]. Half of the students were told to expect some side effects of the shot, while the other half were not. The students were then placed in a room with an actor who pretended to act either angrily or extremely excitable and happy. Those that expected no side effects were shown to experience similar emotions to the actor, while those that were expecting side-effects felt nothing as they attributed their feeling to the drug they had been given.

---

[36] Cognitive, social, and physiological determinants of emotional state | Schachter, S., & Singer, J. E. [1962]

This implies that when the body is in a state of arousal, but the dominant valence is unclear, environment, thoughts, and memory can play a part in directing the brain to come up with an explanation for the arousal, thereby influencing the direction of valence and therefore the *affect*. This can be seen in situations where we enjoy the thrill of a roller coaster or take pleasure being scared during a horror movie. Provided we believe our safety is not in question, our knowledge that these are "pleasurable" experiences helps us construct positive feelings like excitement or exhilaration rather than anxiety or fear. Again, this is all down to perception, learned and experienced memory, and a belief in our safety. A 100m drop in a rollercoaster is likely to produce a very different feeling to a 100m fall from a hotel balcony.

This might suggest, then, that there could be many more people suffering from heightened threat responses than we would anticipate, but the threat response that they experience is simply leading to general arousal and not being attributed to a specific feeling because they have no memory or experience of a feeling to pin it to. It may also be being redirected into anger or excitement, or some other emotion, rather than anxiety. The reason it causes anxiety in so many others, is because that is an emotion with which they are already familiar and one which is being discussed more and more online, and it therefore provides them with that emotion to pin their affect to. The question should be asked though, if people had higher emotional granularity, and more experience in recognising other emotional feelings, might they attribute their anxious states of arousal to something else? Something other than anxiety?

In Part 3 we will look at how we can increase our emotional granularity, especially within the area of anxious emotions, to enable us to assign different emotional feelings to our affect and move away from anxiety, and also how recategorising anxiety has been shown to reduce anxiety and how we can use this to our advantage.

Value Evasion

As we have already seen, anxiety is triggered through the formation of a gap and the mind running through a value process to determine the perceived expected outcomes that will have the most impact on survival. This is the whole point of anxiety and is how it helps to keep us alive and thriving. It is important to note, though, that anxiety is not the only emotion that can be triggered through thoughts and the value processes that follow them. Most of the emotional feelings that we know including sadness, guilt, anger, and joy can be triggered through this same process. When we get angry because someone insults us, it is not what the other person says that enrages us, it is how we perceive what they say, and the thought process that follows that makes us mad. It is very often our own perception of a situation and how our minds value it that produce an emotional reaction.

This also means that when we don't want to feel a certain emotion, very often we will suppress the thoughts and value processes that would lead to that emotion to prevent us from experiencing the resulting negative *affect* and emotional feelings. For example, most people do not like to entertain the idea of a loved one dying. The very thought and the subsequent value process results in a feeling of sadness and anxiety that makes us uncomfortable, so we try not to think about it. The saying "it doesn't bear thinking about" is one that is very appropriate here. The reason that this thought doesn't fill most people with overwhelming anxiety is because the value process will likely assign a very low likelihood to it happening and so we can put it out of our minds without too much issue. Of course, if a loved one is sick, the value process will result in much more anxiety as the chances of it happening increase. This is also true as loved ones grow older.

When thoughts are clear, like in this example, the anxiety triggered is normal and appropriate as real possible loss is considered, but in some cases, when the thoughts and value processes are suppressed, it might not be so. In some cases, often those built upon a low sense-of-self, the possible outcome of a value process could be perceived to be so damaging that the entire process is ignored. For example, a man might think that his wife is too good for him, and he may believe that he is unworthy of her and possibly even unworthy of being loved. The thought of her leaving him and him being alone forever might arise on a day-to-day basis and fill him with unbearable anxiety and sadness, so he tries to avoid the thought and the value process altogether. He pushes the thought away each time it crops up, and through the process of habit formation, the unconscious mind eventually stops the thought appearing at all. The unconscious mind is "protecting" the man. The man is now taking part in value evasion and the value process of his wife leaving and him being left alone may never enter his mind again.

Unfortunately, life, like our minds, is not that straightforward: Just because the thought never becomes conscious again does not mean that the value process is not being run unconsciously. It might not take the same form, as the thought is never clearly identified, but the underlying beliefs and feelings of inadequacy and not being worthy of love still exist under the surface. This will result in anxiety with no clear origin or trigger. There may be more emotional fall-out as well, as the negative *affect* generated can lead to sadness, depression, guilt, and shame. The man in question would not be able to pinpoint the cause of this anxiety and emotional turmoil, but he could suffer tremendously. The anxiety generated could also begin to filter down into all aspects of his everyday life where he would find threats where there were none and fears that he never had before. All because he chose to suppress a thought and evade an unwanted value process instead of trying to deal with it.

The point here is that suppressing a value process to avoid the anxiety does no such thing in the long run. The unconscious mind can function perfectly well without our permission and will continue to run value processes whether we want it to or not. All that happens is that the anxiety becomes non-conscious and harder to detect or tackle.

The Self

As already discussed, it is undeniable that the self and the mind are two sides of the same coin. The unconscious mind develops the self over time and governs it as we go through life, while the self, in turn, influences the mind, the way it thinks, and the decisions it makes. They are inseparable at a base level, and yet appear as separate entities on a day-to-day level. The reason I have separated them here, then, is because self-concepts run much deeper than the average cognitive thought of the mind. Self-concepts cover a wide area that normally we never consciously think about, and may not even have access to, but make us who we are. They can cover such specific ideas as nationality, ethnicity, gender, and sexual orientation, while they can also include those concepts that underlie our personalities, such as whether we are extrovert or introvert, conscientious or irresponsible, kind or thoughtless. Our self-concept of these things may all be perceptions created in the brain, but they have strong genetic, social, and environmentally formed bases which make them different to the things we think about every day. These are things that make us who we are, and, in this context at least, are distinct from the mind. These make up the self.

There seems to be as many ways to talk about and describe the self these days as there are selves to be described, so I am going to boil it down to just three simple concepts of the self that have been shown to play a role in anxiety—the self-image, self-worth, and self-efficacy. Together, these are sometimes known as self-esteem.

Self-Image

Every one of us has a mental image of how we see ourselves and how we believe others see us. We create images based around our physical appearance (height, weight, attractiveness) and how we think others view this appearance, as well as our personalities, characteristics, and values. It is, how we think the world sees us. Whether we view ourselves as having integrity, being assertive, kind, or intelligent, the self-image is created within us, and is based on our own perceptions of ourselves.

Self-Worth

I was going to use the term self-esteem to include both self-worth and self-efficacy here, as it is a commonly used term, but I decided that it was also a very controversial term now as many people associate negative ideas with the term. While these ideas may well be incorrect, the bias is no doubt there, so I decided to leave the term self-esteem on the side-lines for now and use the separated concepts of self-worth and self-efficacy. There are still many different ideas and theories about the structure of these—some simple and some extremely complicated—but I am going to try and use ideas that are simple and elegant, and yet complete enough to show their importance.

Self-worth, then, is very simply how we value and feel about ourselves as people, and therefore how we perceive others feel about and value us. This could also comprise self-respect, and self-acceptance. It is how worthy we feel of being happy, how worthy we feel of sitting at the table of life, how much value we place on ourselves, how generally we feel we belong in society and where we feel we rank within it. It is important to note that it is not how other people value us, as that is impossible to know, it is how we value ourselves and how we *believe* others value us.

Self-Efficacy

Self-efficacy is our feeling of competence at doing certain things, how much control we have over changing our environment, or how well we feel we can cope with certain situations, changes, relationships, and life in general. It is the confidence we have in ourselves to complete life, to be ourselves, and to fulfil our own needs.

This could also comprise self-confidence, and self-awareness. Again, this has nothing to do with how others judge our competence but is only how we perceive our own competence and *believe* others perceive it.

Each of these three senses-of-self combine to form what I am referring to as our whole "Self" in this book. Certainly, there are other descriptions of the self, and there are undoubtedly many different theories of self-esteem and self-image, but these capture the sense of self that I need here and incorporate each of the parts of the self that can affect anxiety. And it keeps everything much simpler.

To understand the difference between self-worth and self-efficacy and the importance of each, we can use the analogy of starting a new job in a new company. For the first few months of a new job, we always feel like the newbie. We don't fully fit into the work culture, and we don't fully understand the job. This is a lack of the work-specific self-worth and self-efficacy. As time goes by, though, we slowly incorporate ourselves into the work culture and social life more and more, and get better at the work, and our work-specific self-worth and self-efficacy increase within the job.

Of course, as we all know, it is possible to have someone who fits perfectly into the office culture, is popular amongst colleagues and liked by management, but is fully aware that they are not really that good at their job. This is what it is like to have a high self-worth and low self-efficacy. The reverse is also possible: There are many people who are exceptional at their jobs, but for whatever reason feel that they are disliked by management and not accepted by colleagues. This is like having a high self-efficacy and low self-worth.

Both examples are common in work or other specific scenarios but can cause huge problems when this is the overriding perception of someone's entire life. Of course, it is also possible to be very good at a job and be at ease within the company regardless of the feelings of management and colleagues. This means that if someone is very secure in who they are they care less about the feedback from others and rely more on their own self-evidence. This is certainly possible, but not common in everyday work culture.

What Does the Self Do?

The first question that is often asked, and the one that is often used to dispute the idea of any sense of self, is why do we have one in the first place? What is the evolutionary reason for keeping a sense of self within us? Many theories have been put forward over the years, and many of them argue persuasively on the difficulties of ranking within a social culture if we did not have at least some sense of how we view ourselves ranking within the society.

Niche Ranking

All social mammals, and certainly most primates have a hierarchical structure, and it is useful for everyone to know where they stand within that structure. Ranking ourselves against others is one way in which we do that, and the Self is one way in which we can rank ourselves against other people, just as other social animals do: An alpha male who does not feel he deserves to be alpha male will not last long, and a young upstart vying to take the crown would never dare challenge the current leader if he did not believe in himself and his own abilities. Both scenarios take some kind of belief in the self.

Of course, ranking is not absolute. Ranking depends on self-worth and self-efficacy and is therefore often niche specific, which means it only applies to certain areas of our lives. A good example of this (at least for people of a certain age) is the movie Saturday Night Fever, which starred a young John Travolta in 1977: Travolta played a young man named Tony Manero who worked as a paint store clerk in New York and did not have much success in most areas of his life. During the week he ranked lowly in general society, but at the weekend, Tony hit the local disco. Here Tony was king. Everybody knew who he was, and everybody wanted to dance with Tony. On the dance floor Tony ranked top dog; here Tony's sense-of-self was huge, but only here. This is not uncommon, and many of us will find that we have a high sense-of-self in only certain parts of our lives.

Identity Verification

A newer theory which I find particularly compelling is that of identity verification: As social animals, we humans understand that we must abide by certain social rules and constraints, and we learn what is expected of us to be accepted in the community. But how do we know if we are fulfilling our social contract? How do we know if our actions are in line with what is expected? Of course, it is easy to know if our actions are skirting local laws, as the handcuffs tend to give it away, but most of the things we do in our everyday life are well within the law but may not be within social expectations.

This is where our sense of self comes in. In social situations, we are continually comparing our actions in society and our behaviour and interactions with others with our sense of self. We compare our actions to see if they are in line with what we believe our own values, beliefs, and self to be. Much like a guided missile finds its target by making constant course corrections each time it veers off target, we do similarly when we act in society. If our actions are out of line with how we view ourselves—our sense of self—then we make corrections by changing our actions and getting ourselves back on course. We want to behave the way we think we should—it is ingrained in us from young as our Self was being forged. Any difference between our actions and the way we feel our self should act will create a gap, which will result in anxiety and a drive to close the gap by making a correction.

When our sense of self is not in line with our actions and the resulting gap needs to be closed, there are two choices of correction that can be made: We can change our actions, or we can change our sense of self.

In normal situations, most people tend to change their actions and behaviours to stay in line with their own self-image and self-worth. If we think of ourselves as a kind person, and we realise that something we have done has hurt someone else, we will take steps to redress the hurt, close the gap, and quell the anxiety inside us. This will usually be by way of an apology or actions that atone for the pain caused. The change is as much to lessen the anxiety as it is to help the other person. This is the way society works, and why anxiety is such an important social tool.

Sometimes, though, self-worth and self-image are the more convenient to change. No person in history started off as a murderer, a criminal, or a corrupt official. A corrupt politician doesn't start his career wanting to be corrupt (in most cases anyway), but over time, small unethical actions and behaviours that go uncorrected due to external pressures or ambitions of power cause slight course corrections in the sense-of-self, and before the politician realises what has happened, the values and lofty ideals they once held have all but disappeared. Small corrections over a long time can put us in a completely different direction to that which we started. This is true for both positive and negative changes.

This doesn't always have to involve clear-cut cases between good and bad, though. Sometimes the actions we take or the work we do, or the behaviours we exhibit are subject to negative feedback from others for many different reasons. If the work, action, or behaviour is difficult to change or we are unable to improve it, then the course correction can be made in our self-image, self-worth, or self-efficacy to close the gap.

If we write a book, for example, and everyone who reads it says it's terrible (it's a real fear), we can try and rewrite it to make it better, but eventually we may start to believe we are not a good writer, and our self-efficacy and self-worth take a hit, and eventually we quit. In fact, I would say that a useful definition of confidence would be to believe in what we are doing and persevere at changing our actions rather than our Selves in the face of criticism and setback. This is different to narcissism where no amount of feedback or criticism will be allowed to affect either.

This means that feedback from others can play a huge role in carving our self-worth and self-image, as it is often the only metric that we have to gauge our success in the social world. Therefore, our identity verification will often depend heavily on other people. This is how social groups work together, rank each other and form hierarchies. If others in our social group respond positively to our actions, then we get a feeling that we are doing well and have something to offer the group and our self-worth and self-efficacy rise. Negative responses from the group, however, prompt us to change our actions to move in line with what the group desires or change our expectations of what we can deliver—the latter being a change in the self. Unless it's social media of course.

The problem with feedback is that it is not always genuine or sincere. There are millions of trolls on the internet just waiting to tear others down because they know there will be no repercussions for doing so and because their own sense-of-self is so low that they know that they could never do anything truly constructive themselves. The only way they can feel good about themselves and 'raise themselves up' is to try and drag others down to their level. This is fake feedback and therefore the kind that we should look to ignore and not let it force either a change in action or in self.

This leads us to another important point of a sense-of-self: We view the feedback we receive from others through the lens of our Self. This means that people with a high self-worth and self-efficacy are much more likely to be able to withstand criticism without folding and are likely to choose more carefully those they are willing to receive feedback from.

Fake feedback isn't always negative though, there are plenty of examples of fake positive feedback, and I'm not just talking about Grandma. We only have to look at the "self-esteem revolution" that took place in the US and across the western world at the end of the last century. Millions of children were told that they were wonderful and that everything they did was perfect in a hope to raise their self-esteem and give them a better chance of success. They were given participation trophies and told they were winners at everything, when it was clear they weren't. This feedback did of course raise the self-worth of the children as they grew up, and indeed gave them the impression that they could take on the world, but of course it wasn't that easy. It never is.

The problems with this came two-fold: First, self-efficacy is less easily fooled by false praise than self-worth and needs good solid results in the most part to rise significantly. Knowing we are loved and valued will help raise our self-worth but being told we're awesome at running when we came last in every race will not fool our self-efficacy into thinking we are a star athlete. And coming last is fine. Not everyone can be a star athlete. Not everybody should be. But when Mom and Dad tell us that we were awesome in the race, it causes conflict between what we are being led to believe and what we know really happened, and this can lead to anxiety in future races and situations. This can of course then lead to lowered self-worth.

The second way that false praise can cause problems, occurs as young people grow up: As they get older, some young people realise they are not as wonderful at everything as they thought. They learn that the world is a much tougher place than they had been led to believe. Identity verification causes them to lower their own self-worth and self-efficacy over time as they are unable to course-correct their actions to match the expectations set by themselves and others. The result is wholesale lowering of their sense-of-self—quite the opposite to what the parents had hoped. In fact, because these children were never pushed to do anything productive or challenging and were often allowed to coast through their early years doing very little of any worth but receiving high praise for it anyway, the resultant self-efficacy is often far below the norm. These young adults expect a lot, but can't deliver, and are forced to course-correct to make up the arrears, tanking their self-worth. They begin to realise they can't compete, so they expect society to fill in the gaps like their parents used to, and they become entitled. Being entitled is a symptom of low self-worth and self -efficacy, not high. I should point out, that although this issue was possibly most pronounced in children from the 90's, it is in no way restricted to that generation.

Social identity conflict

The self-identity that we grow up with will, of course, change over time, but what is often more important in our day-to-day lives is the new social identities that we forge for ourselves that build upon that base self-identity.

Social identities are forged by the different social groups that we identify with as well as the groups that we join as part of our jobs and career world. We all identify with different groups whether they be groups based on gender or race, political or religious interests, or what we do for a living, and these groups can play a significant role in who we view ourselves to be. They also provide us with social rules and norms that we must abide by if we wish to remain part of the group. There is a large body of evidence showing that the rules set by our social groups play a significant role in impacting our behaviour and ensuring our conformity to the group values[37]. While the group rules can be enforced like laws for a time through reward and punishment, they tend to become internalised over time and become learned behaviour[38] and this makes us identify with the group more and more.

There are a few ways that this social identification can cause anxiety: As we will see later, people can become dependent on their social identity, and the prospect of losing it can cause immense amounts of anxiety. But sometimes anxiety can also be caused by conflicts between these identities. We all hold more than one social identity, and sometimes these social identities don't play well together. When this happens, we can find it difficult to reconcile the issues between them, and this can cause anxiety. For example, a doctor may feel affinity to being both a health care professional and a manager as he must run his own practice astutely. This might lead to anxiety between wanting the best care for his patients but also wanting to keep costs down.

Being a member of a religious group that espouses anti-homosexual ideas might also provoke anxiety in a gay member of that group.

Anxiety can also be present when people find it difficult to adhere to the social rules prescribed to their social identity. An example of this might be men trying to adhere to the cultural norm that men are stoic and unemotional, when in fact many men are just as emotional as women. Give me a sad movie and I will sob like a baby, and yet I will often try to hide it from those around me, as sobbing like a baby is not historically considered a very manly trait.

People who are more rigid with the boundaries of their social identities tend to experience much more anxiety than those with a more fluid stance, and it has been shown that conflict between social

---

[37] Asch, 1951; Cialdini & Goldstein, 2004; Sherif, 1936
[38] Miller & Prentice, 1996; Scott, 1971

identity concepts leads to more anxiety and depression and less well-being in general[39].

How Does the Sense-of-Self Change?

The simplest and most elegant way to express how the sense of self is changed is to say that when our needs and values are met, our sense of self increases, and when they are not met, it diminishes. Other people meeting our needs and values tends to raise our self-worth, while meeting our needs and values ourselves tends to raise our self-efficacy. This is a simplification but is a good rule of thumb. As a child, if our needs for love, caregiver bonding, and social connection are not met, we will develop with an incomplete sense of self-worth, and if we are not allowed to face challenges ourselves, we will develop with an incomplete sense of self-efficacy.

Self-worth and self-efficacy, then, have subtly different methods of change: Self-worth, at least in our early years, is most often based on the feedback of others, or, more precisely, our perception of the feedback of others, and portrays how worthy we feel to be a member of our social group. If the feedback is positive, then our self-worth will grow a little; if negative, our self-worth will drop a little. This has led many researchers to state that this means self-worth has nothing to do with the self and is based purely on what people think of us. In my opinion, this is a little short sighted, because it presumes that we know what other people are thinking, which, even when they speak plainly, is impossible. Feedback is always viewed though our own perception and so, therefore, is our self-worth.

Very often the feedback from others is not actually intentional feedback at all, but subtle interactions that we interpret and take meaning from as positive or negative. Every interaction that we have

---

[39] Campbell et al., 1996; Sheldon & Kasser, 1995; S. J. Schwartz et al., 2011

with another person is weighed and measured by the scales of our own perception to determine how it will affect our self-worth.

Even when someone does speak plainly to us, there is still interpretation and bias within us. The feedback that we receive from others, is of course based on our perception, and is viewed through the lens of our self-worth. This, of course, can put self-worth into negative, or positive, feedback loops: If our self-worth is high, we might have a more positive view of feedback, even if it is not meant as such by the other person. Alternatively, if we have low self-worth, we can bias the feedback negatively, and even if comments are neutral or not intended to be feedback at all, we can view them as negative, which can affect our self-worth further.

As already mentioned, not all feedback is verbal. Very often, the feedback received is based solely on our own interpretation of the physical responses or body language of others. This is really where the lens of self-worth plays its part. If the boss walks around with a scowl on her face and does not answer when the staff says hello, someone with low self-worth might think "she hates me, I am rubbish at this job" which will negatively affect their self-worth further, while someone with high self-worth might think "She looks in a bad mood today" which will have no impact at all on their self-worth.

We can see, then, that self-worth is determined by our perception of the views and feedback of other people about us. It is how we feel about ourselves, based on what we think other people feel about us. Of course, the level of our self-worth not only determines the bias we put on feedback, but it also biases which people we choose to accept feedback from. People with low self-worth will often accept criticism from anyone, whereas those with higher self-worth are more likely to choose only those people who are important to them to accept criticism from.

Self-efficacy, on the other hand, is based on self-validation of the successful outcome of an action. If you perceive that you did a good job at something, your self-efficacy in that area will increase. Self-efficacy does not rely on feedback from others as much as self-worth does, as true self-efficacy can only be increased through completing actions well (although someone telling you that you did a good job will certainly help with this). If you win every game of chess that you ever play, you do not need someone else to tell you that you are good at chess, although it's certainly nice if they do. If you complete every task your boss gives you in half the time of everybody else, you know you are good at your job even if your boss keeps tight lipped. If, however, everybody tells you that you're a good driver, but you crash your car at least once a week, then you will realise that everyone is just kissing your behind. Self-efficacy is how competent you feel yourself to be at a task or action, and this can only be truly known through a job well done. Of course, this sometimes requires feedback, but not always.

Self-efficacy, then, is determined through our own belief in how good we are at something. Feedback can help bolster this belief, but it is not enough on its own.

Of course, this doesn't always hold true for actions that are subjectively viewed. For example, if everyone around you tells you that you are the best dancer they have ever seen, you might start to believe them, but if the only dancing you ever did was Morris dancing (if you have never heard of this, please Google, it I implore you) then you probably shouldn't start entering dance competitions anytime soon.

For most tasks, the increase (or decrease) of self-worth through feedback, or the increase (or decrease) of self-efficacy through the perception of an outcome, will only be for that specific niche or area. For example, if we beat the world champion at chess and everybody tells us how good we are, then our self-efficacy and self-worth will increase within the field of chess. This does not mean that we will suddenly feel better at tennis or doing stand-up comedy; it will only make changes at chess. Self-worth and self-efficacy in narrow fields like this are called **domain specific**.

That said, changes in domain specific self-worth and self-efficacy will also make small changes to our **global** self-worth and self-efficacy. Our global self-worth is our overall evaluation of ourselves as members of society and is not based in any specific areas or situations. It is how we evaluate ourselves generally. Our global self-efficacy is how we feel we will cope with life in general, or how confident we would be of tackling the unknown. The more domain specific areas we have and the more we build each of them, the more we build the global levels of self-worth and self-efficacy.

It is easy to see the narrow reach of domain specific self-efficacy and self-worth if we imagine a professional tennis player who is extremely confident in his ability to play the game on the court and is also at ease in the overall tennis environment with all the TV interviews and networking that goes a long with it. His self-efficacy and self-worth in the domain of tennis are sky high. But when it comes to love, or parenting, or finances, or swimming, or whatever other areas of life he might encounter, he may not be so self-assured. Professional levels in a single domain do not necessarily equate to high levels globally, or even high levels in other domains. Many people are world-beaters at their jobs but are car wrecks in their personal lives.

Dependency

One of the biggest causes of low self-worth is dependency. Now obviously not everyone who is dependent on something else will lose self-worth, but it can play a major part in others, and often people can be dependent without even realising that they are. There are three main kinds of dependence and, as we will see in a moment, each of them can create gaps and generate excessive anxiety, but I will look at each of the three types first:

Physical Dependence

The most obvious one that people think of when we mention the word dependence is physical dependence, because they automatically think of addictions such as alcohol, drugs, or gambling. While these certainly do create a lot of anxiety, they are certainly not the only physical dependencies. Many people also depend on others completely for their physical safety, security, and survival. For many people, especially the young, being physically dependent on other people is not a problem and will not cause any undue anxiety. The problems start if being dependent begins to interfere with our own values, deprives us of other needs, or is deemed socially unacceptable in which case self-worth and social connection begin to play a part. Like each of the other two kinds of dependence, there are several things that someone could be physically dependent on, and we call these the dependence centres[40].

A brief list of dependence centres for physical dependence might look something like this:

Spouse
Parents
Family
Children
Work
Friends

As mentioned above, many of us may well be dependent on some of these with no concerns about gaps or anxiety. For example, a teenager may be dependent on his parents, a new mother may be dependent on her husband for financial support, and many of us will be dependent on our jobs to survive. Whether anxiety is felt or not in these situations will depend on how well we accept our situation and

[40] The 7 Habits of Highly Effective people - Book by Stephen Covey

the dependence that is inherent within it, but for these examples the anxiety should be low because each of these is a socially acceptable situation, so there will be no social pressures. Of course, if the teenager is desperate to follow his dream in the city, the mother is resentful that she had to halt her career, or the worker desperately wants to quit his job and start his own business, then an anxiety gap can certainly form around the dependence.

These forms of dependence can be made even more difficult to deal with when they impact self-worth or social status. For example, a middle-aged man living with his parents will enjoy the safety and security of being looked after at home but will suffer the embarrassment and loss of self-worth that comes with being a middle-aged man living with his parents. His losses for staying with his parents will be sizable as they will include possible losses to self-worth, self-efficacy, self-respect, social status, ranking, social connection and likelihood of finding a partner, causing a huge gap and massive anxiety problems. I am not saying this is true of all middle-aged men living with their parents, but I am just using it as an example of a socially unacceptable dependence.

Many might ask, why doesn't the middle-aged man leave his parents' house if the gap is so large? That is a good question. The problem is that whenever he thinks about leaving, a second decision gap is created, and because of his already low, and sadly decreasing sense-of-self, the gap to leave is even greater as his fear of "being out there alone" is too great. The gap for remaining at home is the remaining half of a latent decision gap, and although he may come to terms with it and might minimise the effects by using the cognitive dissonance techniques from earlier, the chances are he will suffer the anxiety from the gap for the rest of his life. Dependency, then, can be a vicious cycle, as low self-worth keeps the person dependent, and by being dependent the self-worth is diminished further, and any alternative gap only gets bigger through time.

Similar gaps can occur elsewhere, such as aged parents who have suddenly become dependent on their children through sickness, people who have been made redundant and are suddenly dependent on their spouses, or people who have been forced to borrow money from friends to stay financially afloat and now feel indebted. The gaps for each of these can range from non-existent to extreme and will only be determined by the perception of importance of the needs or values by the individual.

Intellectual Dependence

Intellectual dependence is when a person depends on someone else to make decisions or tell them what to think. Sometimes they may even have their own beliefs and values hijacked by another person and depend on that person to tell them how to behave or act. Intellectual dependence can even go so far as relying on someone else for the values to live by. Of course, we all gain our original values from others as we go through childhood, but our values and beliefs should become our own as we enter adulthood. Intellectual independence does not mean that we should not learn from other people, but it does mean that we should not substitute the thinking, or judgements, of others as our own. When a person views their entire reality through the perceptions and minds of other people, they are completely intellectually dependent.

Like the physical dependence above, intellectual dependencies can play havoc with the sense of self, and the fear of losing self-worth, social connection, cognitive self-efficacy, and beliefs and values will create a large gap with lots of anxiety. Of course, none of this happens if it is to be expected or is acceptable by the person, such as a young child, but an adult that relies on anyone else for decision making, judgement calls, values, beliefs, ideas, or evaluations of life, is never going to have a full and robust and healthy sense of self and is always likely to suffer from anxiety.

Emotional Dependence

Emotional dependence is where a person depends on somebody (or something) else for their sense-of-self. Very often they see the object of their dependence as the very thing that makes them who they are. This might sound strange, but it is more common than you think, and is usually when self-worth is dependent on self-identity. For many people, being emotionally dependent will cause no adverse effects, but for some, the fear of losing that on which they depend, and therefore losing themselves, their identity, and their sense-of-self, is terrifying.

The dependence centres for emotional dependence include the same ones as the physical dependency but also cover a lot more options than the two other kinds of dependence. For example, a mother may be emotionally dependent on her children and view motherhood as the only role for her in life, and being a mother as who she is. She is therefore terrified of the day that they will fly the nest and leave, as her perceived identity will leave with them. A man might be emotionally dependent on being a policeman, as he sees it not as a job, but who he is, and he is terrified of what will happen when he must retire and become a "nobody". A woman might be emotionally dependent on her looks, as she has always identified with being a beautiful woman and fears the day that they will fade. A man might be emotionally dependent on his sexual exploits, as he has lived his life on the "admiration" and "respect" of his friends, and so fears the day that women will no longer want him. All these things can, of course, happen to anyone of both sexes, but they are just examples.

For each of the above examples, and all examples of emotional dependence, things can be fine for long periods of time, but as soon as the person starts to think that they may lose the person, object, position, trait, or value that they are emotionally dependent on, they will create a gap and anxiety will be triggered. The thought of losing "who we are" is one of the biggest fears we can have and can create huge amounts of anxiety.

Social Media and Emotional Dependence

I think we are in a worrying time in history right now where so many young people have staked their self-worth on the success of their social media personalities. So many young people have tens or hundreds of thousands of followers on social media simply because they look good and have learned to perform a few moves of a popular dance. Depending on this kind of fleeting fame for their sense of self is detrimental in more ways than one: Not only is the fickle view of the internet likely to focus its spotlight of adoration on someone else quicker than a new video can be made and edited, but it also leads to people not truly living their lives. How many people these days go to the most beautiful places in the world, but instead of savouring the beauty of the place they are at, spend the entire time taking photos and videos to show other people that they were there? I have seen people in restaurants order a whole table full of food, take a few photos, and then leave without ever taking a bite simply to impress their followers. Caring more about showing off to other people than enjoying life is a dependence that will not end well.

Self-Doubt and Anxiety

The sense of self is built around belief in ourselves. People with a high sense-of-self tend to believe they can do things and are worthy of good things happening to them, while people with a low sense-of-self often do not. People with a low sense-of-self often have what we call "limiting beliefs" which, as the name implies, are beliefs which limit the person's goals, ambitions, behaviours, and thoughts. These limiting beliefs are at the core of self-doubt.

Self-doubt is the result and the culmination of a low sense-of-self, and the limiting beliefs that come bundled with it, and is arguably the biggest cause of most anxiety disorders. As the name suggests, self-doubt is when we question our own value, our competence, or our ability to cope with a given situation. When the sense-of-self is low, doubt plagues our actions, decisions, and thoughts, and this can lead to anxiety. When the unconscious mind is running through the value processes of any situation to determine the values that are most likely to affect survival, the sense-of-self, and the beliefs formed because of the sense-of-self, plays a pivotal role in the inference and evaluation of each thought. This means that a low sense-of-self, and therefore strong self-doubt, very often results in more negative thoughts, inferences, and evaluations and therefore a more negative gap than does a healthy sense-of-self.

This can lead to two of the characteristics of anxiety disorders:

1. See threats where there are none and cannot distinguish easily between threat and safety.
4. Catastrophising Threats.

Just to clarify, when the sense-of-self is low and self-doubt high, the thoughts and inferences that result will be more negative than usual and will therefore predict the outcome of situations to be more negative than they should be. This will lead to threats being perceived much more often than usual. Also, when self-doubt leads to negative evaluations, this will result in those threats being considered more damaging than they should be. This is catastrophising.

If we look at the value process more closely, though, we can see that self-doubt will lead to higher "perceived odds of happening" for negative inferences than for positive, and more negatively skewed "perceived value if happened" for all thoughts and inferences. This will obviously result in an exaggerated negative "perceived value outcome" and therefore a more negative gap. As you probably already know by now, this will lead to more anxiety.

There have been many scientific studies that have shown clear links between low self-esteem and anxiety where, for example, "the results indicate a clear inverse relationship between self-esteem and anxiety level"[41], but it is clear to see, even without the science, that a negative view of the self is more likely to result in negative predictions of future outcomes and situations that involve the self. This will of course lead to more fear of failure, an exaggerated FFFS response, and therefore increased anxiety.

What is often not so clear is that our sense-of-self can also sometimes change our values. A man who sees a bomb falling on him will certainly not value the bomb, but if he believes himself to be indestructible, he will not care[42], and if he is tired of living, he might welcome it. The way we view ourselves (i.e., our sense-of-self) can help determine our values, and if our values determine our hopes and fears, it is no wonder that our sense-of-self plays a significant role in the construction of anxiety gaps and the triggering of anxiety. If a man's self-image means he sees himself as a low-level worker within his company and nothing more, then when a promotion opportunity arises, he may not even apply, as he does not view himself as

---

[41] Rosenberg, M. (1962)
[42] The psychology of self-esteem, Nathaniel Branden

management potential and doubts that he could do the job. The fear of failure baked in with his self-doubt creates enough anxiety to stop him even trying. This is obviously a self-fulfilling prophecy.

I think it is clear, then, that a low sense-of self and high self-doubt can lead to more negative gaps and increased anxiety, but it can also lead to anxiety in other ways. It can lead to two other characteristics of anxiety disorders that we saw previously:

3. Intolerance of Uncertainty
5. Perceived Inability to Cope

These two characteristics are closely tied together, as both are based around a lack of self-efficacy, resulting in doubt in the ability to cope or deal with the world when the future is uncertain. People who are intolerant of uncertainty tend to be so because they fear that uncertainty leads to negative outcomes, and they believe they cannot cope with very negative outcomes. The fear of negative outcomes, coupled with the uncertainty around them happening, generates large amounts of anxiety, which the sufferer also believes they cannot cope with, and so they try to avoid anxiety as much as they can. Intolerance to uncertainty is an intolerance to anxiety. The problem is, of course, if anxiety is itself the thing we fear, because we feel we cannot cope with it and will "lose our minds", then we are creating a self-fulfilling cycle of anxiety feeding anxiety. Much like panic disorder sufferers suffer from panic attacks because of their fear of having a panic attack[43], getting anxiety because of the fear of anxiety is a difficult cycle to break. Most sufferers fall back into the comforting arms of chronic avoidance. If everything that causes anxiety is avoided, then there will be no uncertainty, and no more anxiety. But this is also the avoidance of life. The only way to beat these two characteristics is through action, as we will see later.

---

[43] The Anxiety Shift: Mind Reset | Neil Breakwell

The Avoidance—Self Cycle

Although passive avoidance is a natural outcome of anxiety and the activation of the BIS, there are two major reasons why it should not be relied upon on a frequent basis: The first reason is that avoidance ensures that we will never see the outcome of what would have happened if we had not avoided. In some situations, this can be a good thing, as seeing the outcome of an altercation with a hammer-wielding maniac might not be beneficial to our future, but in most situations that occur in everyday life, avoidance means not seeing that the outcome was not as bad as we had feared. Avoidance helps maintain the mystique of simple everyday situations and creates a perfect environment for unfounded fears to fester and grow. This compounds the fears and strengthens the desire to avoid again if the same situation arises keeping the whole anxiety train rolling.

The second reason for not giving in to avoidance is the impact it has on the Self. As we have seen already, self-efficacy, and to some extent, self-worth, is strengthened by positive actions and personal successes. Avoidance is neither of these. The constant avoidance of perceived threats results in a reduction in overall levels of the Self, which in turn will result in more self-doubt, bigger gaps, increased anxiety levels and more desire to avoid. This is a vicious cycle that can only be consciously broken.

Both reasons make it important not to make avoidance a habit, because, as we have already seen, avoidance is one of the major players in the formation of anxiety disorders:

2. Increased Avoidance Habits

Being locked in the avoidance-self cycle is a clear indicator that we are suffering from an anxiety disorder, and so breaking the cycle is an excellent way to free ourselves. Again, the only true way to break the cycle is through action, and action can be made possible by increasing the overall sense-of-self and developing the mind to think more appropriately, which we will look at in part 3.

A good example of the pitfalls of avoidance is Carl Jung's description of personality types in his famous brook analogy: A group of people are hiking across the hills when they come across a brook flowing across them blocking their path. The first person views the brook as an exciting challenge and leaps across it with joy. The second person views the brook as an obstacle that must be crossed and takes a running jump and lands safely on the other side. The third person is fearful and a bit intimidated by the brook and fears what will happen if he falls in while trying to jump. He doesn't want to jump, but he knows that if he doesn't, he can't continue with the hike, and he is enjoying the hike too much to stop now. He takes a deep breath, and jumps across the brook, landing safely on the other side. The fourth person is also intimidated by the brook and fears making the jump. He looks at the brook, shakes his head, turns, and heads home. On the way back, he justifies the decision by telling himself that he had walked far enough anyway, or he was bored of hiking for the day, or he needed to get back for some reason. Now every time the fourth man hikes through the hills, he will stop at the brook and turn back. This will become his habit. He will come to think of the brook as the end of his hike and take it for granted that he will go home. He will never get to cross the brook or see what's on the other side. His entire world has now shrunk to within the confines of that brook.

The third and fourth hikers are like anxiety sufferers, but whereas the fourth guy avoided taking the leap, the third guy overcame his anxiety of jumping and did it. While he may still feel anxious the next time he reaches the brook, he now knows he can do it and that nothing bad happened. His anxiety will reduce over time until jumping the brook becomes second nature and he gives it no more thought. There will be other brooks to cross, but hiker number three is now equipped with the knowledge that brooks hold no fear and he can tackle any future brooks that might cross his path. Hiker number four, however, is likely to avoid any future brooks and limit his world still further.

The Inner Critic

The inner critic, or the inner chatter as it is sometimes called, will be found in most respectable anxiety books, and so I wasn't going to leave it out here, although my opinion of it may differ to the norm. The inner critic is the voice inside our heads that mirrors the self-doubt within us. Whether it takes our own voice or that of an authority figure, the inner critic will let us know what it thinks of our decisions or our chances of success. The inner critic, it is thought, develops as we grow, and as our primary caregivers give us instructions. To begin with we repeat these instructions to ourselves aloud to remind ourselves what to do and ensure we are staying within the boundaries of our social group, but over time, these words are internalised and become the inner voice in our heads. This voice is important though, as the inner monologue helps us navigate life as we grow and helps us to find our true beliefs and values.

Everybody's inner voice is different. Some people can hear an audible voice, while others cannot. My inner voice consists of a flow of thoughts, but none of them is audible. I think, but I don't hear. But that's just me. Many people with anxiety, though, have quite severe inner critics that take great pleasure in berating them and letting them know that they will fail at everything.

Of course, the inner critic is just a manifestation of the unconscious mind and is just a way for unconscious thoughts to be brought to the conscious. The inner critic should not be thought of as an adversary, even if it is overly critical. The inner critic can give us insight into the unconscious and help us decipher the needs, values, and gaps that are causing our anxiety. If we use it right, the inner critic can be a useful tool to help us overcome anxiety, even though we may think it is the main cause of it.

Social Media

There are many reasons why limiting social media use is a good thing, but not all of them involve anxiety, and so are not important here. There is no doubt, though, of the link between social media use and anxiety, and there are many reasons for it: First, there is the dopamine hit of notifications and waiting for replies. The dopamine drip is why we become addicted to checking our phones, and unfortunately it can lead to anxiety between checks as we wonder if we are missing out on something important. Taking extended periods away from phones and social media can reset our dependence on the dopamine drip and reduce the anxiety associated with it.

The second way that social media plays havoc with anxiety is comparison. Everyone on social media tries to show their best side. They post their best moments and their top days, and many are more than willing to lie to make their best days look even better. The problem is that most of us look at social media and see everyone else doing better than us. They all look happy, and we are not. They are enjoying a wonderful meal out with friends while we are stuck at home in our pyjamas with a cheese sandwich and a bottle of wine. This fills us with anxiety as we begin to wonder if we have failed at life. But, of course, instead of failing at life, we have failed to realise that those people aren't always happy, just like us. They too sometimes sit at home with a cheese sandwich and a bottle of wine, but they just don't post it. Nobody posts photos of their cheese sandwich in underwear nights, but everyone has them. Or something like them at least. This is important to keep in mind.

I think most people agree that social media is detrimental to a solid sense of self, but if you are still unsure, I invite you to look at this graph of mental health issues in teenagers over time[44].

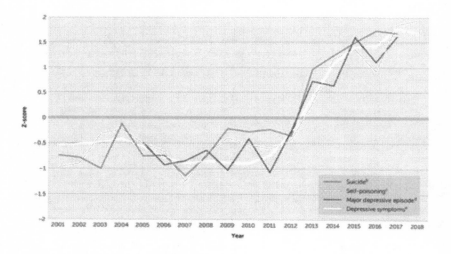

There is a clear rise in mental issues in young girls from around 2012. In young people this is unlikely to be caused by politics, global financial insecurities, or social instabilities, but it does happen to coincide with the rise in popularity of social media apps. Now this is certainly correlation and not necessarily causation, but it does raise some interesting questions and is enough, in my mind at least, to warrant a reduction in social media use.

[44] Indicators-of-poor-mental-health-among-US-girls-and-young-women-2001-2018 |Jean M Twenge

The Body

The Gut

We have already seen the key role that interoception plays in determining our *affect*, emotions, and feelings, but could it also play a role in turning normal *affect*, feelings, and emotions into that of a disorder? As we have seen, the point of interoception is for the brain to regulate resources and to keep the body in tip-top shape. If something is wrong with the body, then the interoception will spur the brain into generating a negative *affect* as it tries to force a positive behavioural change to correct the problem. This is straightforward when we are talking about hunger, thirst, tiredness, or overheating, but not so easy with some of the other, less obvious, issues that the brain must deal with. Many of those issues that can trigger the brain to make *affect*ive changes—but might well go unnoticed by us—can be found in the gut.

The gut, or gastrointestinal tract, which includes everything in the uninterrupted, but varyingly sized, tube from the mouth to the rectum, is an essential part of the body and an integral component of interoception and the overall determination of our wellbeing. The gut not only houses more neurons in its walls than are in the brain of a mouse, giving it the oft-used moniker of "the second brain", but it also contains most of our immune system[45], as well as about 100 trillion bacteria—way more than the human cells that make us up— that seem to play as much a part in our health as any other part of our body. It is no wonder, then, that there are plenty of ways that things can go wrong with the gut that can affect our mood and emotions without our even knowing it.

The bacteria in our gut are diverse and numerous, but get the wrong kind of bacteria, or an uneven balance of good vs bad bacteria

---

[45] Gut feelings: the emerging biology of gut-brain communication | Emeran A. Mayer (2011)

and they can send signals to the brain that can result in negative *affect* and exaggerated anxiety[46]. It has been known for years that the brain sends signals to the gut to regulate digestion and immune processes, but it has been found more recently that the gut sends as many, if not more, signals the other way—to the brain through the vagus nerve— than it receives[47]. These signals form a large part of the interoceptive signals from the gut, informing the brain of the condition of the gut, its overall digestive health, and what is needed to maintain the overall health of the body. If the gut is out of balance, then the signals sent to the brain will be negative, and the *affect* generated will be undesirable.

There are several ways in which the signals from the gut can be negative, and many ways that the gut can affect mood-influencing neurotransmitters like GABA and serotonin, but I will just be looking at an overview here and the main processes that lead to negative *affect*. I already went through it a lot more in my book The Anxiety Shift: Gut Rehab, which goes into much more detail in how the gut can cause anxiety and what you can do about it.

As already mentioned, the first way that the gut can become out of balance, which has now become popular in mainstream media, is the gut bacteria, otherwise known as the gut flora or microbiota. Through the excessive use of antibiotics, or eating the wrong foods, the microbiome—the ecosystem of bacteria that exists within our guts— can become unbalanced. Usually, there is a perfect blend of "healthy" and "unhealthy" bacteria, which allows our guts to flourish, like all ecosystems, in a balanced way. But if we favour foods that feed the unhealthy bacteria, like sugar, then the balance can be tipped in their favour, and the results can be catastrophic for our mental health.

[46] The gut microbiome and the brain | Leo Galland (2014)
[47] Vagal sensory neurons and gut-brain signaling | Chuyue D. Yu et. al., (2020)
The Gut-Brain Axis: Influence of Microbiota on Mood and Mental Health | Jeremy Appleton (2018)
The gut-brain axis: interactions between enteric microbiota, central and enteric nervous systems | Marilia Carabotti et.al., (2015)

The second, and most devastating, way that our guts can influence our *affect* is through **inflammation**. Inflammation is primarily a protection mechanism and most of us will know inflammation from situations where we have been hurt or injured. When we damage ourselves, such as hitting our thumb with a hammer, the body sends cells to the damaged region that will begin to heal the area. This will result in swelling, which is the body's way of protecting the area, and it will go red as the regenerative cells go to work. This is a simplified account, but most of us will recognise this form of inflammation.

Inflammation also occurs when we are sick, of course: If we get a virus or bacterial infection, the body's immune system, which is primarily housed in the gut, will send out other cells to try and attack the virus or invading bacteria. It will also send messages to the brain to raise the temperature of the body and enact other changes to weaken the virus. This results in the extreme negative *affect* that we all know as being sick. It is not the virus that makes us feel bad, it is the body's own reaction to the virus[48]. This is inflammation.

So how can the gut generate inflammation if there is no virus present? Well one of the ways is through what is known commonly as leaky gut[49]. The proper name is intestinal permeability, which, as it sounds, is holes in the gut lining. These holes can be caused by excessive eating of certain foods like wheat, which triggers the gut dissolving zonulin[50], an excess of unhealthy bacteria in the gut, or overuse of NSAIDS—painkilling drugs such as ibuprofen or aspirin which damage the gut lining. Once the gut lining is perforated, this

[48] From inflammation to sickness and depression: when the immune system subjugates the brain | Robert Dantzer et.al., (2008) Cytokine-induced sickness behaviour: mechanisms and implications | Jan Pieter Konsman, Patricia Parnet, Robert Dantze (2002)
[49] Partners in Leaky Gut Syndrome: Intestinal Dysbiosis and Autoimmunity | Yusuke Kinashi, Koji Hase (2021)
[50] Zonulin and its regulation of intestinal barrier function: the biological door to inflammation, autoimmunity, and cancer | Alessio Fasano (2011)

allows bacteria and foodstuffs into the bloodstream. Once these foreign invaders are in the bloodstream, the immune system acts in just the same was as if they were viruses, and attacks them, and inflammation is instigated. If you've ever had a cold or the flu, you will know just how bad you feel during inflammation, and how much easier it is for your anxiety to take hold. The *affect* during inflammation can be much more negative than it should be.

The problems do not stop here, though. Once food stuffs have passed through the gut lining and initiated an immune response in the form of inflammation, they are blacklisted. This is how our immune systems work, and why immunisation is so effective against diseases. It also means, however, that if we ever eat that food again, the immune system will be activated as soon as it touches the gut lining. It does not even have to pass through into the blood stream again, it just has to touch the gut wall, where the immune system is housed, and inflammation will begin. We are now allergic to this food and inflammation will occur every time we eat it. Many of us are allergic to foods without realising it, but because we don't come out in hives or have stomach problems when we eat them, we believe we are fine. Instead, there is a subtle inflammation process that churns out a negative *affect* which changes our mood and our anxiety levels.

The foods we eat can also play a role in the production of the brain's neurotransmitters, as many of these neurotransmitters are produced by the microbiota that live in the gut. For example, about 90% of the serotonin produced in the body and about 50% of the total dopamine[51] is produced by bacteria that live in the intestinal tract, and even the neurotransmitters that are produced in the brain are often generated with the help of gut bacteria or other chemicals from food,

---

[51] Regulation of Neurotransmitters by the Gut Microbiota and Effects on Cognition in neurological Disorders | Chen et. Al. (2021)

such as tryptophan. As both dopamine and serotonin are essential neurotransmitters for the approach drives and therefore positive *affect*, eating foods that allow our bodies to manufacture healthy amounts of both is essential for our mental well-being.

It is important to remind ourselves here of the importance of *affect* on our thinking. *Affect* is not only the result of the physiological anxiety response which we sometimes recognise as the feeling of anxiety, it can also influence the anxiety itself. When the *affect* within us is negative it skews our thoughts in a negative direction. Our thoughts, inferences and evaluations are all more negative than usual because of the negative *affect* inside us. These negative thoughts, inferences and evaluations will lead to an overall negative mental outlook, which of course will lead to more anxiety. This means, then, that even if anxiety was not present to begin with, a negative *affect* can take everyday run-of-the-mill events and turn them into anxiety-triggering ones. Therefore, fixing any issues within the body is very important.

This means that problems with the body should not be considered an afterthought here. With the rise of processed foods and the popularity of sugar-laden foods in the diet, the body could well be the main cause of many people's anxiety and could be keeping the brain in an almost constant state of anxious arousal. In my view it should be the first thing on everybody's list to tackle when trying to beat anxiety disorders. As well as being the most straightforward thing to treat, it could well be the biggest culprit in creating negative gaps in most people and they just don't realise it. I've been saying this since 2013 when I started writing my first book, and I still believe it to this day. Thankfully the scientific community is starting to agree, and more and more studies are starting to confirm it[52].

---

[52] Anxiety and Depression in Irritable Bowel Syndrome: Exploring the Interaction with Other Symptoms and Pathological Factors | Midjenford, et al.[2019]

Do not underestimate the significance of inflammation and the gut in general. Your anxiety could depend on it.

In Summary

Anxiety, then, is a natural emotion that occurs in everybody and has an important role to play in each of our lives, ensuring not only our survival, but also the realisation of our potential. Anxiety promotes action to change things that could be detrimental to our well-being or action to make a decision that is in our best interest. Without anxiety, we would be devoid of meaningful action, content to either stagnate in mediocrity or move unwaveringly to our own destruction. We certainly would not flourish in a healthy society. Anxiety allows us the drive we need for action to change but ensures that the change is the least likely to cause us harm. This is an important distinction between a suicidal drive to succeed and one that plays the odds.

It is important to note, then, that if you suffer from an anxiety disorder, the problem is not the anxiety itself. Anxiety disorders are a symptom of a deeper, unseen problem. Whether that be a problem with your physical health, incongruous values, limiting beliefs, identity conflicts, dependencies of some description, or simply a sense-of-self that needs some work, there is an underlying problem that is causing the anxiety. This might be an unpopular statement, as pitting anxiety as the enemy is a popular mental tool in trying to beat anxiety, albeit a not-so-successful one, and most people prefer to

---

52 Obese Mice Exhibit an Altered Behavioral and Inflammatory Response to Lipopolysaccharide | Lawrence CB, et al. [2012] Randomized Clinical Trial: The Effects of Gut-Directed Hypnotherapy on IBS in Different Clinical Settings. | Lindfors, P et al. [2012]

blame anxiety for their problems rather than look deeper. But being unpopular doesn't make it untrue. The anxiety is NOT your enemy.

The anxiety is a call to action. A prompt for change. It is the gap torn wide inside of you. A conflict raging and steeping you in uncertainty. There is a problem, and anxiety is trying to help. Sure, it may be doing a bad job, but it is doing it the only way it knows how— by getting your attention. Concentrating all your energy on trying to beat the anxiety, is a bit like trying to wash water off your body or trying NOT to think about pink elephants. It's futile and does the exact opposite of what you want it to do.

Your anxiety is trying to spur you into change. It is your job, then, to figure out exactly what it is that needs changing, find the things that you *can* change, and make peace with the things that you can't. This is, as you might imagine, not as simple as it sounds, and is why the next part of the book is given to different ways you can try to change by finding the areas in your life that are out of balance and in conflict. Of course, this can only be a brief look, as entire book series have been created on this kind of thing, but hopefully it will point you in the right direction. But once you accept that anxiety is not the enemy, you are already on the right path.

Part 3: Change

"Life is ten percent what you experience and ninety percent how you respond to it."
Dorothy M. Neddermeyer

Chapter Six: What Can We Do?

Changing the Gap

Although the gap itself is an imaginary construct, I think it serves an important purpose in helping to visualise anxiety, pinpoint anxiety triggers, and therefore to deal with the problem. The uncertainty between hope and fear is undoubtedly what causes anxiety, but as we have seen there is more to it: There are cognitive biases, issues with the sense of self, and unhealthy signals from the body that can all lead to exaggerated negativity and increased fear responses, and therefore an overly negative gap and increased anxiety.

This section is going to concentrate on some of the things that you can do to help tackle any issues that you might have with your mind, body, or self, and put you on the first steps to changing your gaps and reducing your anxiety. None of these things is a miracle cure. They will not lessen your anxiety overnight. Anything or anyone that claims it can do that, without medication at least, which comes bundled with its own problems, is lying to you. This will take time and effort and will result in many steps backwards as you go forward. This is usual and perfectly normal. The trick is to keep moving forward, regardless, and build momentum. Once you have enough momentum, nothing will stop you.

The Mind

Action

The best way to overcome anxiety in general is through action. Doing things that cause anxiety will, over time, result in reduced anxiety as the perceived fear involved will be seen to be unfounded. Do anything enough times and it will appear much less intimidating than it used to. The problem is, of course, that to do positive actions, you must overcome the habits associated with anxiety avoidance and make the decision for action when the opportunity arises. This, of course, is not as easy as it seems. It is made even more difficult if the decision gaps are made non-consciously. As much as we would like to believe in our free will to be able to make any decision we like, it is not as easy as that. Many of our decisions are made in our unconscious mind and then justified by our conscious. As we have already seen with the split-brain subjects, the conscious mind often invents excuses for actions. This is also sometimes true of avoidance behaviour: Sometimes the bizarre thoughts that you might have to avoid something are fabricated excuses made to explain the avoidance that has already happened or at least unconsciously decided upon. Decisions are made based on risk assessment and the unconscious analysis of need/value achievement vs need/value loss, and then justified by the conscious mind and made to feel like a free decision.

Does this mean that we are stuck then? Does it mean that we have become robots and can never change the outcome of our lives? Luckily, no it does not. If we understand what needs or values our decisions are being made upon, we can change the importance of those needs/values to our lives. If our current decisions in anxiety-ridden situations are being won by the avoid side of the decision gap, then we can either increase the value-gain (BAS) motivation of the approach side or increase the value-loss (FFFS) motivation of the avoid side. Ideally, of course, we will change both.

The values that our decisions are made on are determined by our own beliefs and perceptions, so they are certainly within our own ability to change. A father that gives his life to save his children does so because the fear of losing them is greater than his own fear of dying. Giving his life is the smaller of the two gaps. This is a severe example but shows the possibilities that arise to us when we change our gaps. Even the seemingly unassailable need for survival can be overcome.

In a more everyday example, when I quit smoking, I found it much easier to stay strong and not smoke that first "cheat" cigarette if I had told someone else that I was quitting smoking. The idea that the other person would know if I broke my promise or not helped me stick to the goal of not smoking. In goal motivation language they call this accountability, but what it really is, is fear of judgement or losing credibility in someone else's eyes. This fear increases the gap associated with smoking a cigarette, and therefore makes the "non-smoking gap" the stronger choice.

Whatever the reason for someone quitting smoking (or anything for that matter), they can only do so when their smoking gap has become negatively large enough to make non-smoking a preferable choice. This might be through their partner, friends, money issues, health issues, or whatever, but once the possible reasons for not smoking have made the smoking gap more negative than that of non-smoking, the person will quit.

This can be done with all anxiety gaps, and learning the techniques in this chapter, as well as the later tips on changing the mind, self, and the body, will help you modify your gaps in this way making it easier for you to take positive action. Moving forward in life and taking positive action-steps stops anxiety from festering, and, if you find action in certain situations difficult, changing the size of each gap in favour of action like this is the way forward, and this is done by the mind. This will involve work, but it will be worth it in the long run. Once you can overcome your mind's tendency to avoid anxious situations, you will become a more approach-minded person, and will begin to see that the fear that was first there was unfounded. This will, in turn, reduce the avoid motivation in future instances.

Risks and Benefits

We have already seen how *affect* can influence the gaps that determine our decisions and how risk and benefit are inversely correlated. We know that the more you see the benefit in something, the less likely you are to appreciate the risks and vice versa. This means that simply by making a list of the benefits of doing something that causes you anxiety—the benefits associated with the value-gain (BAS) of the approach side of the gap—you can start to nudge the gaps in favour of action. Once you start to see what the benefits are, the negative evaluation of the risks will be decreased, resulting in the positive side of the approach gap increasing and the negative side of the avoid gap decreasing. This will slowly move you in favour of action. The same list can be made with the negatives of *not* acting. Writing down the values and needs that could be lost by not acting will help your mind to build the avoid gap of no action and again help build the overall gap in favour of action.

Making these lists physically on paper can help nudge your gaps in the right direction.

Recognising the Gaps in Anxious Moments

One of the main problems with anxiety is figuring out exactly what it is that you are anxious about. Often anxiety just creeps up like a dark cloud in the soul seemingly without a cause. What is important to remember, though, is that there is always a cause, and, as we have already seen, this cause is the anxiety gap. Even when it seems like no gap is present because the brain is operating through association or habit, or being influenced by negative interoception, there is still an underlying unconscious gap with an uncertain threat of some description. If there is not, then it is simply a case of a negative *affect* caused through issues with the body being assigned to anxiety due to a lack of emotional granularity. This can be fixed by concentrating on issues with the body and increasing your emotional granularity. Both of which we will look at later.

Presuming a value process is present in most people that suffer from anxiety, though, we need to look at the gaps. While each gap in question might be exacerbated by problems with the self, the mind, or the body, the first step in doing anything is to find and recognise the gap itself. This is why I have started this section with the mind, as that is the tool that creates the gap, and therefore the only tool with which we can recognise it. The art of recognising a gap is built on some simplified ideas from CBT (Cognitive Behavioural Therapy). We have already seen how the gap is created by thoughts, populated by inferences, and the size determined by evaluations. These three things, then, are what you need to look for to see the gaps that are generating your anxiety.

The thoughts are the most obvious, but they can still often be too fleeting to grab hold of. Locking down the thoughts takes practice and is a practice I would advise starting as soon as possible. This involves moments of what could be called mindfulness. Observing the thoughts as they wash over you is a skill that can be mastered by ignoring the world around you and looking inwards. Put down the phone, turn off the TV and inwardly observe the thoughts as they pass through your head. Do not try and control them, just observe them as they pop into your mind, and preferably write them down. The most important skill, though, is catching that HOT thought as soon as your unconscious chooses it. It is not so important to catch positive HOT thoughts, as these are not the ones that cause excessive anxiety, and probably play a much smaller role in your thoughts if you are an anxiety sufferer anyway, and so the negative HOT thoughts are the ones to catch. The HOT thoughts are the ones that your unconscious chooses as the most likely "reality" and will often cause your stomach to "drop" or make you feel uneasy. You may not know why you feel uneasy, because the thought itself does not cause that, that is the unconscious inference and evaluation that you are often not privy to, because the thought itself has no true valence attached to it until an inference and evaluation is made.

Faulty Thinking

To help you find the thoughts, it might be useful to look at some examples of different kinds of faulty thinking. Knowing what kinds of thoughts can pass through your mind may help you catch the thoughts more easily. The following faulty thoughts have been taken from my book *The Anxiety Shift: Mind Reset.*

The following list demonstrates the ways in which an anxious mind can distort regular thoughts and make them more negative along with examples of the thought process involved.

All or Nothing Thinking

This involves thinking in black and white where words such as "every, always, or never" are used and everything is either good or bad, success or failure. There is very often no grey area, but generally the negative is emphasised.

e.g., 80% on a test is a failure because I didn't get a perfect score.

"If I don't do something perfectly then I have failed."

"I will never get all this stuff done so why bother starting."

"She never called me back; I am such a loser I'll never get a girlfriend."

This is quite common with panic attacks and panic disorders as people think that anxiety and panic ruin *everything* in their lives and they will *never* get over it.

Make a note of times you talk to yourself and use terms like *always, nothing, all, every and never.* Write down the thoughts and think how you could reframe them without such black-or-white extremes. Is there any grey area? Could there be another option?

Ask yourself "have there ever been times when it was not like this". If there is even only one time, then it is not "Always".

Overgeneralisation

This involves coming to a result or conclusion based on one event or situation, or one piece of evidence. When something bad happens once, you expect it to happen every time.

e.g., You don't get offered a job after an interview and decide that all the jobs are going to say no.

Someone you like turns you down and you think that everyone is going to turn you down.

"I didn't finish my work on time, I never get anything right, I am never going to do well in this job."

"One person said they didn't like my work so my work must really be terrible."

Try to catch yourself overgeneralising and say to yourself "just because something happened one time does not mean that it will happen every time.

Discounting the positives

Discounting positives is all about deciding that if a good thing happens to you, it can't be very important, or very difficult, or even down to you.

e.g., A friend compliments you, but you decide they are just trying to be nice or to get something out of you.

You complete a difficult task at work but decide that anyone could have done it.

You do something well and think you were "lucky".

Ask yourself "what does count?"

When people compliment you, accept it with a thank you and let it go.

Make a list of your positives, your personal strengths, and your accomplishments.

Try to look at yourself through your mother's/father's/best friend's eyes and write the good things that they would see.

Jumping to Conclusions

As the name suggests, jumping to conclusions is when you make a negative interpretation or prediction for a situation with no evidence to support it. This usually manifests itself with how you believe people perceive you and shows as either "mind reading"—making assumptions about other people's thoughts, or "fortune telling"— anticipating an outcome and presuming your prediction is fact.

e.g., I haven't received a call from the team because they think I'm stupid. (Mind reading)

"She talks to John more than me so she must like him more." (Mind reading)

"I could see he didn't like me when we met." (Mind reading)

"This relationship is sure to fail." (Fortune telling)

"I haven't heard back about the interview; I must have failed really badly." (Fortune telling)

"Everyone thinks I look stupid in these clothes." (Mind reading)

Ask yourself "how do I know this?" "What evidence is there that this is true?" "How did I get to this idea in the first place?" "How does this conclusion serve me, and where will I be in 5 years if I continue to think like this?"

Try to catch any mind reading or fortune telling thoughts as you have them and question whether you really know that for a factor or is it just a guess based on faulty thinking or a negative *affect*?

Magnifying and Minimising (Catastrophising)

This is when you exaggerate the importance of negative events (your mistakes, someone's reaction, somebody else's achievements) and down-play the importance of positive events (your own achievements, other people's flaws, your own good qualities). This is usually for yourself, of course; the opposite is usually true when thinking about other people. It is presuming the worst-case scenario will happen every time. Catastrophising typifies anxiety sufferers and can lead to the overly negative evaluations that result in excessive anxiety.

e.g., You make a small mistake at work, but you decide it means you will lose your job, and then your wife will leave you and your life will be over.

"Helping her move to a new house will never make up for making her angry last year. She will always be angry with me."

"My friend didn't ask me to be his best man, he doesn't care about me as a friend, he doesn't want to be my friend anymore."

"Jane is so lucky—she always gets the man she wants. She will always be happy, not like me, I'll never be happy."

Think about what you expect the outcome would be if this situation happened to someone else you know. Do you think the outcome would be disastrous for them? Would it be the same expected outcome for them as you expect for yourself? Make a list of all the possible disastrous outcomes that might happen after this event, and then make a list of all the possible positive (or less negative) outcomes that could happen. Which ones are more likely and why? Which ones have more evidence supporting them? What if it were to happen to someone else, would your response be the same?

Emotional Reasoning

Believing something is true because it "feels" like it is even when the evidence is not there is called emotional reasoning. This can result in self-fulfilling prophecies:

e.g., "I feel stupid around other people therefore I must be stupid." This might make you stop trying to better yourself or studying because "what's the point?" so you do not progress.

"I feel like a failure so I must really be a failure—what's the point in trying to do anything?"

"I feel overwhelmed or hopeless so the situation I am in must be hopeless"—leading to procrastination and quitting.

This kind of thinking is often caused by negative *affect* or limiting beliefs, so it can be worth telling yourself that the feelings that you are getting are either just a result of chemicals being released in your body, or habitual thoughts, and are not a reflection of who you are in any sense whatsoever. *Just because you feel it, doesn't make it true.* This statement should be taught to every student in school.

Making "Should" Statements

This is one of the most common types of faulty thinking, and one that you need to keep an eye on all the time. When you use the word "should" to yourself, it is usually because you are negatively comparing yourself to someone else, or to some unrealistic ideal, with words like "you should have done that" or "you shouldn't have done this", or "you should be earning that now", or "you shouldn't still be working here".

What you really mean is that you *wish* you had done something or *would have preferred* to do it like this or *would have liked* to have been in that situation. It is a form of self-abuse and often called "beating yourself up" about something that happened (or hasn't happened) and often leads to rumination and anxiety.

e.g., "I should have done that better, I am better than that."

"I must stop eating ice cream, I am fat."

"I should have stood up to let that old lady sit down."

"I should have made manager by now."

"I shouldn't still be living in this old house."

Try and catch the "shoulds" and swap for the word "prefer" instead.

Ask yourself "Why should I have done that?" "Who says so?" "What is the worst that can happen if I didn't do it" "Would everyone have done that?" "Why did I not do it?"

Above all, cut the word "should" out of the conversations you have with yourself. If you catch yourself saying it, say "NO! There's nothing I should or shouldn't do, only what I would prefer to do or not do".

Labelling

An extreme form of overgeneralisation, but instead of describing the problem, you attach a negative label to yourself that describes why the problem happened. This is a case of concentrating not on the problem being what you "did" but that you "are" the problem.

e.g., Your children are misbehaving so you tell yourself you are a bad mother.

"I'm a loser" instead of "I lost."

"Why am I such an idiot? I couldn't pass this test."

It can also be a label attached to someone else:

"That guy is such a jerk."

When you recognise that you are labelling yourself or someone else ask yourself:

"How, specifically?" e.g. "How specifically am I a bad mother (or a jerk, or an idiot, or a loser)?"

Is there anything that you could point to in your life that would disagree with this label?

Remember that there is more to you (or the other person) than this one bad behaviour or situation.

Blaming or Personalisation

This is where a person entirely blames themselves or something else for something that could have been caused by a multitude of factors.

e.g., Blaming yourself for the break-up of your marriage. Abuse victims blaming themselves.

"He wouldn't hit me if I didn't keep messing up"

"He always makes me feel bad about myself."

"What does that say about him as a person?"

"My marriage didn't last because my wife is unreasonable."

"I am the reason the office didn't hit the goal this year."

Ask yourself "How do I know I am to blame? Says who?"

"Is the other person solely to blame?"

"Who else is involved in this problem?"

"How much of this problem is my responsibility?"

Inferences

Once you have nailed down your HOT thought or have an idea of what it/they might be, there is a technique in CBT that will enable you to determine your inference and complete the bottom rung of your anxiety gap: It is called the downward arrow technique but is basically a method of consciously inference chaining. The trick to the downward arrow technique is to take the HOT negative thought and ask yourself "what would it mean to me if this happened?" Whatever the answer to the question, you keep asking yourself the same question, until you come to the real underlying belief and the real fear of losing your need/value.

As an example, Let's look at Tom again from earlier. Tom's HOT negative thought was that his wife had not come home because she was having an affair. Tom then asked himself the question "what would that mean to him if it were true?" His answer was that she would leave him, and he would lose the house. What would that mean? That he would be alone and homeless. What would that mean? That he would be lonely, have nothing, and his friends and others would think he was a loser. What would that mean? That he would never have friends and be alone forever. As we can see, Tom not only worries about the loss of love and social connection with his wife, but also the loss of security and connection with his friends, and a loss of ranking and self-esteem that would (in his mind at least) accompany such a loss. These fears of loss would populate the negative side of Tom's anxiety gap. At this stage, in Tom's current state of mind, the positive gain side of the gap would only have the BAS slightly activated for keeping the status quo of current connection with his wife and friends. The status quo is the best that Tom could imagine doing.

Practising inference chaining is a useful tool to try and recognise the inferences that your mind creates. Once you have picked out your common HOT thoughts, run through an inference chaining process to try and get as many inferences as you can from that thought. This takes a lot of introspection, as this is usually done by your unconscious, but the values and beliefs that these inferences are built upon are yours and can be tapped into with some practice. Just be as honest as you can with yourself and keep answering the same question: What would that mean to me if it were true?

Write down all the answers you can think of in the chain until you reach the end, noting particularly those answers that make you feel uneasy. Making this a frequent exercise and incorporating it into your daily routine can really help you to understand your own needs and fears. It can also help you populate your gaps with hopes and fears that could be generating your anxiety. Before you can figure out which inferences are triggering your anxiety, though, we need to know how you are evaluating each inference.

Evaluations

Once you have a list of possible inferences based on possible negative thoughts, it is time to run each of them through the evaluation process to determine which inferences populate your common anxiety gaps. If you suffer from an anxiety disorder, the chances are that as well as generating overly negative thoughts and inferences, you also tend to evaluate your inferences much more negatively. It is the evaluation that is the driving force of the anxiety gap as the thoughts and inferences themselves carry no emotional weight. It does not matter if you have the most negative thoughts and inferences in the world, if you evaluate them positively or neutrally, you will suffer no anxiety from them at all. The evaluation, then, is holding all the cards and is where you need to look to see where your anxiety is coming from. There are four main evaluation types, and four ways in which anxiety sufferers can negatively affect their evaluations of inferences. Each one can create more anxiety when they are based on black-and-white thinking and a catastrophizing mindset.

Overestimating Likelihood

The first evaluation can set the whole evaluating ball rolling and is when you think about a possible negative scenario or situation, and you feel that it is **certain** to happen even though you really wish it wouldn't. This evaluation type is the one that affects the weighting in the "odds of happening" part of the value process. If you suffer from an anxiety disorder, there is a good chance that your mind tends to overestimate the likelihood of negative events and weight them with higher odds of happening than they should rationally receive. An example of this might be Jeremy getting shouted at by his boss for not getting his presentation completed on time and afterwards being convinced that he is going to get fired. "This time it's going to happen for sure", he thinks.

This overestimation of the likelihood of negative outcomes is not rational and will often lead to excessive anxiety. Whether it originates from a lowered sense-of-self, habit, or overly sensitive threat response doesn't really matter as we know that this kind of evaluation can be changed. Like most things in life, it takes time, effort, and practice, but it can be done.

Take a list of all your inferences for each anxious episode and give each one a score out of 10 based on how likely you feel it is to come true. You can do this many times a day, both before, during, and after an anxiety attack, and see what happens to the percentage. Does it change depending on your mood? Time of day? Then for each inference come up with an alternative inference that might make more rational sense. What inferences would a family member who does not suffer from anxiety make? You could even ask them. Give each alternative inference a percentage score for how likely you think it is to happen. This will probably be lower than your previous inference, but if you keep doing this and work on other areas specified in this book, you should see the percentage for the alternative inferences increase and the percentage for your original inferences decrease over time.

Overly Negative Outcome

The following three evaluation types are based on evaluating the impact of the inference if it were to happen. These, as you might be able to guess, can influence the "perceived value if happened" part of the value process.

Catastrophe

This evaluation type is the catastrophe evaluation and is very common and probably very well known amongst anxiety disorder sufferers. In this evaluation, the feeling tends to be that if a situation were to occur, then the results would be catastrophic; it would be awful; it would be the end of the world as you know it. This maladaptive evaluation type leads to an overly negative "perceived value if happened" score. This can mean everyday events can be made into life-threatening dangers. The simplest of situations can be made to appear catastrophic. Jeremy might believe that when he gets fired, that will be the end of his life.

Intolerable

This is the evaluation based on how well you think you would cope if the inference happened. A very negative evaluation of this type might be if you believe that were the situation to occur, it would be unbearable and there could be no way you would cope. This is often grounded in a self-efficacy that needs some work and, when coupled with a catastrophic evaluation, can lead to a very negative perceived value and therefore a very negative anxiety gap.

Imagining an inability to cope with adversity is a sure-fire way to crank up the anxiety.

Worthlessness

This is where the evaluation gets personal and if the situation were to occur you know that you (or someone else) would be worthless, useless, or completely bad. This kind of evaluation can have a seriously negative effect on the evaluation of any inference and can push the "perceived value if happened" score to irrational lows.

Bearing these evaluation types in mind can help you recognise them when they are in force. Keeping a note of your *perceived value if happened* score for each inference can be a useful exercise for you to understand the causes of your anxiety. Thinking about each evaluation type in turn can also be useful as it can lead you to recognise what might be negatively skewing your overall evaluation and what might be the best course of action to fix it, but generally, because the evaluations are based on perceived lack of coping, a feeling of worthlessness, and catastrophizing, these are usually best resolved by bolstering the sense-of-self.

If you want a more in-depth look at addressing your own negative thoughts, inferences, and evaluations and techniques on how to build more healthy versions, then I hope you will forgive me if I shamelessly plug my own book *The Anxiety Shift: Mind Reset* again. It has CBT based techniques to help you tackle issues with your mind with exercises and worksheets to help you along the way that I don't have the space to discuss here. You can find it on Amazon ☺

Journaling

As we will talk about on more than one occasion in this book, journaling can be a powerful tool to help you get in touch with your feelings and fears. Writing just a little bit everyday about how your day went, what anxiety episodes you experienced and what feelings you felt throughout the day, not only helps you be more mindful of these things as you go through your day, but also makes you question the thoughts and feelings that you have. It may not come easily to start with, and chances are you won't know what to write about for the first few days but sitting down for ten or fifteen minutes at the end (or the start) of every day to write about your thoughts and feelings throughout the day certainly gets easier over time and can be an eye-opening introspective experience that can help to discover thoughts and inferences that you might not otherwise have acknowledged. I know you might think that journaling won't help you, but I can assure you that the scientific evidence is quite strong in this area.[53]

Finding Decision Gaps

Finding the gaps involved with decision making follows a similar process to that of the anxious moments. The only difference, of course, is that you have two or more gaps instead of just the one. The reasons for finding the gaps in decisions is not to help you make every decision (you don't need to know the hopes and fears involved with what to eat for lunch) but is instead to help you make decisions that will spur you into action to help you overcome your anxiety. A lot of anxiety is built around avoidance, and avoidance is almost always a "do/don't do" decision gap where "don't do" wins because the fear of doing is too great. If there are things that you avoid that you know would be good for you, then building the anxiety gaps around these avoid decisions can be a useful exercise.

For decision gaps, then, you need to look for both the positive and negative thoughts for both sides of the decision and go through an inference chaining process for each one. This means that if your decision is whether to go to a party, you will need to look for both positive and negative thoughts about going to the party and positive

[53] Expressive writing and health: Self-regulation of emotion-related experience, physiology, and behavior | Lepore, S. J et al. [2002]
Cognitive-behavioral therapy for anxiety disorders: An update on the empirical evidence | Kaczkurkin, A. N et al. [2022]

and negative thoughts about not going to the party. Try to keep in mind that although the positive reasons for staying home may well become reasons against going to the party later when we combine the gaps, for now they should be on different gaps. One gap—the going to the party gap—should have positives for going to the party and negatives about being at the party. The other gap—the not going to the party gap—should have positives for staying home and negatives for staying home and not going to the party. This means there should be four lots of inference chaining to determine the real feelings behind the positive and negative thoughts of each gap. The goal is to discover the values and needs at play in the formation of the decision gaps. Use Maslow's needs and the values from the later section to populate this.

Once you have determined the gaps involved in your anxiety-inducing decisions, you can use your mind to try and purposefully change the gaps in favour of making the more rational decision. Remember, action is the best way to reduce excessive anxiety and so altering the gaps in favour of action is a positive step forward. Even just understanding the reasons behind your decisions can be an empowering process.

Finding a Threat

Sometimes finding the threat during anxiety can be difficult. The feelings of anxiety seem to creep up from behind without our noticing without any threat at all. But there is always a threat. The threat might be well hidden as it is generated by the unconscious, but you can guarantee it is there. Remember that all threats are created about the possible loss of a need or value. Having an extensive list of needs or your personal values can help you find things that could be under threat. If a threat is unknown and the anxiety seemingly unprompted, then the threat is very often either social in nature, or it is caused by the body (which we will look at later).

Social fears and sleights are often subtle and go unrecognised by our conscious minds as our unconscious minds delight in trying to read body languages and predict other people's minds, regardless of how horrendous a job they might do.

Social hints to Look For

Social gaps might not be immediately recognisable in everyday life, but very often the emotional fall-out of such gaps is, and they will lead to anxious feelings. Looking out for these specific social feelings can give insight to when the gaps are being formed and when to start looking for the gaps involved.

A feeling of social isolation
A feeling of a loss of social connection
A Feeling of embarrassment
A feeling of being judged
A feeling of being bettered
A feeling of lowered rank

These are all examples of social fears that can lead to anxiety. Be mindful when you feel that you might be experiencing these feelings as they could be loading up the fear side of your social anxiety gaps. Building a stronger sense of Self can help reduce these feelings over time.

The Spotlight Effect

One of the ways in which these social hints can be caused is through what some psychologists call the *Spotlight Effect*. The spotlight effect is how most people overestimate the amount of time or effort that other people put in to thinking about them or judging them. We are all guilty of mind-reading others and imagining how much they are thinking about us. Usually when we do something wrong, we imagine everybody is talking about us and thinking bad things about us. The reality, of course, is much different, as many studies on the spotlight effect have shown that the amount of time that other people spend thinking about us is much less than we imagine[54].

It is relieving and empowering to realise that most people really don't care what we do and spend very little time thinking about us at all. Most people spend time thinking about themselves or imagining what others are thinking about them. They have very little time for us. This means that most of the negative social feelings that we experience are created by our own minds and have no bearing on reality at all.

Consciously Changing Gaps with Reason

As we saw earlier when discussing "willpower", when attention is brought to bear on gaps, we can change the outcome by consciously focussing on certain aspects of one side of the gap. For example, by consciously building the case against getting fat or unhealthy, or losing face to friends, we can force ourselves to forego the after-dinner doughnut, even though our taste buds are telling us it would be a wonderful idea. This can be done with any gap and with any decision if the reasoning is done correctly.

It would be easy going to a party that you were terrified of going to if your friends or family said they would never talk to you again if you didn't go (provided you believed them of course). This is how interventions work. The fear of losing your friends or family would automatically increase the fear of *not* going to the party and shift the gaps in favour of going. This kind of gap shift can also be done without the need for excessive threats from loved ones. By concentrating on the positives of going to the party and writing down all the good things

---

[54] The spotlight effect in social judgment: An egocentric bias in estimates of the salience of one's own actions and appearance | Gilovich, T., Medvec, V. H., & Savitsky, K. [2000]
Do people know how others view them? An empirical and theoretical account | Kenny, D. A., & DePaulo, B. M. [1993]

that could come from that as well as writing the negatives of staying home and all the negative consequences of doing that, you can slowly start to shift the gap in favour of going to the party.

Bring your future self into play and imagine the consequences to him or her when your decision is made. Sometimes you may need to be creative and think up more needs to be gained from going to the party and more things to be lost from not going. Writing these needs down and spending time contemplating the importance of these needs to your life can help increase the size of the gaps and skew them in favour of action. If nothing else of course, the very fact that you are taking action should be a positive when you suffer from anxiety, and the fear of making your anxiety worse should be a negative against not taking action.

The flip side to this is to look at the fears of going to the party and the needs that you fear might be lost by going. Write down exactly what it is that you fear will happen if you go to the party and try your best to pick out the needs that are at the heart of these fears. Run these fears through the evaluation part of the value process and, as before, try to use reason to reduce your perceived odds of them happening and the perceived value if they happened. If you can skew the gaps enough to favour action one time, the following times will get easier as the perceived odds of happening and perceived value if happened will both naturally decrease the more you experience situations where your fears are not realised.

Limiting The Affect Heuristic

As mentioned earlier, the *affect* present at any given time can have a meaningful impact on the decisions you make. This is called the *Affect* heuristic and is a quick way of making decisions based on feelings. When an *affect* is overly negative, though, it can have a profoundly negative influence over your gaps, and the resulting decisions that you make, moving you towards avoidance. It is important to take note of your mood, then, when making any decisions, and try not to make any important decisions when your mood is low, as the negative *affect* could bias your decision in favour of the more risk averse option. The *affect* heuristic changes the gaps based purely on feeling, and no data, information, logic, or reasoning are brought into play. This is yet another reason why making lists of decision criteria is a useful exercise as it reduces the likelihood that the affect heuristic could be hijacking your decisions.

It is also why it is important to review your lists at several times throughout the day as your mood might change and, therefore, so might your lists.

Using Circumstance

Usually, the logical conscious mind will be overridden by the emotional unconscious even though its thinking might be far less rational. Sometimes we know what we should do, as our conscious mind has weighed all the data and decided upon the most logical course of action, and yet our unconscious mind still wins the day with its decision gaps. A change in circumstance, or a change of perspective, can be used to change the gaps themselves, and alter our decision outcomes:

In May of 1999 I was staying in a small guest house in Medan in the North of Sumatra, Indonesia. My mom was flying to Bali for a holiday with her new partner, and I was due to meet them for a couple of weeks of holiday. Two weeks earlier, I had been in Laos, about 1800 km away to the North and had travelled down on the sleeper train, stopping for a few days in Bangkok, before heading to Indonesia. After a couple of days of disappointment of having one of the most beautiful views in the world—Lake Toba—obstructed by forest fire haze in the North of Sumatra, it was time to begin the trip to meet my mom.

The obvious, most logical, and by far the sanest, choice would be to fly, as there are several flights per day shuttling from Medan to Bali, but my ingrained fear of flying made that option no option at all. My unconscious had thrown together the decision between flying and not flying and the threat of flying (in my mind at least) trumped everything else. My conscious, rational, mind knew that flying was by far the safest way to travel, but my stubborn unconscious was having none of it, and chose the next best thing—to travel the entire three thousand or so kilometres (almost two thousand miles) by land.

The first leg of the trip was going to be by bus. I think it might once have been called a coach, but it had long left that honour behind. The seats were uncomfortable and the air conditioning just strong enough to maintain a light film of sweat. Thank goodness I only had to suffer the bus for 42 hours. Sadly, the journey ended up being slightly longer than that, because it seemed that the forest fire haze that had enveloped the beautiful caldera of Lake Toba, had also formed a thick blanket of smog over the small backroads of North Sumatra. These were not the best driving conditions and not the best roads. The bus crawled around blind corners and teetered along fogged escarpments as it made its way down the length of Sumatra.

The close shave occurred about twelve hours in. The fog had worsened, and our driver, worried about losing time and possibly emboldened at still being alive, had begun to drive faster, honking his horn, and flashing his lights as he rounded the blind corners. On one corner, though, he turned to find a fallen tree blocking the road. As he swerved around the fallen tree, he moved the bus into the path of oncoming lights. Out of the fog came another bus, straight towards us.

It was bus-chicken. Who would blink first? One side was the fallen tree. The other side a ditch. Just before our two buses became one, the other bus swerved suddenly and tipped over in the ditch at the side of the road. I will never forget driving past the fallen bus and seeing the frightened faces of passengers looking out of the forty-five degree-angled windows as we drove off into the night. I have no idea how those poor people managed to get out of that predicament as it was in the middle of nowhere, I just really hope that they did. I must confess, though, to feeling a small guilty pang of "I'm glad it wasn't me" as we drove into the haze.

We finally made it to Jakarta after about 48 hours of travelling and precious little sleep. It is difficult to sleep when you're not sure what will happen when you close your eyes. My journey wasn't done of course, but after a welcome night's sleep in a cheap Jalan Jaksa guest house in the middle of Jakarta, the next 24 hours spent on a train journey through the beautiful rice fields of Eastern Java, and a ferry to the island of Bali were luxury compared to the previous few days.

It is easy to see that my taking the bus from Medan to Jakarta was in no way the best of decisions and was orders of magnitude more dangerous than flying would ever have been. It was a decision made by my unconscious through anxiety gaps based on my aversion to flying. Of course, I had flown to Asia to begin with, but I was more than happy to limit the flying to the necessities only, and I guess I figured that 72 hours of overland travel did not make flying a necessity in this case.

Looking back, it should have been easy for my conscious mind to weigh up the chances of dying in a flight versus the chances of dying in a 48-hour bus ride through smog filled winding forest roads, but I didn't use it, or at least if I did, I completely ignored it. This is usual for most of us when it comes to this kind of decision. We use our emotions; we use our gut feelings; we use the affect heuristic; we use our unconscious.

I'm happy to say that I do now fly instead of driving—although I still need a couple of beers to get going—but I can't let my rational conscious mind take as much credit as I would like, if any at all: Once I got married and discovered that there was no way my wife was ever going to take a bus or a train when she could take a plane, I didn't really have much choice. My unconscious just shifted the decision gap in favour of flying and that was that. When you're married, the FFFS has much more to worry about than simply the small chance of dying in a plane crash.

The reason I tell you this story is to highlight exactly what I was willing to endure to avoid flying in my younger years, but also how quickly this avoidance changed when my circumstances did. Using a change in circumstance to shift the gaps and change a decision is often the way we break our habits and our fears in favour of a more positive action.

Some of us may start flying because the perceived value of upsetting our partners becomes greater than the perceived value of dying in a ball of flaming fuselage, others may overcome their fear of elevators because they landed their dream job on the 62nd floor, while others might start going to the gym because they have a holiday coming up and want a six-pack, not a keg, to show off on the beach. Circumstance is important.

Of course, it is not always easy to change our circumstances on a whim, but it is possible to trick the mind into thinking that our circumstances have changed: If our friends are a little upset that we won't go to the party, we can imagine that they will never talk to us again if we don't go. This will, of course, generate more anxiety, but that's the point. If there is more anxiety about not going to the party than going, then the decision will swing in favour of action—going to the party. And once we have gone to the party, the fear of going will be decreased the next time. It is important to realise which side of the gap your anxiety is on.

The conscious mind is smart, rational, and logical, in most people at least, but it's not usually very persuasive, and so most of the decisions we make, especially those steeped in anxiety, are made by our unconscious minds, and can be modelled using the decision gaps.

And this can be taken advantage of by consciously changing our own gaps.

Don't be afraid of purposefully generating more anxiety if that anxiety leads to action. This will be a good beginning to decreasing your overall levels of anxiety in the long-term.

Be Honest with Yourself

As we have already seen, evading the value process, and trying to suppress any part of it, is never an effective way to avoid anxiety. All it does is push the entire anxiety producing process from the conscious mind to the unconscious, leaving the conscious mind with no knowledge of the issue whatsoever and depriving it of the little knowledge it ever had in the first place, thereby making it much more difficult to pinpoint the source of the anxiety and making it infinitely more difficult to tackle the problem. Being honest with yourself, then, is critical to figuring out what are the causes of your anxiety.

Making Habit Your Friend

While this may sound a bit strange after talking about how habit can cause all kinds of anxiety earlier, habits can be powerful in both negative and positive aspects of our lives. People who go running every morning don't want to go running *every* morning. Even *they* sometimes wake up and their bodies are telling them it would be better to have another hour of snoozing that alarm. But they don't. Well sometimes they might. But normally they don't. And why? Because they have built up the habit of waking up every morning and going for a run. Without the habit, the chances are the snooze button would be used a lot more.

This means that you can use this to your advantage too. Of course, building a habit doesn't happen overnight, and the first few times you try to do anything positive, it probably won't be easy, but the very point of habit is that over time the action becomes automatic, and by utilising this to your advantage, you can change your life and create something much better with less anxiety. The basic steps of building a new habit, then, involve one thing—action, and lots of it.

Listening to the Inner Critic

As we have already seen, the inner critic is the voice inside our heads that mirrors our unconscious and provides (often non-constructive) criticism on our decisions and the actions we are taking. Most people try their best to ignore their inner critic as it often takes the form of a stern authority figure and is fond of criticising their every action.

The inner critic, though, can be a useful insight into the mind and the unconscious and should be used not ignored. Instead of trying to ignore your inner critic and push it from your mind, try and listen to what it is saying, and write it down. The criticisms of the inner critic hold valuable information about the needs and values that you fear losing. Listen to what it says, write it down, and then try and figure out what it is trying to say. What needs is it trying to help you avoid losing? What values is it trying to keep intact? Very often the inner critic is the only window to the unconscious that you will have, and so using it to your own ends not only gives you vitally important information on your unconscious thought process, but also allows you to see the inner critic in a different light: It no longer acts as an angry authority figure trying to bring you down and make you feel small, it becomes a useful accomplice to your goals, offering you important insight into the thought process of your unconscious mind and giving you ammunition with which to help you beat your anxiety.

Emotional Granularity

Earlier in the book, I talked about the new theory of constructed emotions, whereby the feelings of emotions that we experience, the things most of us would term fear, anxiety, sadness, guilt, anger etc., because they are the things we tend to experience consciously, are emotional feelings that are actually learned and then constructed based solely on our recognition of the patterns of *affect* that are created inside us.

This means that what you experience and call anxiety, might be slightly different to what I experience and call anxiety. Sometimes, the label that we give feelings can be overly broad and would be better served being broken into smaller and differently labelled chunks. For example, if every time you have a negative *affect* with a hint of adrenaline you associate it with anxiety, you will start to believe you are experiencing anxiety in situations where you really might not be. You might begin to associate normal everyday feelings like nervousness or anticipation with anxiety and start to feel that anxiety is taking over your life. More anxiety can then be produced just through the fear of experiencing this "anxiety" or the thought that you will never be anxiety-free. You may even begin to associate other feelings like pangs of guilt or flashes of anger, and even tinges of excitement, with anxiety, which can make the problem worse.

This means, then, that working on increasing your emotional granularity—building up your vocabulary of feelings—can help you isolate the real anxiety that is causing you problems and concentrate on it. Increasing emotional granularity was shown in studies to help with better emotion regulation, which can help to alleviate anxiety.

Of course, increasing emotional granularity is not easy and it can take time to separate out your feelings and recognise them as distinct and different. One way that I would suggest trying to separate your feelings of anxiety is to spend a lot of time noticing your anxiety in different situations and times throughout the day and trying to feel what makes each form of anxiety different to the others. Think about the valence and arousal in each case and try to notice how they differ from case to case. Once you can notice the difference in feeling between different cases of anxiety, you can assign each of them a colour. The colours do not have to relate to any aspect of the feeling of the anxiety, they are just labels. The reason I suggest beginning with colours instead of different feeling words is because it is often difficult to recognise the exact differences between each anxious feeling to begin with and there may be resistance to naming it anything other than anxiety. Naming individual cases of anxiety "blue anxiety", "green anxiety", or "teal anxiety" has no emotional bias and so is easier to accept at the start.

Once you have labelled the anxiety episodes you experience with your chosen colours, spend some time (a week or more) observing your own anxiety as it arises and calling it out with the colour that you recognise. If there is one that you do not recognise, give it a new colour, or assign the colour that most closely resembles it. Eventually you should end up with a list of coloured anxieties that cover the anxious feelings that you experience day-to-day. Continuing this practice of naming the anxiety episodes with colours when they arise will slowly lead to you noticing the differences between them more and more. Where once they were all just "anxiety", your mind will begin to see them as distinct feelings of "purple anxiety" or "pink anxiety" and the differences between them will become more pronounced over time and they will become much easier to spot. This is what the brain does, and how it works, as it likes to place things into categories.

Once you are happy that you can easily tell the difference between your coloured anxieties it is time to make the more difficult leap of assigning values of valence and arousal. This would be extremely difficult to do with anxiety normally as it would change so often but is made much easier when you have many different colours of anxiety to compare against each other. You may not know the exact numbers for valence or arousal, but you might well be able to recognise that green anxiety makes you feel much worse (valence) than purple anxiety, or that gold anxiety fires your body up (arousal) much more than magenta anxiety. This comparison of all your colours can help you rank and rate each one for both valence and arousal and then you can either assign actual values and put them in a list or you can plot them on a valence-arousal graph if you are a more visual person.

Once you have done this, you can compare your list or your graph to the valence-arousal graph below and see which feelings your colours match most closely. It should be noted that valence-arousal graphs can vary wildly and no two are usually the same, but this is to be expected when emotional feelings are constructed by individuals, and so no two people experience the same emotional feeling anyway. For this activity, though, the actual names on the graph matter less than the fact that they are different. Much like giving your anxiety colours, assigning different names to your experiences of anxiety will grow your emotional vocabulary and your granularity and it matters less what those actual names are and more that they are not all called anxiety.

If your yellow anxiety most closely resembles nervousness, then from now on, when you experience that episode of anxiety, you can recognise it as nervousness. While you may believe that this is just semantics and is simply changing the name (and you would be completely right in thinking this way) the act of viewing the emotional feeling as something else is extremely powerful to the mind, and just like you could separate the coloured anxieties from each other over time, your mind will allow you to separate the feeling of nervousness from anxiety completely over time. It will start to view it as something completely different. This will be taking a chunk out of your anxiety, and if you do this with each of your coloured anxieties, eventually your mind will dissociate your anxiety and break it apart into different feelings that will no longer be characterised as anxiety. There will of course be some anxiety left, as it is a real emotional feeling and has its place on the valence-arousal graph, but it will be a much smaller set of emotional feelings and will give you much fewer examples to deal with. If you find you end up with no feelings called anxiety, then great, just carry on with your new set of emotional feelings and move on. Your emotional feeling vocabulary, and your emotional granularity will have been increased and it will make it much easier for you to tackle the rest of your anxieties head on.

Arousal

Valence	Concern [1]	Hesitation [3]	Restlessness [5]	Agitation [7]	Nervousness [9] 10
-1 / -2	Concern	Hesitation	Restlessness	Agitation	Nervousness
-3 / -4	Doubt	Anticipation	Apprehension	Trepidation	Alarm
-5 / -6	Unease	Tension	Anxiousness	Distress	Panic
-7 / -8	Discomfort	Worry	Dread	Fear	Panic
9 / -10	Sadness	Despair	Dismay	Horror	Terror

Using the Granularity

Once you have disassociated your anxiety into more finely grained categories, it is important that you use them on a regular basis. This means calling out your feelings with as many varied descriptions as possible, as a growing body of research is showing that labelling a feeling, or putting that feeling into words, can help to "downregulate that *affect*"[55]. In one such study, researchers tested three different approaches on spider-fearful individuals. First, they used re-appraisal,

---

[55] Feelings into words: contributions of language to exposure therapy | Kircanski et al (2012)

where participants described the spider in a non-threatening way. Second, they tried distraction, by diverting the participants' attention elsewhere. Third, they tested using emotional labelling where participants vocalised their feelings when near to the spider. A week later, while all three groups still reported feeling similar amounts of fear in the presence of a spider, the labelling groups showed greater improvement in being able to approach spiders and their physical threat response measurements were lower— "Additionally, greater use of anxiety and fear words during exposure was associated with greater reductions in fear responding." Using a wider vocabulary built through an increased emotional granularity really does work. Using an expanded vocabulary of anxiety and fear words in your everyday anxious moments could help you reduce the anxiety that you feel, especially once your expanded vocabulary includes more positive (or at least less negative) words than just anxiety and fear.

But it doesn't stop there. As well as consciously labelling your feelings with your new, more positive, words, it has also been shown to reduce anxiety if you believe that a certain amount of arousal is good for your performance in any given task, which of course, it is. If you remember, the Yerkes-Dodson law states that a certain amount of anxious arousal is a necessary ingredient for optimal performance in difficult tasks. It is not too great a leap to recognise that the "nervousness" or "trepidation" (or whatever new vocabulary you use) that you feel, is not only a positive for you, but is in fact a necessity for you to achieve your best results.

This can be seen in a couple of studies that researchers did to test this: In the first,[56] they asked a group of volunteers to take part in public speaking, a very stressful activity as we all know. A third of the participants were instructed to "interpret arousal as a tool that aids performance", the second third were given instructions that "the best

---

[56] Improving Acute Stress Responses: The Power of Reappraisal | Jamieson et al [2013]

way to cope with stress was to ignore the source of that stress", while the final third was given no instructions at all. The first group that were asked to reappraise the stress as helpful performed better than the other groups in the task, exhibited much fewer physical signs of anxiety, and exhibited fewer attentional biases to threats in a subsequent test, which means they were less likely to see threats that weren't there. It was also shown that this group's physiological state of arousal returned to baseline much quicker after the task than the other groups.

In the second study, the same researchers took students studying to take the GRE and told half of them that "signs of physiological arousal (e.g., increased heart rate) that accompany testing situations predict better, not worse, performance". These students were shown to have performed better on the quantitative section of the GRE than the other group and reported that arousal on the day of the test aided their performance[56].

It has been known for years that a certain amount of anxiety is needed in order to perform difficult tasks, so if you can view your anxious feelings as a positive instead of a negative, and a tool to help you get better at the things you want to do, then not only will it reduce the anxiety that you feel, but it will also improve your performance, A win-win situation.

"Trick" Your Mind with a Placebo

As you probably already know, there is a tonne of evidence out there that shows that placebos can work for easing both physical and mental ailments and why any drug trial worth its salt will be double-blind and involve a placebo[57]. Placebos can be as simple as a sugar pill,

---

[57] Effect of Propranolol Prophylaxis on Headache Frequency in Children with Migraine Without Aura: A Randomized, Double-Blind, Placebo-Controlled Trial | Keerthana et. al. (2022)

but the belief that the medicine is real can make it effective as a treatment. This is why, if a new drug can't do significantly better than a placebo, then the drug is simply acting as a placebo itself and is not worth pursuing.

Placebos have been shown to be effective to a degree in helping reduce anxiety, but they come with two major drawbacks: Firstly, they have certain ethical issues when not involved in a trial. A doctor can't really tell you that he is giving you a good anxiety medicine, then give you a sugar pill. While it may well work, the lie is unethical for a doctor. Secondly, conventional wisdom says you can't really self-medicate a placebo. If you give yourself a sugar pill, you know full well it is a sugar pill. That said, new evidence suggests that this might not be as big a problem as previously thought:

Recent studies have shown that purposefully taking a placebo, even when you know it is not real medicine, can reduce anxiety. In science these are called *open placebos* and a test was done to show that open placebos reduced the anxiety in high-school test takers when compared to a group that took nothing[58]. Obviously, this test could not have a placebo control, as the placebo was the variable being measured.

To be honest, this doesn't come as much of a surprise to me, because when I was a kid, I suffered from allergies. It was mostly the cats, but the sneezing, and itching eyes and nose was torture. One year we got some homeopathic allergy tablets, which worked wonders. When we checked the ingredients, they turned out to be not much more than sugar pills, but I didn't care. I knew they worked for me, so

Placebo response in depression: bane of research, boon to therapy | G Andrews [2001]
What influences placebo and nocebo responses in Parkinson's disease? | Witek et. al (2018)
[58] Open-label placebos reduce test anxiety and improve self-management skills: A randomized-controlled trial | Schaefer et al. [2019]

I continued taking them. I knew it wasn't real medicine, but they worked...for me.

Taking a sugar pill of sorts and telling yourself that it will reduce your anxiety, could reduce your anxiety. Belief is a strong tool indeed. And that's based on science.

The Self

Improving your sense-of-self and overcoming your anxiety is not like changing the oil in your car. You can't just spend thirty minutes in one almighty overhaul and be good as new. The brain (or the body for that matter) doesn't work like that. Many people live with anxiety in the hope that one day it will suddenly go. One day, they hope, they will wake up and feel better about themselves and the anxiety will have disappeared. Or they long for the invention of a panacea sometime in the future and take away all their pain. The point is, most people with anxiety imagine that someday their lives will make a major change for the better, and their anxiety will be gone. Just like that.

Unfortunately, it doesn't normally work like that. The only real way to change direction in your life enough to influence your Self and your anxiety is by changing a little bit at a time. Tiny incremental changes, almost imperceptible to anybody else, but changes that will compound, and build upon each other, to make massive changes over time. Unless you get forced into saving the world, this is going to be your only real option.

We can all appreciate the difference in time needed to build something as opposed to the time needed to destroy it. Building a high-rise tower block can take months, even years, but a controlled explosion will bring it down in seconds. This can be the same for much of the mental processes that create anxiety disorders. Although much of the wrong thinking and Self issues that form the foundation of anxiety disorders in general can be formed over many years throughout childhood, they can just as easily be generated quickly and abruptly through trauma, upheaval, or bereavement. The shock to the system in these situations can happen quickly in the grand scheme of things but will usually need much longer to set right. It doesn't take long to shatter the Self, but it can take a lifetime to fully build it up. But building it to a degree that prevents excessive anxiety is certainly possible, and it does not take a lifetime.

Uncertainty breeds anxiety. Having choices to make and giving yourself the freedom to make these choices comes inherently bundled with anxiety. If you make the decision and move on, then the anxiety is normal. What causes the anxiety to be out of control and to build up to unmanageable levels is when the decisions are not made. When there is no "moving on". It is this lack of direction, when all the decisions and options in life are overwhelming but never acted upon, when anxiety becomes its most powerful and damaging. This, then, becomes a vicious cycle, as the build-up of anxiety can prevent you from making any decision at all, but as life progresses, more decisions and options present themselves which will result in more anxiety. This is the problem with anxiety avoidance.

There would, of course, be much less anxiety if there were no uncertainty in life. If you knew for sure exactly how your life was going to pan out, then there would be no need for anxiety. Sure, there might be fear because you knew of impending pain, but not anxiety. Anxiety relies on uncertainty. The problem is that uncertainty is a fact of life, and so, therefore, is anxiety. There are only two ways to relieve the anxiety of uncertainty: 1. Avoid everything that is not certain, which as we have seen means avoiding life itself; and 2. Act and see what happens. Once you act, there is no more uncertainty. You know the outcome, be it good or bad. Of course, in some situations, with latent decision gaps, you will still have a gap remaining that causes anxiety, but one gap is always better than two, and they usually reduce with time anyway. This means that there is only really one healthy choice to relieve anxiety—action. *The only true way out is choosing a direction and following it.*

Even opting to remain with the status quo is a decision and can calm the anxiety associated with having a decision to make, but as we have already seen, if the choice is made because of dependency, or the status quo is socially unacceptable, then a brutal latent gap will remain, and the decision is certain to arise again in the future. This is not a good long-term solution.

Even if the decision is socially acceptable, choosing the status quo too often means you are ignoring growth, and without growth you are destined to stay as you are. You are ignoring the possibilities given to you, and shirking the responsibility you have to yourself, and you will stagnate. This breeds guilt, and shame and self-blame over time, and will result in dents in your self-worth and self-efficacy, which can then, of course, lead to anxiety in other ways. And of course, there will still be the original anxieties that were there in the decision to begin with. They may have gone away temporarily when the decision to remain in the status quo was made, but it doesn't mean they won't resurface again later.

Choosing a path and taking action is certainly not easy, and of course is much more difficult when you suffer from an anxiety disorder. We can make the task of action easier over time by increasing and strengthening the sense-of-self, thereby reducing self-doubt, and eliminating limiting beliefs.

It is important when trying to tackle out-of-control anxiety to not think that once you have beaten anxiety you will be able to do all the things that you always wanted to do. Action is the antidote to anxiety and so needs to be present at the beginning of the journey as well as the end. Every journey begins with a single step, but even a step is an action going forward. Doing things that you want to do, and things that are positive for you—albeit slowly and in tiny amounts to begin with— is how you begin the journey of beating anxiety.

The strategy for beating anxiety, then, is to achieve your values one-by-one; step-by-step. The litmus test to see if you are on the right track to overcoming your anxiety is not to ask yourself the question "do you feel less anxiety?" but "what are you doing differently from before?"

This next section, then, will focus on a few ways that might help to rebuild or strengthen your sense-of-self. This is not an in-depth look at building self-esteem as that is not possible here. Many books have been written and devoted to this subject, so it is impossible to do it justice here. That said, I will discuss a few things that I think might have the biggest impact on reviving a flagging Self and point you in the right direction, but I would suggest you do as much research as you can to help build your global self-esteem and overall sense-of-self.

Action

As well as being the perfect antidote for relieving anxiety, taking action, and doing positive things, is also the perfect way to build a solid sense-of-self. The good news is that building up the self does not require you to take action on your most anxiety triggering activities (although that would certainly produce a good boost), because taking action and completing the smallest of tasks can still lead to a building of the self.

Everyone completes tasks every day, but most people don't even realise it because they take the tasks for granted and consider them easy. A stay-at-home mom might risk damaging her sense-of-self when she compares herself to her career-minded peers as she considers her tasks mundane and "easy", but in reality, she can do many things that many people (including her career-minded buddies) could not do, and I would have no idea how to start, and these actions are no less important just because they don't create money. People tend to believe that if their actions don't create money, then they are worthless, but this is patently untrue and a dangerous perspective for the sense-of-self.

This action blindness can happen in any walk of life, any job, and any person. Many people believe the actions they take in a regular day are mundane and easy and that everyone could do them, but in fact this is often not the case. Even those that are commonly termed "unskilled workers" will do things in their jobs that most people, even their bosses, would have no idea how to do. Even getting through the day when you suffer from debilitating anxiety should be considered a win.

For this reason, then, it is important to take notes of the tasks you complete. Every evening, think through what you have done during the day, and write down any task that you completed. It doesn't matter how small or insignificant you view the task to be, just write it down. The act of writing down the tasks will help you recognise what you accomplish each day, often without realising it, and help you concentrate on the positive actions in your day. This will help boost your self-efficacy. It will also help push you into trying new things to add to the list. It is a kind of accountability to yourself. It will help you to realise that you don't have to perform open heart surgery or design a rocket submarine to be meaningful. Every action that you take is another step towards higher self-efficacy and self-worth, and so keeping track of the steps helps you see it. Building up your list of actions, no matter how mundane you may think they are, can only be a positive for your sense-of-self. And always remember that making money has no bearing on the true importance of an action, and even often overlooked things like dealing with anxiety, demonstrating restraint, or being kind and compassionate, should be considered wins.

Making Goals

It is difficult to take action, complete tasks, and meet needs without first having a goal in mind. A goal gives you reasons to act and helps you build on previous actions to keep you moving forward. In fact, goals, no matter how big or small, are always needed for you to fulfil your needs. If you have a need for more financial security, then you may create goals of going to university or getting a better job, but these goals always need to be broken down into smaller bite-sized goals before any real action can take place. Most people have some sort of major goal in their lives, some grander than others, and having goals can certainly help relieve anxiety. Often the feeling of uncertainty and the sense of things spiralling out of control can spike anxiety while goals can help focus the mind and bring things back in perspective. The problem is that sometimes the goals themselves can cause anxiety or can be set in a way where motivation is quickly lost, so choosing the right goals and learning how to follow them positively is important.

Identifying Goals

The first thing to do is identify areas of your life that you would like to improve, such as relationship, health, or career, and write down what changes you would like to see made in the long term. These are your long-term goals and are simply markers to help guide the direction of your other goals. Always remember that long-term goals can change over time, so don't worry if you find yourself going in a completely different direction after a few years. You should reassess these long-term goals on a regular basis anyway, maybe once per year. Next, you can break your long-term goals into steps that you can take over the next six months to a year to help you achieve your long-term goals. These are your medium-term goals and can be thought of as checkpoints along the way—smaller things that you can achieve, that when grouped together will help you reach your end goals. Then, of course, come the short-term goals, which are things that you can work on over the next few days, weeks, or months that will drive you towards achieving your medium-term goals. These can be small incremental steps with easily obtainable goals which will funnel you in the direction of your bigger goals.

If anxiety restricts your scope of long-term goals, then you can do one of two things: Either imagine a future without anxiety and think of the things you would do if you were anxiety-free or skip the long-term goals altogether and focus on making short and medium-term goals only.

Research shows that having clear goals and a sense of purpose is strongly correlated with well-being in life[59], and progress towards goals helps to generate a positive *affect*, but it also shows that setbacks when following goals can lead to negative *affect*, so how you choose and follow your goals is important. There are a few things you can do to help maximise the positives of goal setting and minimise the negatives, while making the outcome of your goals more achievable:

Approach vs Avoidance Goals

You may not realise it, but every goal you make in life is either an approach goal or an avoidance goal. Approach goals are those that will expand your life, keep it moving forward, and make your standard of living better. Avoidance goals, on the other hand, are those that aim to avoid or change the bad, or negative things in your life. The difference between approach and avoidance goals is mostly mindset, and often the same outcome can be used for approach or avoidance goals

---

[59] Goal striving, need satisfaction, and longitudinal well-being | Sheldon, K. M., & Elliot, A. J. (1999).
Goal setting with young people for anxiety and depression: What works for whom in therapeutic relationships? A literature review and insight analysis | Jacb et. al. (2022)
An integrative study of motivation and goal regulation processes in subclinical anxiety, depression and hypomania | Dickson et. al. (2017)

depending on the view of the person creating the goal. For example, one person might think "I want to be slim so I can look and feel good", while another thinks "I don't want to be fat anymore, people laugh at me". Both involve losing weight, but one is an approach goal, and the other is an avoidance goal. The difference between them is the *affect* outcome for success and failure: In approach goals, progress leads to joy and setbacks lead to sadness, while in avoidance goals, progress leads to relief, while setbacks lead to anxiety and fear. It is clear to see which one is better for the sense of self and overall anxiety levels.

In planning your goals, then, it is important to frame the goal as an approach goal and not an avoidance goal. While avoidance goals can be effective motivational tools for some people as fear of loss is often stronger than joy of gain, the added anxiety involved is restrictive to an anxiety sufferer and can result in a lower sense-of-self. In fact, studies have shown[60] that anxiety levels are correlated with an increase in avoidance goals, so the more avoidance goals you have, the higher your level of anxiety. It was also found[61] that people reporting more avoidance goals evaluated themselves more negatively on measures of self-esteem, which is another good reason for building the sense-of-self.

Growth-Seeking vs. Validation Seeking

The reason for your goals can also play a part in how well they bolster your Self and change your anxiety levels, so you must ask yourself why you want the goals that you are planning for. There are two opposing reasons that are often used for choosing goals—growth-seeking, and validation-seeking. Growth-seeking is choosing goals that will help you grow as a person or as a social group, while

---

[60] Dickson/mcleod 2004
[61] Approach Versus Avoidance Goals: Differences in Self-Evaluation and Well-Being | Coats et al. (1996)
Perceived consequences underlying approach goals and avoidance goals in relation to anxiety | Dickson [2006]

validation-seeking is choosing goals that will help you prove your self-worth to the world. Again, this will often come down to mindset and how you view each individual goal. If you choose to learn a language to make yourself a more versatile person and grow your career, then this is a growth-seeking goal, but if you choose to learn a language to show off to your friends at how smart you are, then this is a validation-seeking goal. Both have the same outcome—learning the language—but very different reasons behind the initial goal. These subtle rationale differences can play a significant role in anxiety. Studies have shown[62] that validation-seeking increases anxiety, while growth-seeking decreases anxiety. It can be important for your anxiety levels, then, when planning your goals to think about the reasons that you are making those goals and ask yourself is it for personal or social growth, or is it for self-validation?

Find The Needs of Your Goals

When you have set your goals, it may not be obvious at first what needs are involved in each goal. You may have set a goal for something you want, but knowing the reason behind it is important. We have already seen how important needs and values are to our decisions, and our anxiety gaps, and so figuring out the real reason you have chosen your goals is important. It allows you to consciously create gaps around your goals and see the anxiety associated with them.

Finding the needs involved with goals is easy: All you have to do is ask yourself the question "why?" after each goal. Why do you want that goal in the first place. Why do you want to lose weight? Why do you want to find a new job? Why do you want to learn Chinese? This was already done to determine if your goals were approach or avoid, or growth seeking or validation seeking, but being more specific with

---

[62] Integrating cognitive and motivational factors in depression: initial tests of a goal-orientation approach | Dykman (1998)

the reasons will give you the values and needs that you hope to achieve from the goal when reached. This is important and will allow you to see the gaps that might be formed around your goals later.

Understanding the true needs and values that you are trying to achieve through a stated goal is important and should not be underestimated. Too many people make goals without truly understanding the reason they are doing so. Nobody really has a goal of owning a sports car. There is always an underlying reason, and therefore need, for why they want a sports car in the first place. These needs are important to know,

Make Your Goals Realistic

It is all very well reaching for the stars and wanting the best life you can have, but if it is impossible to achieve then you are unlikely to get off the ground. If something is difficult to achieve, then even when broken down into steps, the steps themselves are not going to be easy. Of course, there is nothing wrong with having a few big goals, but if all your goals are too big and unattainable then they are more likely to cause more anxiety and lower your sense-of-self than achieve the desired result. Try and keep your long-term goals big enough to be something to strive towards, but not so big as to be unrealistic. Of course, don't be too restrictive though, everyone should have one crazy dream in life. Just don't make it your only goal.

Make a Plan

As Baumeister and Tierney discussed in their book "Willpower", the Zeigarnik effect of undone things can create tension and anxiety as the unconscious mind badgers the conscious to form a plan. Forming a plan is like making a decision and will quiet the unconscious down and therefore dampen the anxiety created by the open gap. There is also the fact that no goal can ever be achieved without a plan laid out on how to achieve the goal.

Forming a plan involves four main parts:

1. Be specific about your goals. If your goal is to eat healthier, then to make a plan you would need to make this goal more specific, such as "I will eat five fruit and vegetables every day". If your goal is to lose weight, then a more specific goal would be to lose 10 kg. If your goal is to travel more, then a specific goal would be to travel around Thailand.

2. Break it into chunks. Goals of losing weight or eating healthier are medium-term goals, so to make a plan you need to break these medium-term goals into short-term goals. This means breaking the goal into smaller steps that you can accomplish daily or weekly—e.g., buy vegetables at the weekend, cook them all, and then freeze them for use throughout the week.

3. Make time constraints and build a schedule. If you want to lose 10 kg, when do you want to lose it by? 1 week? 1 month? 1 year? If your smaller goals for weight-loss are to exercise, then set a schedule of when you want to go to the gym. You need to have your smaller step-by-step goals always assigned to times and dates.

4. Write it all down. Make a schedule with a calendar, so you can see immediately what your plans for the day, the week, and the month are. If it is not on a calendar, it will not happen.

Having a concrete plan of written goals with a step-by-step schedule of how to achieve each goal not only offers more chance of reaching your goals, but it is also more likely to build a stronger sense-of-self and reduce anxiety in the process.

Execute the Plan

No plan is worth anything on its own without the action to make it happen. Here we have come full circle to the very thing that started this chapter—action. Implementing ideas and plans is crucial for building a solid sense of self and for reducing overall anxiety. If you find taking action on your goal is difficult, then maybe your steps are too large. Look at breaking everything down into even smaller steps. Even trivial things can be broken down into individual actions, and this can sometimes help when anxiety has taken hold. You can also try and make life easier for yourself by anticipating your own obstacles. If you find it difficult to get to the gym in a morning, then put all your gym gear ready the night before so you cannot use that as an excuse the next day. Call a friend and ask them to be your gym partner, so they will give you some accountability and pressure you into working out. This can apply to any goal—if you are trying to be more sociable and get out more, then ask a friend to be your social partner and make it a little more difficult to give in to avoidance.

Be Patient

The most important thing about making goals is patience. Nobody achieves their goals overnight, and everyone, I mean everyone, has setbacks along the way. It is important to remember that the aim of your goals at this stage is not to make you a world beater, it is to build your sense-of-self and reduce your anxiety and your avoidance behaviours. The larger goals, then, are just somewhere to aim. It is the journey that makes the difference. The journey of taking small incremental steps of action towards achieving and surpassing a series of micro goals that you laid out in front of yourself. Each goal met is a small bump to the self. You may find yourself going backwards on some days, everybody does, but if you strive to move forwards and tick off your succession of tiny goals as you go, then there is only one direction you can go, and that is forward. So be kind to yourself. Be patient. Have compassion. And your goals will fall into place. And if you are achieving your goals, your Self can only get stronger, and your anxiety will run out of places to hide.

Remember, There Is No Failure

Although you may get setbacks, and may find yourself going backwards on occasion, it is important to tell yourself that this is not failure. It is normal. In fact, tell yourself that you cannot fail; there is no failure. This does not mean, of course that you will win, or succeed at everything you do, it is just that the fear of failure is such a potent adversary that it is best to try to remove the idea of failure altogether. The fear of failure results in the avoidance of failure, which results in the avoidance of action, and as we have already seen, the avoidance of action is the avoidance of life.

When you really boil it down to the bare bones, though, you will see that the only way to really fail is to give up. If you don't succeed at something the first time, then you can keep trying. Every time you don't succeed, you learn more. So, there is no failure, only feedback. Every time you don't succeed you gain more knowledge about what it is you are trying to achieve, and you will get better at what you are trying to do. If you never try, you will never learn, but if you strive to fail as many times as you can, you will learn more than most people ever possibly could, and eventually you *will* succeed.

But, of course, if your values change, then even giving up can be a positive experience, and should not be viewed as a failure. When values change, the change of direction is simply realignment. But this should not be used as an excuse if it is not true.

Avoid Multi-Tasking

Although many of us like to believe that we are expert multitaskers, the fact of the matter is that most of us are not. Multitasking, or the act of doing more than one job at the same time is a lot more difficult than most of us realise. In fact, what most of us think of as multitasking is task-switching, where we switch from one task to another and back again. Studies have clearly shown that not only is task-switching less efficient and slower[63] than doing each job in turn because of the time it takes for our brains to get back up to speed with each task, but they also show that switching between tasks, and the mental interruptions that this involves, can directly lead to anxiety[64]. The moral here is simply to do one thing at a time.

Missed Needs

As we have already seen, not meeting needs that we were expecting to meet can be seen as a threat. This is why writing down goals, no matter how small, can be an extremely important part of your daily routine. Knowing what it is that you want to achieve in the short term will prevent you from missing out on goals and needs that you weren't aware you were striving towards. This will make it less likely you will miss out on important needs on a day-to-day basis. It is also the reason why making short-term daily goals is as important as the long-term goals that most people concentrate on. Journalling goals for each day is an extremely powerful practice.

---

[63] Rubinstein, Evans, Meyer [2001] | Yeung, Monsell [2003] | Meuter, Allport [1999]
[64] The Cost of Interrupted Work | Mark, Gudith, Klocke [2008]

Values

The values that we live our lives by are clearly important in the way we view our needs and therefore play a pivotal role in the formation of our gaps. If our actions are not in line with our values, anxiety will result. The problem is that sometimes the values that we hold are those of our younger selves and no longer hold true within the life we live today, or they are the values of a parent or other important player in our childhood and are no longer compatible with the person that we have become. Sometimes we hold onto values with no idea why.

This is why it is useful, as we grow as people, to occasionally re-evaluate the values that we hold dear. Values can, and do, change as we reach milestones within our lives, and it can be useful to assess what our core values are to have a clear roadmap for our actions going forward.

Discovering Core Values

Finding (or choosing) your core values is not a straightforward process and can take a lot of work and introspection. I cannot really do it justice here, but there is wealth of information online for doing this if you care to look. I will give a quick overview here to give you an idea of what is involved, and you can get an idea of what your values might be without going through all the work. It is important to note the distinction between your true core values, and values that you, or your family and friends, think you ought to have. Choosing values that you think you ought to have because they are noble, popular, or cool, or because your social circle says that you should have them, will only lead to more anxiety, not less, if they are not in line with your true self.

Knowing your true values, then, is important, but also very difficult, because there are so many social, cultural, and family pressures pushing you to have values that you don't really value. The aim is to find your real core values. The true values that make you tick, and the ones that truly make you who you are. Finding these values is a goal then.

Three Steps to Finding Core Values

The idea here is to try and find the values that you really care about in your life.

1. Go through the list below (or another list if you have one) and choose 10 - 15 values that you feel resonate with you. Values that talk to you
2. Once you have a list of values that you can relate to take some time to narrow that list of values down to a list of 5 that you feel are the most important values to your life in general.
3. Rank the values in order of perceived value and importance to you and your life.

Abundance	Courage	Freedom	Knowledge
Accountability	Creativity	Friendship	Leadership
Adventure	Curiosity	Fun	Learning
Affection	Decisiveness	Generosity	Love
Ambition	Dedication	Gentleness	Loyalty
Appreciation	Dependability	Goodness	Mercy
Assertiveness	Detachment	Generosity	Moderation
Art	Determination	Gratitude	Modesty
Balance	Devotion	Growth	Morality
Beauty	Dignity	Happiness	Motivation
Career	Diligence	Hard work	Objectiveness
Care	Duty	Harmony	Open mindedness
Change	Effectiveness	Health	Openness
Charisma	Eloquence	Home	Optimism

Charity	Empathy	Honesty	Order
Cheerfulness	Endurance	Honour	Organisation
Civility	Energy	Hope	Originality
Clarity	Enlightenment	Humanity	Passion
Cleanliness	Enthusiasm	Humility	Patience
Comfort	Equity	Humour	Patriotism
Commitment	Excellence	Independence	Peace
Communication	Excitement	Innovation	Perseverance
Compassion	Exploration	Integrity	Positivity
Competence	Fairness	Intelligence	Power
Competitiveness	Faith	Intimacy	Preparedness
Confidence	Fame	Intuition	Pride
Connection	Family	Invention	Professionalism
Conscientiousness	Finances	Involvement	Punctuality
Contentment	Fitness	Justice	Prosperity
Cooperation	Forgiveness	Kindness	Purpose
Quality	Realism	Relationship	Reliability
Remorsefulness	Resourcefulness	Respect	Responsibility
Risk-taking	Security	Self-discipline	Self-esteem
Sensitivity	Serenity	Sincerity	Skill
Spirituality	Strength	Success	Support
Teamwork	Tolerance	Trust	Truth
Virtue	Wellness	Willingness	Wisdom

You Do What You Value

Another way to look at this that can help to see the values that you hold dear is to look at how you act and what you enjoy, and conversely what you hate, doing. If you think long and hard about what actions make you happy and what makes you unhappy in your life, very often the things that you do that make you happy will show you the values that you truly hold, and while you might not realise it, so can the things that make you unhappy. Often when actions make you unhappy it is because you are doing things against your values, so looking at what you do, whether it makes you happy or unhappy, can give valuable insight into the values that you hold dear.

Changing Values

It is not unusual to want to change our values. It is not unusual to sometimes feel that we NEED to change our values. This is the whole point behind the oft-ridiculed *mid-life crisis*. People laugh at the middle-aged man buying himself a sports car, dressing in garish suits, or looking for younger partners, but the whole exercise is brought about through anxiety from changing values. As we grow older, and our children leave home, our values about life are forced to change. The things that were most important for years have now moved out of our sphere of influence and left us with a vacuum. We have to fill that vacuum with new values and new goals, but it's not as easy as it sounds, and if it is not done with purpose, the wrong values can fill the void. The activity above, if done with care and honesty, can help with this.

It is important when choosing values, though, that you don't choose values designed to relieve anxiety. you should choose values that define who you are and not because of anxiety. Values that are used to protect from anxiety I have called "protective values". These can be morally righteous values, but if the reason you have them is solely to dissipate anxiety and allay fears, then the value is not a good one and is more likely to lead to more anxiety, not less, in the future. Values should be those that improve your life and let you truly live the way you want.

Another Way at Looking at Values.

Another way that you might find useful for finding your values is to look through the list of needs from Maslow's triangle and assign values that you can relate to for each one. Here is the list in case you forgot:

Basic Physiological Needs
Self-protection
Social Connectedness
Status/Esteem
Cognitive
Aesthetic
Parenting
Self-actualisation

If you can create a list of a few values that you associate with each of these need groups, you can then try to whittle the list down to 5 main values and rank them like before. The reason this can be useful is that all our values are built around needs that we want to gain or fear losing, and it can be very enlightening to view the values through this lens. Why do you value honesty? Why is respect important to you? What does wealth mean to you? Thinking about the needs that these values fulfil and questioning the reason for choosing them can be an eye-opening experience.

Ways to Grow

Growth in self-worth and self-efficacy is, as we have seen, a path to reducing anxiety, as they provide more certainty in both action and outcome and can reduce self-doubt in decision-making.

Here are a few simple examples of areas in life that you can look at to grow as a person and strengthen your self-worth and self-efficacy:

- Be conscious of unnecessary conformity.
- Take responsibility for your emotions.
- Practise gratitude every day.
- Respect yourself.
- Accept compliments.

- Acknowledge your achievements.
- Don't people please.
- Admit mistakes.
- Accept disapproval.
- Practise self-compassion and compassion for others.
- Don't put off until tomorrow what can be done today.
- Question your beliefs.
- Limit social media.

Conformity

Conformity, to a degree at least, is not only a good thing, but is essential for our survival as a species. Humans are, by our very nature, social animals, and by far the main reason we have been able to reach the heights that we have is because of our social harmony. We work together, we look after one another and we share stories, learning, and ideas with others within our social group. Without adherence to social norms and expectations, we would have no laws, no decorum, and certainly no social harmony. This is why, to conform to social rules and expectancy is normal and hard-wired into our brains. Social rules and correct behaviours are the cornerstone of societies, and our civilisations, and are essential to our growth and progression. In fact, as we have already seen, the fear of ostracization from a group can cause anxiety through the loss of social connections, and so conformity is a way to ease that anxiety by ensuring we remain part of the social group.

Many times, when people think they are being independent thinkers and breaking away from the social group, they are in fact just following a different group that better follows their values. Conformity, then, is an essential component of being part of a social group and keeping social anxiety low. So, what's the problem?

One of the downsides of conformity is that it takes away from individuality. Conforming to social norms is fine and important, but when it starts to impinge on our values and ideals as individuals, it can cause problems, and it can result in anxiety. Most of us conform with no anxiety at all when we don a shirt and tie for work (maybe a little begrudgingly) or when we use designated toilets to relieve ourselves instead of the supermarket freezer section. These are social conditions that lie in parallel with our own values as people, but if you find yourself in situations that conflict with your values, then you need to either look at changing the situation or the value, as anxiety will be a consequence. If peer group pressure from friends is making you do things that you do not agree with, then you might want to look at changing your friends or take a firmer stance on your values. Likewise, if your work is leading you to do things that contradict your values, then you need to decide on which is more important, the job or your mental health.

Sometimes conformity is not as drastic as violating your core values though. More often it is simply following the crowd when you would rather not, verbally agreeing with the group when you disagree, or getting swept along in a decision that you did not want to make. Sometimes, this is just called marriage, but in most other situations it can lead to a damaging of the Self. Much like the problems with dependence, conforming against your better judgement can lead to a loss of a sense of self and so should be questioned at the very least.

This does not mean that you should go out and do whatever you want, though. As already stated, rules and social norms are important, and conformity to them is what keeps society running, and without them you are more likely to suffer from more anxiety, not less. Often, then, it is in your best interest to conform even if you don't really want to. We do it all the time in our jobs, social lives, and to keep on the right side of the law. And this is good. But you should be mindful when conforming if doing so is really in your best interest. Are you doing things that are not in your best interest because you are worried what other people think? Are you following the crowd, not because you believe in the direction they are going, but just because you want to fit in? This kind of conformity can be stifling and damaging to the Self. Again, choosing the right times to conform and not conform comes down to introspection, being mindful of your true values, and questioning your decision gaps.

Responsibility

Many people advocate viewing anxiety as a separate entity— something to fight against and view as an adversary to be beaten. This is certainly the way many people view their anxiety. The problem with this is, although it may relieve some of the guilty feelings and will certainly instil an urge to fight, it is also simply a tool for avoiding any kind of responsibility. It is always easier to shift the blame to this foe whatever crops up. This might make it seem easier to beat anxiety if it is seen as a dangerous enemy, but what ends up happening is every little problem that appears, every little obstacle that presents itself, will be blamed on anxiety and put to the back of the queue of things to beat, making the enemy grow over time.

Taking responsibility is vital. It is also vital to understand that responsibility is different from blame or guilt. Responsibility itself carries no intrinsic emotional content but taking responsibility can help grow the sense-of-self.

It is liberating to accept that you are responsible for all your emotions: Nobody can make you angry, nobody can make you sad, and nobody can cause your anxiety. It is the way your mind perceives the world around you, and the value processes that follow, that determine your emotional responses. You make yourself angry, you make yourself sad, and you trigger your own anxiety. This also, of course, means it's up to you to make yourself happy. Nobody can do that for you.

This doesn't mean, of course, that a cheating husband doesn't cause pain to his partner, or a romantic gesture can't trigger happiness. He can and it does. The value processes that trigger the emotions in these situations are based on real and valid thoughts, inferences, and evaluations. The problem is that most things in everyday life are not as clear cut, and taking overall responsibility of emotions leads to less passive acceptance of outside influence and more introspection on the value processes involved. This allows you to distinguish between those emotional responses that are helpful and valid and those that are not.

Practise Gratitude

Being grateful for things in your life doesn't sound like it could have any meaningful effect on your sense-of-self, or anything else for that matter, but science has found that daily acts of gratitude can have profound effects on many areas of your life from improved relationships, higher levels of self-esteem[65], less social comparisons[66], and even a direct reduction in anxiety levels[67]. In fact, in one study it was shown that "gratitude significantly predicts less depression and anxiety symptoms in the general population"[68].

There are many ways that gratitude helps to reduce anxiety, and some of them may be as simple as gratitude being an easy positive emotion to conjure. Positive emotions in general can help people to cope with stress and anxiety more readily[69] and can help return anxious physical responses to baseline levels more quickly[70].

There is another way that gratitude could be helping to reduce anxiety, though, and this one has a direct impact on the gaps

[65] Lin (2015) | Rash, Matsuba & Prkachin (2011)
[66] Winata & Andangsari (2017)
[67] Petrocchi & Couyoumdijian (2013)
[68] The impact of gratitude on depression and anxiety: the mediating role of criticizing, attacking, and reassuring the self | Nicola Petrocchi & Alessandro Couyoumdjian (2015)
[69] Aspinwall, 1998, 2001; Folkman, 1997; Folkman & Moskowitz, 2000
[70] Fredrickson et al., 2000

produced: Delay discounting. Delay discounting is the tendency of people to put less weight on rewards in the future than they do in the present. For example, in one study, volunteers were asked if they would prefer to receive $50 now or $100 in a year's time. Almost all the subjects took the $50, so the researchers began to decrease the amount given now to see how much people would accept to not have to wait. In the end the researchers found that most of the subjects, on average, were willing to accept *$17* now rather than receive $100 in a year's time.

While delay discounting is easy to see with financial offers, it holds true for all future rewards. This means that the BAS for future rewards is much less activated than for rewards in the present, while the FFFS really does not care when the threat is. Therefore, the threats involved have more chance of winning, creating anxiety and avoidance.

It has been shown[71], though, that people who are grateful tend to be more patient than those who are not, and therefore are less affected by delay discounting and the anxiety of the future that it can bring.

So how do you practice gratitude? Well, the easiest way, is again to make use of journaling (I told you it would crop up a few times). Every evening, or morning, make a note of all the things that you are grateful for. Write them down. It might be people in your life, things you have, or things that have happened to you. Anything that you feel the least bit grateful for, write it down. This will allow you to "practise" gratitude, rather than just feel it. It brings it to the fore of the consciousness and makes it more real. It also brings all the things together and lets you see everything you are grateful for in a single place.

---

[71] The grateful are patient: Heightened daily gratitude is associated with attenuated temporal discounting | Dickens, Destano 2016

Respect Yourself

Having self-respect goes together with having high self-worth, as it is difficult to value yourself if you do not respect yourself. It is even more difficult to imagine someone else respecting you if you do not first give yourself that respect. Most people equate having self-respect with having dignity as people will often say something like "have some self-respect" when someone does something ridiculous. While this might be true, in some cases people doing ridiculous things will have nothing to do with self-respect.

Self-respect, like self-worth, involves knowing your worth and expecting others to treat you well and value you. You do not stand for being treated badly. Another reason others might tell you to have some self-respect, is if you allow others to walk all over you or treat you unfairly.

It is not only others that are allowed to treat you unfairly when you have low self-respect, but also yourself. Most people, when they arrange to meet friends at 7pm, they will arrive at around that time because they have respect for their friends. If your boss tells you to have that report finished by Monday, you will more than likely comply. If your partner asks you to pick them up at 4pm you will probably be there early so they do not have to wait. This is because of respect for that person and their relationship with you, or because of their authority. But when you tell yourself you are going to go to the gym after work, or you will write 10 pages of your book before 10 am, or you will start your new business by July, and you don't, this is showing disrespect to yourself. If someone you respect told you to do these things, you would more than likely do them. So why does listening to yourself seem so much more difficult?

Once you can show yourself the respect you deserve by listening to yourself and following through on the things you plan to do, not only will you be more likely to fulfil your goals, but it is also much more likely that other people will show you the same respect that you are showing yourself.

Accept Compliments

This is something that many people struggle with. For some reason when we receive compliments or praise, many of us suddenly feel very uncomfortable. This is often, itself, due to a low sense of self, and learning to be more gracious in accepting compliments can help to bolster those deficits. People with low self-worth will usually respond to compliments in one of three ways[72]:

1. Deflection: "Oh it's nothing really", "I didn't really do much", and "anyone could have done it", are all deflections of a compliment of a job well done.

2. Reciprocation: Why do we always feel the need to return a compliment? It's almost like a compliment becomes a transactional process and the debt must be repaid. If someone compliments your new hairstyle, it is not necessary for you to say that theirs also looks very nice.

3. Discounting: This is one I have struggled with most of my life. If someone said I like your haircut, I would feel it necessary to reply with discounting terms, such as "It's a bit shorter than I wanted really", or if someone complimented a dinner that I had cooked, I would feel the need to qualify the compliment with "the carrots could have been cooked more", or "needed a bit more salt I think". Now while these things may well have been true, it is not the time to bring them up after a compliment.

Trying to avoid these three responses to praise or compliments will help you become more confident and build your self-worth. If you're

---

[72] Happy Together: Using the Science of Positive Psychology to Build Love That Lasts | book by Suzann and James Pawelski

not sure what to say when someone compliments you, then just say "Thank you" and leave it there. Nothing else. Move your mind on to something else and stop trying to find the most gracious words you can find. The more you hunt for the right words, the more uncomfortable and anxious you will feel, and the more likely you will be to respond with one of the three choices above.

Acknowledge your Achievements.

A natural extension to accepting compliments is to acknowledge your achievements and strengths. Many people think it is boastful to state what you are good at and what you have achieved, and it certainly can be if you walk around shouting "I am awesome" at the top of your voice. But being honest about what you are good at and stating your strengths matter-of-factly is not boasting and can have a positive influence on self-worth. Just make sure that you really are good at something before you make the assertion, the Dunning-Kruger effect makes a lot of people believe they are better than they really are at many things, and it does not help with social connections if you make talent assertions that are demonstrably untrue.

Try to Stop People-Pleasing

When someone has a strong desire to please others, they will often prioritize others' needs and opinions over their own, even if it is not in their best interest. This can lead to a chronic sense of anxiety, as they may feel like they are constantly walking on eggshells, trying to avoid upsetting others or being rejected.

People-pleasers may also have difficulty setting boundaries, saying "no" or standing up for themselves, which can lead to resentment, burnout, and feelings of being taken advantage of. This can contribute to a cycle of anxiety and stress, as the person may feel like they are always putting others' needs first, to the detriment of their own well-being.

Research has shown that people-pleasing behaviour is associated with a higher risk of anxiety and other mental health issues, including depression and a low sense-of-self[73].

Trying to stop people-pleasing is not easy, but being aware you are doing it and making a constant effort to do the things that are in your best interests can help you break away from the practice. It is important to make a distinction between being selfish and not people-pleasing. Sometimes being selfish is a good thing as it is important to look after ourselves before we can truly help others effectively, much like an airline instructs its passengers to affix their own oxygen masks before that of children in the case of an emergency, but it is also true that being a people-pleaser is not based on being unselfish. It is usually based on a low self-worth and a need to be liked.

Admit Your Mistakes

The brutal fact of life is that we all make mistakes. We all mess up and do something wrong, whether that be at work, or in our relationships, none of us is perfect. The important thing is not the mistakes we make, though, but the way we respond to those mistakes. Some people try to avoid responsibility and either blame others for their own mistakes or deny blame at all costs. This can lead to both anxiety and a loss of self-worth and self-efficacy as they realise that they are escaping responsibility and not doing the "right thing".

Taking responsibility for our mistakes and standing tall and owning it when we mess up not only bolsters our sense-of-self, but it

---

[73] When Making Others Happy is Making You Miserable: How to Break the Pattern of People Pleasing and Confidently Live Your Life | book by K Ehman (2021)
How Attachment Theory Can Explain People-Pleasing Behaviors | Xintong Li

also makes us seem more trustworthy in other people's eyes as they know we are willing to take the spotlight when we mess up.

Studies have been done on this and have shown that individuals who avoid responsibility for their mistakes tend to experience more guilt and anxiety as well as a lowered sense-of-self, while those who take responsibility tend to experience more forgiveness and a greater sense of well-being.[74]

Accept Disapproval

Receiving negative feedback or disapproval from someone is never a pleasant experience, but it's a common one. Whether it's from a boss, a friend, or a family member, we all experience disapproval at some point in our lives. However, how we respond to disapproval can have a big impact on our sense-of-self.

When we receive disapproval, our natural reaction may be to become defensive or avoidant. We may feel hurt, ashamed, or embarrassed, and our self-worth may take a hit. However, research[75] has shown that accepting disapproval can help us maintain a healthy sense-of-self and emotional resilience. By accepting disapproval, we are demonstrating a level of emotional maturity and self-acceptance. We are acknowledging that we are not perfect, and that it's okay to make mistakes. When we respond constructively to disapproval, we can learn from our mistakes, make positive changes, and improve our relationships with others.

---

[74] Accountability as a Key Virtue in Mental Health and Human Flourishing | Peteet et. al. (2022)
Accountability and self-evaluation: Social cognitive and neuroscience approaches | Scholer, A. A., Higgins, E. T., & Dumas, D. [2013]
[75] Acceptance of Disapproval and Emotional Resilience | Sarah E. J. Hill, Jessica M. Salerno, and Jennifer A. Crocker [2014]
Disapproval Sensitivity and Self-Regulation: The Role of Mindfulness and Self-Compassion | Sarah E. J. Hill, Alison E. Butler, and Jennifer A. Crocker [2011]

On the other hand, becoming defensive or avoidant in the face of disapproval can harm our sense-of-self. By denying or minimising our mistakes, we are not giving ourselves the opportunity to learn and grow. This can lead to feelings of shame, guilt, and low self-worth.

So, the next time you receive disapproval, try to approach it with an open mind and a willingness to learn. Remember that everyone makes mistakes, and that it's okay to receive negative feedback. By accepting disapproval and responding constructively, you can improve your relationships, achieve personal growth, and maintain a healthy sense-of-self.

Here are some things that can help you accept disapproval:

- Acknowledge your feelings. It is normal to feel hurt, angry, or disappointed when you are disapproved of. Allow yourself to feel these emotions, but don't let them control you.
- Put things in perspective. Remember that one person's disapproval does not mean that you are a bad person. Everyone makes mistakes and everyone has different opinions.
- Focus on the positive. Think about all the people who do approve of you and who believe in you. Remember all the things that you are good at and all the things that you have accomplished.
- Learn from your mistakes. If you have made a mistake, use it as an opportunity to learn and grow. Don't dwell on the past but focus on moving forward.
- Don't take it personally. Remember that the person who disapproves of you is not necessarily disapproving of you as a person. They may simply disagree with your actions or your choices.
- Remember that you're not alone. Everyone experiences disapproval at some point. You're not the only one who feels this way.

- Determine if the person who is disapproving is important. Accepting disapproval is a good thing, but if the person who is disapproving is an internet troll or someone behind you in the supermarket check-out line, then it is often much better to ignore the disapproval altogether.

Practise Self-Compassion and Compassion for Others

Following on from accepting disapproval, whether that be from others or ourselves, is practising self-compassion. Self-compassion is an important factor in dealing with anxiety as it allows us to forgive ourselves for some of the things that we otherwise might beat ourselves up for. It allows us to not only accept disapproval from others but also from ourselves.

Practising self-compassion involves three main points:

- Self-kindness: Treating ourselves with the same kindness and compassion that we would treat a friend or loved one.
- Commonality: Recognising that suffering is a part of the human experience, and that we are not alone in our struggles.
- Mindfulness: Observing our thoughts and feelings with an open and non-judgmental attitude.

Here again, journaling can help, as it allows us to see where we are being harsh with ourselves and gives us insight into where we can try to be more compassionate towards ourselves. There is a lot of evidence to show that self-compassion can help reduce anxiety directly[76].

While compassion for others is obviously different, it can have equally profound effects on anxiety. First, it can help us to feel more connected to others and less alone in our own struggles. When we see that others are also experiencing pain and suffering, it can help us to feel less isolated and more understood. This can lead to a decrease in anxiety and an increase in feelings of well-being.

Second, compassion for others can help us to develop a greater sense of empathy. Empathy is the ability to understand and share the feelings of another person. When we can empathise with others, we are less likely to judge them or ourselves harshly. This can help to reduce anxiety and promote feelings of self-compassion[77].

There are obviously many ways to show compassion for others. One of those is simply kindness. Another way is to be more tolerant towards people who have different values. An important obstacle to practising compassion in this way is the media. The media today thrives on fear. It survives solely through making you hate or fear other people. Every week they come out with a new target for their spotlight to keep people in a state of fear, but more importantly for them, also tuning in for more information. This is designed to increase anxiety and does a fantastic job at it. If you really want to start tackling your anxiety, then limit your news and media

---

[76] Effects of self-compassion interventions on reducing depressive symptoms, anxiety, and stress: A meta-analysis | A Han, TH Kim (2023)
Does a short self-compassion intervention for students increase healthy self-regulation? A randomized control trial | Dundas et. al (2017)
Self-criticism and self-compassion: Risk and resilience: Being compassionate to oneself is associated with emotional resilience and psychological well-being | Warren et. al. (2016)
[77] Self-compassion may reduce anxiety and depression in nursing students: a pathway through perceived stress | Luo et. al. (2019)
The Effects of Compassion-focused Therapy on Anxiety and Depression in the Mothers of Children With Cerebral Palsy | N Khoshvaght et. al. (2021)

consumption. And I'm not just talking about the media that you don't like.

Don't Put Off Until Tomorrow That Which Can Be Done Today

As we have already seen with the work of Zeigarnik, as well as that of Baumeister and Tierney, undone tasks can generate anxiety. From tasks with the smallest of importance to the largest, each will generate a corresponding amount of anxiety, and the more tasks you put off doing, the more this anxiety will compound and grow, adding to the anxiety that is already there. It is unnecessary anxiety and anxiety that can be prevented.

Preventing this buildup of task-anxiety is simple: If it is a basic task, then just do it. Today if possible. Procrastination is not your friend when it comes to anxiety. If it is a more difficult task, then plan to do it as soon as possible. As we have already seen, a concrete plan to complete a task quietens the anxiety and calms the unconscious. Of course, you still must follow through on the plan, but making the plan in the first place will prevent the anxiety from building. This brings us back to the very place we started: Action.

Question Your Beliefs

As we have already seen, misplaced beliefs or values can lead to anxiety when they are out-of-line with actions or social expectations. Cognitive dissonance relieving techniques are often used to minimise the fallout but can leave latent gaps that produce underlying levels of anxiety. It is easy to see the anxiety and fear created in the world today through sensationalist news stories and partisan propaganda, and this can create beliefs that have no basis in reality. These beliefs can generate immense amounts of anxiety, which is, of course, exactly what they are designed to do.

Constantly questioning your beliefs and their validity is an essential part of growing as a person and reducing unnecessary anxiety. Question beliefs that you have held since you were young, but also question any beliefs that people have thrust upon you later in life. Question everything rationally, and not believe everything you read or hear or are told as "truth". It is important to note, though, that questioning rationally does not mean simply changing your source material and following a different crowd. Confirmation bias is an important and common issue to watch out for when doing this.

Limit Social Media

The best advice for social media is simple: if you're going to use it, then use it proactively. Be social, talk to people, catch up with old friends, and make new ones. This way of using social media has been shown to be helpful for general mood and anxiety. The problem is that too many of us don't use it this way. We like to lurk and live vicariously through others and compare ourselves to the people we see online. This is a failsafe way to build anxiety. We see how well others are doing and compare ourselves to them negatively and perceive that we are failing somehow.

Cutting down on social media use is a good way to allow yourself to grow at your own speed without comparing yourself to others. Remember, nobody's life is the same as their social media suggest, and so taking time away from it, or at the very least minimising your use of it, will give your growth a much better chance of taking off.

The Body

As we have seen, issues with the body can lead to anxiety through several different pathways, and if you have ever experienced excessive anxiety with no thoughts involved, just an all-pervasive feeling of dread with your whole body on edge, then the chances are that your body is trying to tell you something. It is this kind of anxiety that began my journey of researching and writing about anxiety in the first place, so I understand it all too well. The problem is that the body and mind have been separated for so long in medical circles that we forget how much they influence each other. We have psychiatrists and psychologists for the mind and doctors for the body, and they are separate from each other. This is not helpful, because we already know that the gut plays a huge role in the functioning of the brain, so separating them so completely makes everything just a little bit more difficult. We are who we are, not just because of our brains, but because of our whole bodies as a complete unit. It is important, then, to treat the body as much as the mind if you want a fully functioning and healthy mental experience.

You could write an entire book on changing the body to create a more positive *affect* from interoception (and I did), so here I will just give a snapshot of some of the most important things you can do to maintain a healthy body and gut to decrease your levels of anxiety. The simplest suggestion here is the most well-known: Eat healthily and exercise. This is a good rule of thumb for everyone and will certainly do most of the heavy lifting in addressing issues with the body that might be leading to negative *affect*, but often there are certain foods that should, or should not, be eaten to maximise the good, and minimise the bad, effects on our anxiety, and sometimes people might think that they are eating healthily but these foods are causing subtle problems.

The Gut Bacteria

The microbiota or intestinal flora are the one hundred trillion or so bacteria that make up the bacterial ecosystem, or microbiome, within our guts. If one hundred trillion sounds like a considerable number, that's because it is—there are more bacteria living in our intestinal tract than cells in the rest of our bodies, and these bacteria play a significant role in the functioning of our bodies, both in relation to digestion, and our overall *affect* and mental health. Get the wrong blend of bacteria and it can lead to anxiety in several different ways. Not only can the bacteria affect the mind directly through the vagus nerve, but they can also release chemicals that can cause leaky gut and inflammation which can lead to anxiety more indirectly. Getting the right mix of bacteria is important to keep your anxiety at normal levels and so there are a few things that can be done to help maintain a healthy microbiome and make your gut a positive influence on your mental health:

Use Antibiotics Only When Necessary

Antibiotics are wonderful things, and the fact that we no longer have to worry about small cuts killing us is fantastic, but it is no secret that antibiotics are being overused around the world. Many people take antibiotics as the first line of defence against sickness when they are not really needed, and this can play havoc with the gut bacteria. The very point of antibiotics is to kill bacteria, and they are, on the whole, incredibly good at this. While this can be lifesaving when deadly bacteria have invaded the body, it is detrimental to health at other times, as all the healthy bacteria are killed along with the bad. This means the gut must start again from scratch repopulating the microbiome and this can lead to too many bad bacteria, fungi or yeasts entering the gut.

Please note that I am not saying that people should always avoid antibiotics, they are essential drugs at the right time, I am just saying that you should only take them when necessary and prescribed by a competent doctor.

Limit Sugar Intake

Over the last few years sugar has slowly become the villain of the food world and more and more people are shunning it to lose weight, but it is important to understand that losing weight is not the only reason to cut down on sugar. Most people realise now that sugar is unhealthy and eating as little of it as possible is better for their overall health, but this is, unfortunately, not everyone. Sugar is bad for gut health, and therefore, mental health. In a nutshell, bad bacteria thrive on sugar, good bacteria not so much. Therefore, the more sugar you eat, the more you are encouraging the flourishing of bad bacteria in your gut.

Sugar intake can also lead to anxiety-like feelings more directly through significant spikes and crashes in blood sugar levels, and so it is just best, in general for anxiety, to limit sugar as much as you can.

Alcohol

As an anxiety sufferer, it can sometimes be tempting to use alcohol as a crutch to help with anxious episodes or to ease the anxiety associated with social interactions. This is not unusual, and if the alcohol consumption is kept within limits, should not be a problem. However, too much alcohol can lead to anxiety in several ways: If you've ever had a bad hangover, you have probably experienced the anxiety that often comes inherently with the morning after, as withdrawal symptoms can lead directly to decreased *affect* but also to anxiety through a drop in essential vitamins and minerals.

Excessive alcohol consumption can also aggravate the gut lining and make leaky gut easier than it otherwise might be. Reducing alcohol, then, is a good way to reduce overall anxiety in the long term. It might feel like alcohol helps with anxiety, but it really doesn't.

Probiotics

You may well have heard of probiotics as they have become a popular subject both in scientific studies and popular media. If you haven't heard of them, probiotics are friendly bacteria that you can add to your gut to help tip the balance of the microbiota in a way that promotes good health. The best way to get probiotics is eating foods that are naturally rich in them. This tends to be foods that have been fermented such as kimchi, live yoghurt, kefir, kombucha, sauerkraut, fermented pickles, miso, and tempeh. Each of these foods will provide your gut with healthy and anxiety friendly bacteria.

If you can't find, or simply don't like, fermented foods (and I can understand that), then you can also find probiotics in supplement form. They are easy to find online, now, but often not cheap, and you will need to be careful which you buy, as there are many jumping on the bandwagon with sub-par products.

Prebiotics

As well as taking probiotics to add extra friendly bacteria to your gut, you can also eat food that feeds the friendly bacteria that you already have and help them flourish. Just like bad bacteria like eating sugar, good bacteria like *prebiotics* such as inulin. Some of the foods that are high in prebiotics are garlic, onions, leeks, asparagus, bananas, barley, apples, Jerusalem artichoke, dandelion greens, chicory root, chickpeas, lentils, beans, oats, and savoy cabbage. Eating some of these foods will help keep the friendly bacteria in your gut well-fed and flourishing.

Leaky Gut

Having a leaky gut, or intestinal permeability, can lead to food and bacteria entering your bloodstream and triggering immune responses that can result in negative affect and therefore anxiety. Healing a leaky gut or preventing one from forming in the first place can lower the risk of systemic inflammation that can cause generalised anxiety. If you have a leaky gut already, avoiding or treating the following things that can damage your intestinal lining will give your gut time to heal itself.

NSAIDS

Non-steroidal Anti-Inflammatory Drugs are common drugs often sold over the counter to reduce pain or inflammation, and include names such as aspirin, ibuprofen, and naproxen. While these can be effective pain killers, they can also be very abrasive to the stomach lining. Taking NSAIDS can cause stomach ulcers, bleeding, and leaky gut. If you think you might have a leaky gut and you have a headache, then taking paracetamol instead of an NSAID will be better for your gut.

Harmful bacteria

As already mentioned, harmful bacteria can also cause leaky guts, and they do this through the activation of a chemical called zonulin in the body. Zonulin, as discovered by gastroenterologist Alessio Fasano in 2000[78], helps to regulate the opening and closing of the spaces, or "tight junctions", between cells in the intestinal lining to control the flow of fluids through the wall of the gut. If you eat something that has gone bad, zonulin is triggered, and the opening of the spaces in the gut lining allows water to flow through, and the resultant diarrhoea washes out the offending morsel. In these cases, zonulin is helpful, but if the gut is populated with too many harmful bacteria, zonulin production can be increased and cause the gut to be overly "leaky". Balancing the gut flora with probiotics and prebiotics and reducing sugar intake can help reduce the excess harmful bacteria that can cause, or worsen, leaky gut.

Gluten

As with the harmful bacteria above, gluten has also been shown to trigger zonulin levels in some people[79]. These people are what we now call celiac disease sufferers, or gluten sensitive people, but even if you don't already know that you are gluten sensitive, the gluten in your body could be triggering zonulin and causing leaks in your intestinal lining. If you suspect that you might be suffering from a leaky gut, then you might try cutting down on high gluten foods for a while, such as bread and pasta. Anything that is made with wheat flour will have gluten in it and could be triggering zonulin in your body and causing a leaky gut and therefore inflammation.

---

[78] Zonulin and its regulation of intestinal barrier function: the biological door to inflammation, autoimmunity, and cancer | Alessio Fasano [2011]
All disease begins in the (leaky) gut: role of zonulin-mediated gut permeability in the pathogenesis of some chronic inflammatory diseases | Alessio Fasano [2020]
Zonulin, a regulator of epithelial and endothelial barrier functions, and its involvement in chronic inflammatory diseases | Craig Sturgeon, Alessio Fasano [2016]
[79] Zonulin Upregulation Is Associated With Increased Gut Permeability in Subjects With Type 1 Diabetes and Their Relatives | Sapone et.al. (2006)

Inflammation

As we have already seen, inflammation plays a key role in keeping us safe, disease-free, and alive, but it can also cause problems when it arises unnecessarily. Science is beginning to show that out-of-control inflammation, or systemic inflammation, could be the root cause of many diseases and physical ailments. But as we have also seen, the issues that inflammation gives rise to, can also result in overly negative *affect*, and therefore increased anxiety.

The problem with inflammation is that it is caused by many different things. We have seen how it is repeatedly triggered by having a leaky gut, and a badly balanced intestinal flora, but there are other things that lead to excessive inflammation like too much omega-6 fatty acids. Luckily, there are things you can do to reduce the inflammation directly. As always, one of the most important of those things is to eat healthier. This is always a good first step. The second is to reduce the omega-6 fatty acids, which increase inflammation, and increase the omega-3 fatty acids, which decrease it. Omega-6 is mostly found in seed and nut oils, while omega-3 is found primarily in fish oil, and olive oil. This is a simplification, but is sufficient here, and leads to a simple first step of limiting oils like sunflower, soy and corn oil and increasing consumption of olive oil and oily fish like salmon and mackerel.

Other things that can help reduce inflammation are berries, cherries, green tea, broccoli, beans, avocados, turmeric, ginger, and dark chocolate to name just a few. Eating things that reduce inflammation and avoiding things that can cause inflammation, such as sugar and processed foods, can be a first step to a healthier body, a more positive affect, and less anxiety.

Finding Food Triggers

If you believe that something in your diet is triggering an immune response and causing systemic inflammation, but you are unsure exactly what it is, then you might want to follow an elimination diet for a while. Elimination diets are not easy and take a long time, but they can be very effective. You basically cut out everything that could be triggering an immune response from your diet for several weeks and then begin to introduce foods back into your dietary routine one at a time while observing and recording the effects. This not only gives your body the time it needs to reset and heal any leaky gut issues, but also allows you to pinpoint the foods that trigger inflammation.

The process of the elimination diet is too involved to include here, but you will find the process broken down in detail in my book *The Anxiety Shift: Gut Rehab*. You will also find plenty of information for free online. I did the elimination diet in 2013 and found it very effective. It wasn't easy, but it was effective.

Exercise

As well as maintaining a healthy and fit body, which can help build a more robust gut, exercise can also help build mental fitness, help build a more solid sense of self, and it has been shown in many studies[80] that exercise can reduce stress and anxiety directly.

There are both short and long-term benefits to the brain to be had with regular exercise. The short-term benefits can be felt immediately and are through the release of chemicals like endorphins. Endorphins are natural painkillers and are what allow long distance runners to break through the "pain barrier". These, and other short-term

---

[80] A meta-meta-analysis of the effect of physical activity on depression and anxiety in non-clinical adult populations | Rebar AL et. al., [2015]
The Effect of Exercise Training on Anxiety Symptoms Among Patients | P. Herring et. al. (2010) | Lederman O, Groves A, Jorm AF [2015]

chemicals released in the brain during exercise, can give a positive feeling, and reduce stress and anxiety, hours after exercising.

The long-term benefits include the actual growing of new blood vessels in the brain and increased levels of brain derived neurotrophic factor (BDNF), which was found to be reduced in anxiety sufferers in some studies[81].

Another long-term effect of exercise is the formation of neurons in the brain that are specifically designed to release the neurotransmitter GABA that inhibits brain activity making sure that neurons don't fire when they shouldn't be firing, and effectively reducing anxiety.

One last benefit of exercise is that it has been shown to reduce cognitive attention biases and cognitive interpretation biases[82], and as we have already seen, these cognitive biases play a role in pushing the anxiety gaps in a more negative direction than is appropriate and therefore increasing anxiety.

As well as helping keep the body and mind fit and having a positive effect on mental health, it has also been shown that exercise helps to directly reduce inflammation in the body[83]. Inflammation, in my view, is a major player in many physical illnesses, and, as we have shown, also a major player in creating a negative *affect* and therefore leading to increased anxiety. Exercise plays a vital role, then, in keeping the whole body and mind package in tip-top condition.

---

[81] Brain-Derived Neurotrophic Factor (BDNF) protein levels in anxiety disorders: systematic review and meta-regression analysis | Suliman et al (2013)
Investigating the Role of Hippocampal BDNF in Anxiety Vulnerability | Janke et al (2015)
[82] Cognitive Interpretation Bias: The Effect of a Single Session Moderate Exercise Protocol on Anxiety and Depression | Clarke, Cooper, Rana, Macintosh (2018)
[83] Exercise as a means to control low-grade systemic inflammation | Mathur, N., & Pedersen, B. K. (2008).
Debunking the myth of exercise-induced immune suppression: Redefining the impact of exercise on immunological health across the lifespan | Campbell, J. P., & Turner, J. E. (2018).
Exercise and the regulation of immune functions | Simpson, R. J., Kunz, H., Agha, N., & Graff, R. (2015)

It is evident, then, that exercise is good for combatting anxiety and should go together with any anxiety regime that you try, including following the suggestions in this book. Remember, the aim here is not to develop a short-term process to temporarily quiet your anxiety, but to create a whole new lifestyle, and set of habits, that will keep you anxiety-free for the rest of your life. Exercise is an important part of that lifestyle.

Now before you start panicking, and the thought of spending hundreds of dollars on gym memberships and hours a day on the treadmill make you quit the whole thing, please remember that exercise does not have to be a scheduled and structured activity. Exercise can be as simple as going for a walk instead of driving or taking the stairs instead of the elevator. If you can muster around 150 minutes of exercise a week, then you are on the right track for a healthier body and brain. That's about 20 minutes per day, and if you can break that into two 10-minute walks, you will barely notice it. But your brain and your body will.

Sleep

While sleep almost seems the opposite of exercise, and most of us would much rather sleep than go to the gym, it is a fact that too many people in the west do not get enough sleep. In fact, it is estimated that about one-in-three people in the US do not get enough sleep each night. The amount of sleep we need depends on our age, and the National Sleep Foundation determined that for teenagers 8 to 10 hours was considered appropriate, 7 to 9 hours for young adults and middle-aged adults, and 7 to 8 hours of sleep for older adults[84]. Unfortunately, due to work commitments or lifestyle, many of us do not get these number of hours every night.

---

[84] National Sleep Foundation's sleep time duration recommendations: methodology and results summary | Max Hirshkowitz et al., (2015)

A regular lack of sleep can lead to increased inflammation[85] within the body as well as lead directly to anxiety[86], and as we have already seen, inflammation can lead to anxiety through increased negative *affect* in the body. Of course, the problem is that this can lead to another vicious cycle, as a lack of sleep leads to increased anxiety, and too much anxiety, with the worry and the rumination that accompanies it, can make it difficult to fall asleep in the first place.

The best place to start, then, is to try and get at least 7 hours of sleep a day if you are an adult. Go to bed earlier than normal and make sure you do not look at your phone or tablet before you sleep. The National sleep foundation also found that using a phone or tablet within an hour before sleeping made sleep more difficult[87] and led to less sleep than was needed. If you struggle to sleep because of anxiety and overthinking, then maybe consider adding more exercise to your routine to tire your body and your brain out before bed, or you can take up yoga or meditation to help quiet your mind. Another trick that you might want to try is to make use of the Zeigarnik effect that we saw earlier. If you remember, Baumeister and his colleagues used the Zeigarnik effect to show that anxiety remains in the mind until a plan is made. You can use this to your advantage by making a plan to concentrate on whatever is worrying you at a later date. For example, if you were worrying about paying your credit card bill, you would tell your unconscious that you will deal with that at 11:00 am the next day,

[85] Sleep loss activates cellular inflammatory signaling | Irwin, M. R., Wang, M., Ribeiro, D., Cho, H. J., & Olmstead, R. (2009) Sleep and immune function | Besedovsky, L., Lange, T., & Born, J. (2019).Vgontzas, A. N., Zoumakis, E., Bixler, E. Adverse effects of modest sleep restriction on sleepiness, performance, and inflammatory cytokines | AN Vgontzas et. al. (2004).
[86] Effects of acute sleep deprivation on state anxiety levels: a systematic review and meta-analysis | GN Pires, AG Bezerra, S Tufik, ML Andersen (2016) Relationship between sleep deprivation and anxiety: experimental research perspective | Gabriel Natan Pires et al., (2012)
[87] The sleep and technology use of Americans: findings from the National Sleep Foundation's 2011 Sleep in America poll | Gradisar, M., Wolfson, A. R., Harvey, A. G., Hale, L., Rosenberg, R., & Czeisler, C. A. (2013).

and so it should stop trying to find a solution now and wait until tomorrow. It is a simple technique, but you might be surprised how effective it can be. As a last resort you could see your doctor for medication to help you sleep, but trying to do it without medication is preferable as dependency is a real possibility.

In summary, then, getting a full night's sleep of 7 hours each night is essential for both a healthy body and a healthy mind and should not be overlooked as insignificant. If you are watching Netflix instead of getting your seven hours, then you need to look at your choices and your lifestyle before you can start to look at tackling your anxiety. Of course, if you have no time for 7 hours each night due to work or family commitments, then you need to try and work around it as best you can. Many people get by perfectly well on less than 7 hours of sleep per night, but as an anxiety sufferer, it is another thing that could be adding to your anxiety triggers and something to bear in mind as best you can.

In-Closing

There are a few things that I hope stay with you when you put this book down: The first is that anxiety is not the enemy that you have been told it is. It makes no sense that your own body would be trying to sabotage your life, and I hope the idea of the anxiety gaps show that it is not. Anxiety is on your side. It is like a nagging friend trying to make you quit something that they believe is bad for you, but you have not yet been able to see what that thing is. Anxiety is trying to make you aware of a problem within yourself that maybe you are not yet aware of.

The second is that anxiety is not an accident. While the brain does make mistakes, anxiety is not the result of the brain creating fears that don't exist. The fears within you are real and important, and, while you may well not be aware of them now, it is worth trying to nail them down and find out what is causing your anxiety. Blaming anxiety for creating fears that don't exist is too easy, and frankly lazy, and will be detrimental to your recovery, as it is real fears within you that are causing the anxiety. The whole "anxiety is a leftover remnant of the lizard brain that has no place in society today" is a trope that no longer holds water.

The third thing is that the problems within you that are causing your anxiety are all within your own ability to solve. It is certainly not easy, but it is possible, and understanding that is empowering. While no single book, on its own, is enough to help you beat anxiety, I can assure you, that once you get into the habit of viewing your anxiety in terms of anxiety gaps and are able to pinpoint the needs and values involved, your anxiety will never look the same again. It will change the way you view your anxiety and the way you view every decision you make. It will help you understand what happens to your body during anxiety and that will result in a profound change to your life.

This book was never really intended to be a self-help book in the usual sense; it was intended to allow you to see the true face of anxiety and be able to face it head on, because once you understand something, it is much easier to tackle it. Once you get used to breaking your anxiety down into gaps and understand why it is there, then you can start to beat it.

The rest is up to you.

Appendix

These are a few things that I originally wanted to add to the book but thought they might make it more confusing and weren't necessary for understanding the content at the time, but thought they were either interesting enough (for me at least) or might answer some questions that arise in the minds of overthinkers like myself.

Continuous Line (Non-Discrete) Gaps

Most of the time, decisions are made because of double decision gaps, that, as we have seen are based on two or more regular approach vs avoidance gaps. There are occasions, of course, where decisions must be made that are not between two, three, or even twelve individual things, but are instead decisions between an infinite number of things on a continuum. These are decisions such as how much to sell a car for, or how much salary to ask for at an interview. There are no specific choices to choose from, so instead we must determine our own figure. These types of decisions are not always based on money, but often are in everyday life. There are entire courses in economics built around these kinds of decisions, but I want to simplify things to build a model for anxiety.

If we take a simple example of being asked how much salary we want, we can imagine that in anxiety terms, the FFFS will be triggered most if we perceive our decision to be too low or too high. If we perceive our bid to be too low, we might fear people view us as weak or incompetent and we will lose people's respect, or we will feel like pushovers and feel weak ourselves and fear losing self-esteem. If we perceive our bid too high, however, we might fear people view us as greedy and think we don't deserve that, thereby losing their respect and our ranking among them. Of course, the BAS will be triggered by more money as this could raise social standing and standard of living outside the workplace. It is clear, though, that the decision is not simply a two-horse race between too low and too high, the decision is to find the sweet spot where the anxiety is at a minimum between too low and too high.

For this we need a continuum gap, or as I like to call it, the anxiety gradient:

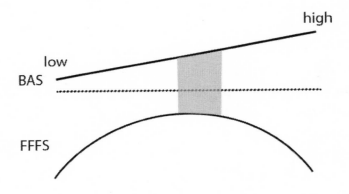

Anxiety gradient for asking for a salary.

This is a rather crude model, but it shows how the BAS line increases with more money and how the FFFS line bends from a negative maximum when the money is too low to another negative maximum when the money is too high. The anxiety at these two extremes would be too great to choose, but between them is a sweet spot area, shown by the box, where the anxiety is lessened. This box indicates what a person might consider a "fair" number to ask for. Where within this box the person would choose their exact figure would depend on their own risk aversion and anxiety tolerance. While the net negative of each point in the box is roughly equal, indicating similar anxiety valence levels, the overall amplitude differs and therefore so does the arousal of the anxiety. How much arousal a person can cope with will ultimately determine the final figure.

While this model might not be particularly practical, it can be useful to show that not all gaps are built the same and not all are simple parallel gaps but that all anxiety can be turned into a gap of sorts. Of course, these are very specific situations, and most gaps can be presumed to be of the regular parallel type, and that is why I decided to add this to the appendix rather than the main body of text. I wanted to include it, though, mainly to illustrate the versatility of the anxiety gap model, even if not all situations follow the regular parallel decision gap. This is a gap that I'm sure will be familiar to anyone who hates haggling with market traders.

In most situations, though, we will find that the regular anxiety gap model works well enough to allow us to figure out what is causing our own anxiety.

Alternative Gap Model for Valence & Arousal

When I first devised the gap model I made the valence the net of the approach (BAS) and avoidance (FFFS) gaps as I showed earlier, but I had the arousal calculated as the sum of the absolute values of the two gaps, as I felt that both the BAS and FFFS release chemicals into the body and both can release adrenaline and therefore both should contribute to the overall arousal of an anxiety episode. This would make the total arousal value out of a possible score of 20 as both the BAS and the FFFS have maximum absolute values of 10. The problem with this is that it does not allow for anxious episodes with very high negative valences and very high arousal. If we look at an example, such as a BAS score of 0.5 and an FFFS score of -10, this would give us a very high negative valence score of -9.5/10 but the overall arousal would only be 10/20 (9.5 + 0.5), which isn't very high at all. The only way to get a very high arousal score is to have a high

BAS (eg., 9) and a very high FFFS score (eg., -10), but this would then only have a valence value of -1 (9 + -10)

This was a problem that did not fit with my overall model concept as we all know that we have can have anxiety with very negative valence and very strong arousal.

For this reason, then, I developed a second arousal model that was also out of 20 but involved a calculation of adding the sum of the absolute values of both gaps to the absolute value of the net of both gaps. This would then mean that even during anxiety, the size of the BAS can influence the amount of arousal, as I think it should. It also means that you can have emotions with low valence but high arousal, which certainly does happen.

As an example, If the BAS is 4 and the FFFS is -10, then the valence in this system would be -6, as usual, but the arousal would be 20 ((4+10) + 6). This system certainly gives the model more range, but I considered the extra step in calculation to be an extra step in complication and I wanted to keep it as simple as possible. This is why I opted for the simplified version I used for the book. If you like a bit of extra maths, though, this might appeal to you and make your arousal values different. If not, then I guess you probably stopped reading way before you got this far anyway. In the long run, it doesn't really matter, though, because as already stated earlier when you are creating your own gaps with valence and arousal, yu don't need the maths because you will be relying on your own feelings and judgement anyway.

Valence and Arousal of Decision Gaps

As decision gaps involve two gaps working against each other, the calculation of the valence and arousal caused by them would be more complicated than a simple anxiety gap, which is why I decided to put this section here. The valence cannot be taken from the resulting combined gap because quite often both decision gaps can be quite FFFS heavy and therefore fear based decisions, which is not necessarily reflected in the combined gap. The anxiety in the original decision gaps is greater than the latent gap that is left behind though, as the BIS always chooses the gap with the least amount of anxiety associated with it. That's the point. By making the decision you reduce the amount of anxiety felt. If you do not make the decision, then the anxiety will remain high.

The valence of a decision gap, then, is determined by the gap that has the largest valence individually i.e., the largest net negative, and the arousal is given by the absolute value of the largest gap. This sounds very similar to the regular method of calculating valence and arousal, but the difference here is that the two might not come from the same gap.

If we look again at the example of John buying his house, we can see the anxiety involved in the decision.

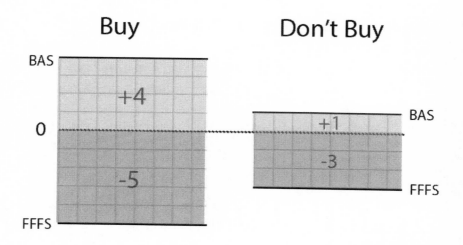

The biggest valence of both gaps is from the "don't buy" gap with a valence of -2, while the arousal is from the "buy gap" with an

300

arousal of 5. This gives the overall decision gap the anxiety levels of the following: valence: -2, arousal 5.

Immediately after John buys the house, however, his latent gap will provide the following: valence -1, arousal 5 as the 'Don't Buy' gap is collapsed. This is an automatic drop of anxiety levels, which, as already mentioned, will also reduce over time.

Supporting References

Using Bis and Bas Sensitivity to Predict Psychopathology, Emotion Regulation and WellBeing | Walker Scott Pedersen University of Wisconsin-Milwaukee (2013)

Emotivational psychology: How distinct emotions facilitate fundamental motives | Alec T. Beall, Jessica L. Tracy

A Theory of Self-Esteem | Cast, Burker (2003)

A two-dimensional neuropsychology of defense: fear/anxiety and defensive distance | McNaughton, Corr (2004)

Approach and Avoidance Behaviour: Multiple Systems and their Interactions | Philip J. Corr (2013)

The Reinforcement Sensitivity Theory of Personality Questionnaire (RST-PQ): Development and Validation | Corr, Cooper

Promotion and Prevention: Regulatory Focus as a Motivational Principle | E Tory Higgins (1998)

The Meaning of Anxiety | Book by Rollo May

Reinforcement Sensitivity Theory of Personality Questionnaires: Structural survey with recommendations | Philip J Corr (2016)

Reinforcement Sensitivity Theory and personality | Corr, McNaughton

The behavioral inhibition system and the behavioral approach system: Sensitivity, temperament, and cognitive style. Psychological Science | Dawson, E. A., Schellenberg, E. G., & Filion, D. L. (2007)

Anxious: Using the Brain to Understand and Treat Fear and Anxiety | Book by Joseph Le Doux

How Emotions Are Made: The Secret Life of the Brain | Book by Lisa Feldman Barrett

The Six Pillars of Self-Esteem | Book by Nathaniel Branden

The 7 Habits of Highly Effective People | Book by Stephen Covey

Other Books by the Author

The Anxiety Shift - Gut rehab

The Anxiety Shift – Gut Rehab builds and expands on the idea that our bodies, but more specifically our guts, play a huge role in creating or adding to our anxiety through a variety of ways. It discusses in detail how the gut can trigger anxiety, how it can make it worse, and what we can do about it. It includes a step-by-step guide on performing an elimination diet to root out anxiety triggers in the foods we eat.

The Anxiety Shift - Mind Reset

The Anxiety Shift – Mind reset discusses the way our minds trigger our emotions through the value process. With exercises and worksheets, it offers an in-depth look at how these thought processes can be broken and the triggers stopped.

Both books are good companions to this book and offer additional information that supports and complements this book perfectly. You can find them both on Amazon.

Made in the USA
Columbia, SC
20 October 2024